I0187504

Putting It Wright

* * *

The Autobiography of
Captain Walter Graham Wright (K.M.) B.A.(Hons)
Royal Australian Navy (Retired)

* * *

Graham Wright

First Edition

ISBN: 978-0-9924657-0-4

Printed in Melbourne, Australia

Cover Photo: 1960 Commander Graham Wright then Executive Officer HMAS Cerberus

Photo scans by Bytes n Colours, Canberra
Book compilation, design, layout, PR, marketing by www.nannetteholliday.com

This book is dedicated to Nannette Holliday who, after talking with one of my skiing friends in August 2013, Group Captain Mal Hurman, Royal Australian Air Force (Retired),
thought it was too good a story not to be told.
My thanks go to her, without her skill and patience
this book would never have eventuated.
Also to my wife Marie for her endless hours of typing
and editing my handwritten notes,
she understands me so well – thank you darling!
GW

Contents

"Sir, my concern is not whether God is on our side; my greatest concern is to be on God's side, for God is always right."

Abraham Lincoln

— 1 —

Reflection - 93 Years On

Glancing at the bedside table, the new digital clock illuminates it's green numerals, 06:45. My inner alarm clock never misses a beat, unlike my old travelling alarm clock that gave up many moons ago, I keep soldiering on and out-living just about everything and everyone around me.

Stretching under the warmth of the duvet, I see the pink tinged sky visible through the gap in the heavy beige curtains. Another glorious day is dawning. Even though it's now late spring the air remains crisp, my nose is telling me so. But this is Canberra, known for cool mornings and warm sunny days during the shoulder seasons.

The rose of my life for the past 42 years sleeps peacefully beside me. Her soft breaths, golden curls and delicate facial features warm my heart. Folding back the duvet and placing my feet on the floor, she doesn't move. My day begins. She will surface in an hour or so.

I've been blessed in so many ways. I am a very lucky man. When we married many said it would never last, her being 25 years my junior, and my third wife. But we've proven them all wrong and I'm so grateful for the joy and pleasure she's brought me over the years—and still does.

Opening the lounge room curtains exposes the colourful rose garden she's developed during the past 15 years since we moved to Yarralumla. She's the green thumb. I've never been good with plants, perhaps because ships don't have gardens. The kitchen is my domain, even prior to retiring in 1985, but since then all the meals and shopping has happily been my main domestic responsibility. I enjoy my trips to the supermarket, then cooking up a storm. Perhaps I would've made an excellent chef in another life.

Happily, I cut the fresh fruit, line up the cereal jars, place a tea bag in the mug ready for my wife, before preparing my own bowl for breakfast. It's now time for the morning's news on ABC radio. The headlines herald more boat people trying to reach our shores, the new government measures, the countries soaring debt and much more.

Gazing out the bay window from the round timber dining table I'm mesmerized by the surrounding beauty of the garden, the birds and bees enjoying it too, oblivious to the dramas of the news.

Reflecting on life, I've certainly seen and experienced so much and it's not over yet. I don't feel the 93 years I've lived, so perhaps there is truth in the saying: *'You're only as old as you feel.'*

I reckon I owe my fitness, first and foremost to having a younger wife and a full and mentally active life; secondly a good wine with my nightly dinner (with a wine cellar to match); and thirdly, to my attendance at the Hyatt Hotel Canberra gym several days a week. If nothing else, I enjoy catching up and chatting with other attendees and the instructors.

Recently I was asked, "If you could have your time all over again, what would you change?"

The simple answer is nothing. While my life hasn't been perfect and many a time I wasn't happy with the outcome, truthfully I could not imagine my life being any different. I admit to wishing I'd gone further in the Navy. I'd always dreamt it, but then again I'd always dreamt of being as good, if not a better batsman than Bradman — the latter more a pipe dream of course. However, after topping virtually every Naval examination, naturally my expectations were high within my first chosen career.

As my wife loves to remind me, "You're a very good team player, as long as you're the captain." This is so true. All through life I wanted to be the best in everything, not just scholastically, but also sportingly.

I wasn't just a bookworm or educational nerd, I excelled in my chosen sports, captaining many a team over the years. In fact I only played my last I Zingari cricket match in 2011 in London and enjoyed two weeks of skiing with military friends at Thredbo this past August 2013. Throughout life I've been committed to putting in 110% effort in all my undertakings.

Always one for speaking my mind, it probably got me into more hot water than ever imaginable. Perhaps I should've taken more notice of one of my Royal Navy (RN) posting officers comments in 1947, "Wright you're a difficult officer. You've got this feeling that you're always right, but you've gotta remember that sometimes it might be 51 – 49, rather than 95 – 5. I'm going to send you to one of our most difficult officers, as I think you were both made for each other."

But holding my tongue just wasn't in my nature, if I thought I was right (and I usually was), I said so and stuck to my guns. Now having survived 93 years of life and having seen many of my predictions and early statements to fruition, there's a gratification in proving to my doubters that I've been at least 90 per cent right. It's a strange feeling, as most people never have that opportunity.

And as for the particular posting under Captain Wynne Edwards (RN), it was one of the best I ever experienced. Not a cross word was ever spoken. We worked magnificently together. The work done during that year in developing the future of sea command laid the foundations for naval warfare as it's practised today.

It was the same when I worked with Sir Arthur Tange in the 70's. Everyone said how difficult he was, but we worked magnificently together in producing the Defence Department structure as it operates today. "I'll do the thinking, you do the arithmetic's, Wright," he'd say. There was no way that *The Tange Report* was going to be read by Service personnel, so he had me condense the main points of my thesis into a special document published under my own name to be distributed to each of the Staff Colleges of the Navy, Army and RAAF for study by their students. He clearly had faith in me.

I still remember the pride of being chosen as an officer in the ceremonial party for Mustafa Kemal Ataturk's funeral during my early days in the Mediterranean. Today, I believe I'm the only Australian still living who attended the funeral of the great, forward thinking president of the Turkish Republic in 1938. Because of this involvement, each year on 10 November I'm welcomed to address Turkish children from Sydney attending the Ataturk Memorial.

Then there was our mission to Archangel in 1941. Where in the frozen north we became privy to one of the major secrets of World War II – escorting Sir Walter Citrine to a meeting with Stalin, with the Nazis virtually knocking on the dictator's door. Time now allows me to be able to set the record straight and tell the real truth of the mission.

I don't know if there any characters still living, but I can assure you that I am the only soul to whom Citrine revealed the true purpose of his visit to Russia. Before leaving for Moscow Sir Walter confided in me.

Imagine if you will, the state of mind of a man without military training or experience, faced with the uncertainty of flying from Archangel to Moscow, hedge-hopping all the way and practically in sight of the deadly enemy. No wonder he wanted someone to know why he was doing it.

On 28 June 2013 I received the Arctic Star campaign medal for my involvement in that mission. It was a pleasant surprise, as was the British High Commission ceremony in Canberra, especially coming 71 years and seven months after the actual event.

One morning during my 70's I remember waking with the words, or at best some of them, going through my head:

They say there's a Corvette just leaving Milne Bay,
Bound for the survey ground.
Laden with tide poles and theodolites,
And any junk that's around.
You get no promotion, surveying the ocean
So cheer up my lads, Bless 'em all.

I very much doubt whether any of those who sang this ditty with me in *Shepparton, Whyalla* or *Benalla* in 1943, while eating giant asparagus spears from Edgell's largest tins (by courtesy of then Leading Stores Assistant, Crowle), are around. Perhaps one of them may have left a copy behind. It was the worst of all doggerels, but it boosted morale! George Tancred got a Distinguished Service Cross (DSC) for his time there. And I have a coral patch named after me. I sighted it, and we avoided it!

I'm sure everyone agrees that life consists of three parts: the present — a race of events competing for our attention that tick by at some alarming rate; the foggy and unfathomable future — for which we dream and plan, and over plan and worry about, as most of it never turns out as

Australian Defence Force Vice Chief of Defence Air Marshal Mark Binskin at the award of my Arctic Star campaign medal in Canberra 2013

At home with one of my early journals and war medals 2013

we expect it to anyway; and thirdly, the past — the realities of what actually occurred, the foundations of one's present life, and the memories brought back suddenly by some scribbled lines in a diary, a smell, an old song, some triviality that makes you think, 'Ah, I remember …' making our heart skip while reliving that inexplicable pleasure.

It's possibly one of the most enjoyable things about 'old age' — one's memories. Unfortunately while I enjoy remembering, I repeatedly remind myself that telling other people about the memories is often boring. After all, why should they be interested in what I've done in my life — it's not theirs? The younger ones, however, do present a certain historical curiosity. I personally think that one's memories represent moments of, as insignificant as they may seem, one's inner and most real self.

To me life has always been exciting, from my earliest memory to today —almost 94 years on. I still enjoy living. And each day presents something different. I have experienced almost every form of high and low, from pain, despair, loss and defeat, to joy, happiness, fulfillment and contentment, but through it all I still know, quite certainly, that just to be alive is a grand achievement in itself.

As A P Herbert wrote:

When men grow old and their blood runs cold,
And the tips of their toes turn blue;
They look back on a life of trouble and strife,
They can tell you a tale or two.

And that I can surely do.

Along with the encouragement and assistance from a young ex-Defence lady and writer, Nannette Holliday, and the excellent typing and computer editing skills of my wife, Marie, I'm going to indulge in the pleasures of my memory, reminisce over my diaries and papers, to now create my autobiography while at the same time putting right a few historical facts.

I'm told the urge overtakes most people sooner or later. And while an autobiography is usually the purposeful study of one's whole life, with lists of names, dates and places in tidy chronological order, I won't be keeping up perfect chronological continuity, but I will at least begin at the beginning.

So having settled that, I'm going to enjoy myself and now begin — provided I can stop every weekday afternoon at 16:30 to indulge in my one obsession since retirement, watching *The Bold and Beautiful*. And I'm not alone. It was also reported recently that it's the one show Derryn Hinch admitted he was going to miss while in prison.

— 2 —

Early Days

It was a warm 10 March morning 1920, in Newcastle when I burst into the world changing the lives of my parents forever. Even though my birth certificate shows my father is aged 25 and my mother 20, they were both only 20 when I was born. My father, John Graham Wright, and mother, Edna Lyall Hanford married in Sydney on 9 July 1919. They'd grown up together in Broken Hill. My father was, at that time, an electrician and mother, like most women of that era, was a housewife.

Newcastle, like its namesake in England, was a coal mining and industrial city. BHP established a large steelworks factory there in 1915, which became the largest employer of the region. However as with most large industry, it also brought pollution to the pristine surf beaches and port.

Thankfully as a youngster I didn't experience too much of this and was happiest at the beach. My earliest memory was from twelve months old with my parents. We'd spend the cooler evening hours down there, as my mother was heavily pregnant at the time. Unfortunately my brother was later to be still born, leaving me an only child.

During a period of marital discord my mother took me back to Broken Hill, where I became more acquainted with distant relatives. She was the youngest of eight, so I had a large extended family in both Broken Hill and Sydney.

To me, school at Broken Hill was marvellous. But I suffered the torment from a handful of the 'damned' local children who took great delight in informing me that, "Come tomorrow you'll be dead."

I think it funny now, as I've probably outlived them all.

Eventually my parents reconciled and we moved to Sydney, firstly living with my grandmother and then in our own place with other relatives, sharing to reduce the costs.

The cultural excursions and experiences around Sydney left a lasting impression, particularly to the Botanical Gardens, occasional concerts at the Sydney Town Hall — especially the 1812 Overture with real cannon fire from outside — the Alan Wilkie Shakespearean Tour at the Newtown Theatre and Sunday School with the Salvation Army.

Me in the garden at North Bondi 1924

My mother Edna Wright and Grannie Hanford

My father Jack Wright and sisters Greta and Etta

The highlight of my boyhood experiences though were the multitude of train tours through New South Wales with my father — so many I lost count. My father worked for the New South Wales Government Railways for many years and was entitled to a holiday pass. Occasionally my mother came along, but only if the journey wasn't too arduous. Mostly it was just the two of us.

Our father–son trips included Moree; where we swam in the mineral baths; Albury, where the train passed through a bushfire along the way; Murwillumbah via the inland route; Grafton along the coastal route; to Nowra, Condobolin and Canberra for the opening of Federal Parliament — each leaving a memorable and lasting impression. I felt extremely lucky as most of my classmates only saw the beach, or a nearby caravan park during their holidays.

'Love and marriage, love and marriage, go together like a horse and carriage', these song words have always stuck in my mind, but

fortunately at a very early age I discovered that, *'it just ain't necessarily so'*.

When I was six at Newtown Public Primary School, I honestly thought I was in love with a girl. So much so that I took myself to the Salvation Army Sunday School in case she should turn up. Alas she didn't, but here began my long road of scriptural education. I was asked to read aloud to the assembled class, the first line of the second verse of a famous hymn: *'Run the straight race through God's good grace'* – which I then decided to do as fast as possible each day of my life.

Before Christmas in my eighth year, a Bexley teacher took us on an outing into the city heart of Sydney. We saw the newsreels in the State Theatrette and had lunch in a nearby cafe. It was a wonderful day. My heart had been doing cartwheels all day, but I had to be honest, she was too tall for me.

Then my father suggested I follow the advice of Lord Baden-Powell and join Wolf Cubs preparatory, prior to joining the Boy Scouts later on in life. In no time at all I'd become a Sixer in charge of five other boys and then the Senior Sixer in charge of the whole pack.

I also loved cricket and at ten years of age I was Don Bradman. I had seen him briefly in December 1928 in Sydney when he fielded for the injured Ponsford having been dropped for the only time in what was to be a twenty-year Test career.

As an only child I naturally became self-taught in all sports that captured my interest. My father was not a games player having excelled as a boxer and swimmer in his youth, until he took to tennis, which he played badly in his late twenties.

Not for me the corrugated iron water tank, golf ball, and cricket stump. Even with the financial stringency during the Great Depression my father and mother managed to encourage my interest in cricket with

My father Jack Wright with the Governor-General

'Don Bradman's Book' and a size six Gunn and Moore Autograph bat, which was to be part of my travelling gear, together with a Hit tennis racquet until the end of World War II. I was also fortunate that my uncle Stan Harris, a Dental Technician, happened to have a two-piece leather cricket ball with raised stitches that he showed me how to grip. When pitched at the right length it proved invaluable as an alternative to the military medium bowling to which I was subjected throughout my career in Service cricket.

When the Great Depression hit it caused the entire family, headed by Grannie Hanford, to alter living arrangements.

My father had been persuaded to join a Swiss firm of Electrical Engineers and move to Europe when their contract to electrify the railway between North Sydney and Hornsby had been completed. When this project came to an abrupt halt, it forced him to borrow Grandfather Walter Henry's T model Ford and set up business as an electrical contractor. One of my father's World War I mates living in Kensington was moving to Adelaide and offered the occupancy of a block of twelve units with garage. It was opposite what was then the Kensington Racecourse, now part of the University of New South Wales.

I know you are now doing your maths — yes my father was 20 when I was born, which would surely render him too young to have participated in World War I. Correct and incorrect. He did participate. At 13 he became a boy seaman in HMAS *Tingira*. However three years later when World War I broke out, he absconded with a few mates and saying he was 22 he enlisted in the AIF, thus negating the need for parental permission. By the time he was 19, or as they thought 25, he'd risen to the rank of Regimental Sergeant Major (RSM) of a combined Battalion at Villers Bretonneux and was about to be commissioned when they discovered his real age, which was unfortunately far too young for a commission.

Anyway, at Maroubra Junction I completed the last two years of Primary School, joined the Church of England as a choirboy, and its Wolf Cub Pack as a lowly member of a six. This didn't last long, as I set out to get as many Efficiency Badges as I could and soon had control over five others as a Sixer again.

With Bob Watkins at Coopers Bent

All this activity rendered me far too busy to have anything to do with the daughter of one of the other tenants. Her mother was a sole parent with strict rules about what she could and couldn't do and with whom. On one occasion I was allowed to take the daughter swimming to Maroubra Beach, but truthfully she was too skinny to be interesting.

Involvement in cricket, Wolf Cubs and as a church choirboy filled in the rest of my childhood years. Some years later I was fortunate to meet and spend some hours with Claud Philcox at the Adelaide Cycling Club, where most of the members had probably never seen, let alone ridden a two-wheeler. As a Councillor and leading Solicitor, Claud had a wide circle of friends, but the remark I will never forget was one concerning his own son, "I would never let him join the Boy Scouts or go to church. I have acted for too many Scoutmasters and Clergymen."

Thankfully my only abnormal experience back then was the way in which my immaculately white surplus that I wore to Matins would disappear after the service and in its place would be a grubby substitute for Evensong. My mother, who was a devout Methodist, would then wash, starch and iron it for me for the following Sunday. As for Cubs, it was the annual adventurous camps at Austinmer, near Wollongong, or Camden, that I found every bit as memorable as the books on my bedroom shelf.

Every Sunday there would be a Navy ship in Farm Cove open to visitors from 14:00 to 16:30. In those days people didn't travel as much as they do today and by the Government opening the ships to the public it allowed the taxpayer to see where their money was being spent. It also gave small boys, like myself, the opportunity to imagine what it would be like to be on the bridge of a fighting ship. Every Sunday I'd take myself down to Stannards Wharf and go aboard, spending as long as possible on the bridge, pretending I was the Captain. Anything less never crossed my mind. Hence grew my yearnings for a Naval Officers career.

Through my own father's love of books he'd encouraged me to read from a very early age. I devoured everything in sight and I'm certain this assisted in topping most of my examinations. But then came my greatest test, the NSW Qualifying Certificate.

My Arithmetic teacher was marvellous and subsequently became a Sydney University Professor of Mathematics, but I still had problems with my maths, particularly percentages and profit and loss.

I'd hoped for a Pass in the exclusive Higher Bracket to qualify for entry into Fort Street, a school famous for producing doctors, lawyers, and notables of just about every worthwhile occupation. However my results only gave me entry to Randwick Intermediate High School, but luckily in the A stream, which included Latin, French, Mathematics I and II, Physics, Chemistry, English and History, eschewing anyone for a career in business.

While I was disappointed with myself, during the next few years I flourished at Randwick.

Now any dictionary will tell you that the word 'tragic' is an adjective. As nobody seems to be taught grammar any more we find the term 'Cricket Tragic' has come into general use without anyone bothering to define what is meant by it. Certainly it is not a tragic cricketer. In my last year at Randwick High School the Captain of the School's First Eleven took an interest in the way I batted. He spent his adult life in England as a County Cricketer until his untimely death in a level crossing accident on the way home after a match. Without doubt he was a Tragic Cricketer.

So perhaps the term must be confined to non-players like Bob Menzies and John Howard who were regular attenders at Test Matches involving Australia against anyone else no matter where they were taking place. Bob Hawke played for Oxford University as a Rhodes Scholar, but tried to keep playing long after losing whatever skill he may have had.

Anyway, at High School every Wednesday afternoon was devoted to sport, but as I was two to three years younger than most of my classmates and invariably top of the class in all subjects these times were devoted to special tuition in the hope that I would bring credit to the school in the Intermediate Examinations at the end of third year.

The highlight of my make-believe games followed the low point of being bowled first ball by Bowes during the Second Test in Melbourne at the end of December 1932. My 103 not out won the game for Australia and levelled the series at one-all.

Reality in 1933 took the form of three broom sticks cut to the size of stumps and intense practice with a colleague from Wolf Club days in a park near home. Faced with two examinations at the end of the year, both of which would have an impact on my future, study had to take priority over cricket. One of my teachers was of the opinion that I should repeat third year in order to do better at the Intermediate next year. My family had decided that I should take the examination for entry into the Royal Australian Naval College contested by 500 odd candidates vying for a maximum of twelve places. As one of the subjects in the exam was not part of my school curriculum cricket had to come a poor second.

In the event I became Dux of the School and obtained the highest pass in the public examination that had been achieved during the headmastership of Mr E Nettleship MA who had been Headmaster when both my father and mother were at school in Broken Hill.

In addition I'd passed the examination for the Navy, completed a successful interview by the top brass, had my adenoids and tonsils removed, and was awarded a Cadetship to join the Royal Australian Navy as a Cadet Midshipman.

This photo accompanied my entry to Royal Australian Naval College

At that time there was Elma, a girl I'd met while swimming at Coogee Beach. We'd never really gone out. All I knew about her was that her father, as a Travelling Salesman, was only home at weekends, and her mother disapproved of boys in general. She promised to write to me at the Naval College, and she did. While it was only one letter, I kept it locked in the top left hand drawer of my chest of drawers. I supposedly had the only key. This was a fiction that was maintained throughout the four dormitories of the College building. Remarkably a number of Cadets incurred the serious displeasure of the Captain of the College, who was also the Captain of Flinders Naval Depot, which was in effect a small town, and at that time hadn't received the ship's name that it bears today. Cadet Captains were disrated on several occasions for things discovered in the so-called 'Private Tills'.

On 1 January 1934 I entered the Royal Australian Naval College. It was time to grow up.

With my mother Edna in first year of life in the Navy

— 3 —
Royal Australian Naval College

In 1934 there was no doubt that Australia was preparing its Navy for war. The normal flow of Cadet Midshipmen from the Naval College to the Australian Naval Squadron had been interrupted by Government economy measures which had closed Jervis Bay and forced the transfer to the existing Flinders Naval establishment (HMAS *Cerberus*) at Westernport Bay.

With no annual intake of Cadet Midshipmen during the period of transition the 1932 examination and selection was opened to a wider field. Twelve of the older group were selected for entry to the College late in 1932, while the remaining successful candidates entered at the beginning of 1933. The 1933 examination and selection were normal, in that 500 applicants from all parts of Australia sat for the entrance examination.

Those chosen for interview were required to pass a medical beforehand. The interview endeavoured to establish such intangible factors such as motivation, general awareness and adaptability. In reality it did no more than allow the Captain of the College to see whether he liked the cut of your jib and the Director of Studies to gauge whether the examination results matched the candidates potential for future learning.

Each State's local District Naval Officer also formed part of the interviewing panel. However ultimate selection for entry lacked something in the assessment of comparative ability. While this was never an issue for us, there was a last minute decision to increase our intake from twelve to fourteen to make up for the wastage in the 1933 entry. I was the 410th Cadet Midshipman to enter the Royal Australian Naval College since its establishment in 1913.

Victoria Barracks Melbourne is an historic blue stone building on St Kilda Road and where many a promising military service career has begun. On a hot January afternoon in 1934, after an exhausting overnight rail journey from Sydney, the buildings beauty and surroundings were lost on the eyes of the gathering thirteen year old boys. Each were more intent on apprehensively eyeing off each other and watching in awe as the six foot plus god-like figures, soon to be revealed as Chief Cadet Captain Crabb and Cadet Captain Brown, stood out front.

Both these men had been at the Royal Australian Naval College (RANC), HMAS *Cerberus*, Crib Point on Victoria's Westernport Bay for a year and three months. They were now in the third year of the four year course and were destined to reign over us for longer than any of us would care to remember.

Unlike these two Year Officer Cadet Captains, the building didn't leave a lasting impression on me. It was to be the centre of my life for the next four years and I simply accepted it for what it was, resolving that I would strive to do what others had done, as well, if not better. And so the slow process of turning out another Naval Officer to be, had began.

John Bell, Ian Cartwright, Tony Cooper, R A H 'Dusty' Millar and A W 'Bish' Savage were also in my entry. But today as the only surviving member, I'm in no hurry for the next reunion of Cook Year 1934.

On our second day all fourteen of us were beaten. Not that we'd done anything to deserve it. But as Chief Cadet Captain Crabb said,

"You're going to get a lot of this in the future, so you'd better get used to it."

The standard beating was six with the sole of what used to be called a sandshoe, or gym shoe, before jogging became popular.

There were six Cadet Captains altogether and their main responsibility was enforcing College discipline, reporting the more serious infractions such as breaking windows and damaging property to the two Year Officers, who in turn would parade the defaulters before the Commander. Heinous crimes such as ungentlemanly behavior would result in being paraded before the Captain of the College, who was also the Commodore Superintendent of Training, Flinders Naval Depot. This would usually lead to a letter being sent to the offenders parents strongly suggesting they remove their son forthwith — shades of naval cadet Archer Shee and the five shilling postal order expulsion back in 1908, which was later immortalized by Terence Rattigan in *The Winslow Boy*.

My attitude to College discipline was philosophical to say the least. In my grandfather's time sailors were flogged, in my father's time they were caned, and we were simply whacked. I looked forward to the day when I could put it all behind me as merely a necessary experience.

I'd been brought up on the shibboleth, "He who wishes to command must first learn to obey." I'd also been greatly influenced by the Greyfriars code expounded weekly in those admirable and well-written stories of English Public School life in the Gem and Magnet. Even today *Chums* and the *Boys Own Annual* have a place on my bookshelf and serve as a reminder of how gullible a teenage boy can be.

For six years my life was to be governed by alphabetical order. In a society where all members are equal there has to be some way of deciding who should be more equal than others. With all due deference to

George Orwell, the device of alphabetical order of surnames is probably human nature at its least inventive.

Nevertheless, constant repetition of lists of Cadet Midshipmen past and present served to give me a feel for the career on which I had embarked. This, coupled with the group photographs taken early on in initial years, made me feel that I had a common identity with more people than I'd ever been associated with previously.

Due to economic circumstances my parents had moved many times and I'd attended at least five different schools prior to Naval College. At each school I tended to establish a close rapport with my teachers rather than class members. My allegiances had been towards learning, to the detriment of friendships, with the exception of Olive Pine, who I was deeply in love with at age seven.

The only names I can recall from my school days are those of the local heroes — Ricky Creighton who broke a leg in a soccer match at Maroubra Junction, Chocca O'Donnell who lost the mile by a lap at Coogee Oval, the Lembke twins who were not identical, Max Wiber who swam and captained the school and Vic Jackson who first recognized my fierce determination to be a cricketer.

Two years ahead of me at College were G J B 'Buster' Crabb, Bill Dovers and H D (David) Stevenson; D C Wells was one year ahead. One year later came D A H 'Nobby' Clarke, Geoffrey Gladstone, R C Savage, D H Stevens and J P Stevenson; two years later Neil Mc Donald, J L W 'Red' Merson, R J Scrivenor and N H S 'Knocker' White.

However, friendships between Cadet Midshipmen weren't encouraged, especially between those of different ages. Every activity was fiercely competitive and each Cadet strove to shine in whatever field gave him an edge over his fellows.

Cook Year 1934, I'm standing at the back right with hands behind my back

As Australian Naval Officers were to be trained to be interchangeable with those of the Royal Navy, sport was to figure prominently during the next four years. Arriving at Westernport in the middle of the cricket season I was asked had I played cricket, and if so where did I bat, and did I bowl. My answer was predictable. Yes, I batted at No. 3 (being Bradman's number of course), and bowled occasionally. As the RANC First Eleven had already been selected from the two senior years left after the departure of the 1930 Entry there were no vacancies for anyone from the First Year to take part in representative matches. There was, however, a great domestic competition. Cadets from all years were divided into three watches, Red, White and Blue and allocation was made seemingly on alphabetical order of surnames. Being a W, I always ended up in Blue for no other reason. In cricket this worked to my advantage on one particular occasion.

At the end of my first term I had become disenchanted with both Cadet Captains responsible for the maintaining of the discipline of my year. One was a natural bully, and the older one a thoroughly unlikeable character who delighted in imposing upon us extra drill which occupied what spare time we might have had otherwise in our lunch hour. During the short leave in September I had considered the possibility of introducing some ground glass into their diet, but as this would have meant grinding up a couple of my favourite taws (marbles that is) I gave that idea away. My revenge came early on return to the College as in the first match of the Watch competition I bowled the older one, who was a left-handed batsman, around his legs with my third ball. I took 9 for 90 that day, a performance that guaranteed my place in the First XI in subsequent years.

Throughout 1935, 1936 and 1937 I continued to bat at No. 3, finally getting my colours for bowling. Two occasions at the crease stand out in my memory of those years. Playing against Scotch College on a veritable 'sticky' wicket having been sent in to bat, as No. 3 I remained undefeated at the end of our innings, a feat that I was not to repeat until I was 60 years of age. The other was a match against the Harlequins whose captain was Ben Barnett, then the Australian XI wicket keeper. With him behind the stumps advising me how to play every ball bowled by L O'B Fleetwood-Smith I made 50. I repeated this performance against the Harlequins on the same wicket unaided some 20 years later against some bowlers less renowned.

In 1934 at the start of the winter sports season the College Boxing Championships took place. Warrant Officer Monty Merton, a pugilist of some renown, was technically in charge of the whole event, plus the judge of the award for the best exponent of the art of boxing, the Shelley Cup. It wasn't a weight for age event like horse racing, but matching was decided by height and reach. In practice for the event David Stevenson and I met in the first round of our division. Being two years my senior, David left me in no doubt as to what was going to happen. It didn't turn out that way though. In the Red corner I won handsomely, and came into contention for the best exponent, only to be pitted against a bruiser from Second Year, Rex Thompson, a born street fighter with no knowledge of the Queensbury Rules. So I ended with a jolly good thumping. Thompson had left College by the start of the next boxing event, but I was never to win in the ring again. I always said, "That was my father's thing. I seemed to have more of the Hanford genes."

Year Officers and College Chief Petty Officers came in for special scrutiny and they in turn strove to exhibit excellence in their particular activities. One had been Chief Cadet Captain during his time at Jervis Bay, because as he said, he could spit the length of the cricket pitch, which was more than any of his contemporaries could do. Another had played scrum half for the Royal Navy, and as rugby was the only game for which we could produce more or less evenly matched sides, he was something of a living legend.

But it was in the classroom that competition was to be seen at its fiercest. With such small classes and teachers of genuine excellence the process of assessment was continuous. The range of subjects studied was inflexible. The curriculum was designed to ensure that when we came into competition with those who'd been through Dartmouth, we'd be able to stand our ground.

Of all the subjects it was navigation that captured my imagination. Hence at a very early stage I resolved to be Navigator. It was mere coincidence that the Commander of the College, the Executive Officer-in-Charge of the day-to-day activities was a Navigating Officer. But starting with him I traced the careers of other Navigators in the Royal Australian Navy to see if that was the pathway to the top.

The results were quite inconclusive. Of the ten RAN Officers who'd headed the Navy during those years, four were Gunnery Officers, three Navigators, one a Torpedo Officer, one an Observer and one a Salt Horse (non-specialist). Of the ten, only one was not a graduate of the RANC. A similar study of the Royal Navy produced much the same result. Nevertheless my mind was made up and I never deviated from my chosen course.

As the four-year course progressed those of us who'd firmly decided the type of career we intended to follow let the others know in unsubtle terms, mainly to ensure that they would choose something else when the time came.

For many years it had been customary for the graduating class to go to sea in the Australian Squadron for some months before proceeding to the Royal Navy for two years sea service as Midshipmen. Generally two cadets, who'd chosen to specialize as engineers, left at this stage to undergo a four-year course in Naval Engineering at Keyham, the UK Royal Naval School of Engineering. Along with doctors and dentists, engineers were considered to be among the intellectual elite of the Senior Service at the time, but their lack of executive status, together with a penchant for wearing oil stained cap covers and overalls on all but ceremonial occasions, hardly made their careers appealing to those with an itch to get to sea and get on with the job of command.

As the final year of College life approached there was the fear that if no volunteers for engineering were forthcoming, two would be drafted and it was quite clear that they'd come from the top, rather than the bottom of the class list.

It was during my third year at the Naval College that I had my first contact with members of the Naval Reserve. One of these had been a former Cadet Midshipman at the College. He'd had a burning desire to be an engineer, but amidst the fierce competition for places he'd missed out. Then when he was offered retirement, as Naval numbers had to be reduced for financial reasons (similar to the Royal Navy of the late 20s that went under the sobriquet of the Geddes Axe), he took the opportunity and decided to study law. He was now in practice as a barrister, but was keeping his hand in as a Saturday afternoon sailor at Rushcutters Bay. His friend, also a barrister and Naval Reservist, had a brother who was a serving officer in the RAN who'd survived the retrenchments. From these two I was to learn that the System had another side to it, one that I was to encounter more frequently the longer I served.

Briefly, it was the difference between being 'in' and being 'out', even though you might think you were still 'in'. And this had nothing to do with the venerable institution, the Naval and Military Club in Piccadilly called the 'In and Out' Club, because of the traffic direction notices at its front door.

The Confidential Report (Form S206 back then) and the Flimsy, so called because of the texture of the paper on which it was written, were the visible clues as to one's standing in the 'in' and 'out' stakes. The Confidential Report didn't have to be shown to an officer, nor discussed with him, but there was an obligation on reporting officers to underline in red those portions of a report considered unfavourable and which were within the officer's own power to correct. However many reporting officers couldn't face this prospect, so they relied on the device of 'damning with faint praise' instead.

The trouble within a small organization is that everyone knows, or thinks they do, everything about everyone else. The result was something akin to the chain of cane monkeys produced in the Philippines, where each is holding the hand of the lower down in order to give him an upward boost.

When the time came I took my position as Chief Cadet Captain, but vowed I'd never be caught in the mould of those before me and now hope that my form of leadership helped those below me.

On 10 December 1937 I graduated Dux of my year, receiving prizes for Grand Aggregate, the Otto Albert Memorial Prize for Seamanship and prizes for Mathematics, Physics, Chemistry, Engineering and Navigation. And most treasured, Colours for Cricket, as well as for Rugby. I also received the King's Medal. It was a Gold Medal awarded annually by the Sovereign to the Cadet Midshipman who during his period of training exhibited the most exemplary conduct, performance of duty, and good influence among his fellows.

The First XV Royal Australian Naval College – I'm the Captain 1937

In second year uniform with my mother Edna Wright

My mother, who was present at the Graduation Parade and Prize-giving Ceremony which followed, was told by Alan Saltmarsh, a Chief Petty Officer of some 30 years experience, that I was destined to become one of the Australian Navy's future Captains.

Years earlier she'd actually been quite miffed by the last sentence of my first quarterly report at the College when it read: 'He needs polishing.' Many years later on National television I remember remarking, "They polished me so well for three years and nine months after that that they gave me a gold medal."

However the four years spent at the RANC, (later dubbed the Crib Point Tech by a new breed of Naval Officers who formed the backbone of Australia's Fleet Air Arm), transformed me from a self-reliant boy prepared to follow the leadership of local heroes, into a self-reliant young man incapable of following any leadership but my own. The battle lines were drawn. The only activities that really seized my imagination were those in which I could take the lead.

I'd chosen a hard row to hoe, and in hoeing it made many people uncomfortable. As one of my Captains in a wartime destroyer said, "If I were to report on you now I'd say that you are insufferable; the only thing I couldn't say is that you are inefficient."

Or, as the officer appointing me after I'd completed my First Class Ship Course at the Royal Naval School of Navigation put it, "The trouble with you Wright is that you think you're always right, but you've gotta remember that sometimes it might be fifty-one to forty-nine, rather than ninety-five to five."

It took me nearly 30 years to work out that being right is no guarantee for success; in fact it's a non-attribute.

Those years also made me realize that there is an essential paradox in the selection and training of officers for the Armed Services. The qualities so admired in senior officers are fatal flaws in the character of junior officers. I've always been perplexed why this is so. At what stage does the metamorphosis of subordinates conforming in every aspect of conventional wisdom transform to the national leaders imaginative solutions take place? Perhaps what was said of one of the earlier Australian Naval Captains summarizes the position:

> *'As a Lieutenant he was hopeless; as a Lieutenant Commander barely adequate but somehow achieved promotion; as a Commander he was efficient; and as a Captain he was brilliantly successful.'*

Those were the days when the highest positions were occupied by Flag Officers on loan from the RN, whose expectations of capability by the native-born Australian officers was not highly regarded.

Speaking of ambition, even the late Earl Mountbatten of Burma said that it must never interfere with getting on with the job at hand.

This is all very well for those in positions of power, with influence over others in positions of even greater power, but the perspective is somewhat different for those on the lower rungs of an excessively long ladder, especially when it always appears to have more people than foreseeable vacancies.

One of the most popular toasts in Nelson's day was to a short and bloody war, which made prospects for promotion so much better for the survivors. However things never quite worked out that well, because in the aftermath of war came an inevitable reduction in the strength of the Fleet, a diminution in appropriations and career stagnation.

Looking back over the years I spent in the RANC I can honestly say that they were an improvement on what had gone before.

However one of the best outcomes from all the letters I'd written home, usually including details of practically every cricket event, was that my father, who numbered among his friends Mr. Garnsey, then coach of the NSW team in the Sheffield Shield Competition, arranged for me to have a net at the Sydney Cricket Ground in January 1938 before joining HMAS *Canberra*. I fronted up and spent the allotted time at the crease. On completion Garnsey's comment was, "These fellows bowl a lot faster than you are used to." From that moment on Bradman left me.

— 4 —

Sea Training

In 1938 our sea training began. The then Australian Squadron consisted of the 8 inch Gun Cruisers *Canberra* and *Australia,* the 6 inch Gun Cruiser *Sydney*, the Destroyers *Stuart, Waterhen* and *Vendetta* and the Sloops *Swan* and *Yarra*.

Cadet Midshipmen were only carried in HMAS *Canberra* where the gunroom was open, and three Sub-Lieutenants were aboard. Two were from the previous Cook Year at Naval College and four years older than the ten of us who'd survived the physical and academic rigors of our College Course.

Squadron ships had a fairly standard routine. The summer cruise was south to Hobart for the Regatta, the winter cruise was north to Hervey Bay and of course the ships were always in Melbourne late October, early November for the Melbourne Cup.

On Wednesday 26 January 1938 the *Canberra* was berthed at No.1 Buoy, Farm Cove, Sydney. Prior to joining the ship in the afternoon I'd the good fortune to be one of the million or so people to witness Australia's romantic history unfold in unforgettable pageantry through the city. Float after exquisitely decorated float depicted our march to Nationhood and Australia's 150th Anniversary.

This was only the beginning of three months of national celebrations that would last until 26 April.

Training with other Cook Year Cadet Midshipmen, I'm left carrying gun in HMAS Canberra 1938

Training with other Cook Year Cadet Midshipmen, I'm behind the gun in HMAS Canberra 1938

Five other excited Cadet Midshipmen and I joined the ship at 17:00. After unpacking we then witnessed the illumination of the city and harbour for the first time. It was breathtakingly spectacular. Multi-coloured lighting surrounded Farm Cove. Sydney Harbour Bridge was awash with flood lights, as were prominent city buildings in the background. As an impressionable young man it felt like this was an omen to my enlightened future.

Reality hit the following day as we gained elementary experience in shipboard life. Later in the day lectures in the Gunroom included allocation and description of our duties and responsibilities, followed by a tour of the ship, upper deck and bridge.

The *Canberra* was the Flagship, but with no separate sea-going stations for the Commodore Commanding and his staff.

Stepping onto the bridge my boyhood memories and dreams came flooding back. But this was real and excitement swirled in my stomach. I stood in awe as the Navigating Officer moved unrestricted from the-Pelorus to the Chart Table and back again. He appeared to be the only person who knew what was going on as he passed wheel and engine orders down the voice pipe. The Yeoman of Signals made great play with a telescope, interpreting the signals being sent from the Commodore Commanding, with flags being flown on the starboard yard arm being answered by the Captain with the answering Pendant on the port yard arm.

I couldn't help thinking that it would've been much easier if the Commodore had merely told the Captain, who was never more than ten feet away from him, what it was he had in mind. Or better still, left it all to the Navigating Officer who did what had to be done without any prompting. I was clearly going to be in for a hard time.

Each day consisted of various drills and exercises. Cadet Midshipman had been assigned an action station on the Ship's Watch and Quarter Bill. Many hours were spent closed up at our actions stations, but this served a dual purpose. Not only did we learn some useful on-the-job task, we also had the opportunity to listen to the men talking to one another. Rarely would any of them speak to us, or would we have been welcomed to converse with them. The gulf between us was as absolute as it had been in the days of Nelson.

My action station was in the 8 inch Transmitting Station where I presided over a magnificent contraption of rods, wheels and what looked remarkably like bicycle chains on which the range of an enemy ship, as deduced by a number of optical rangefinders located in different positions, would appear as perforations on a rolling paper. My task was to select the range most likely to represent the true range and follow the range changes to produce the rate of change of range from which it was possible for me to deduce whether the enemy ship was in fact altering course towards or away.

Above deck others were watching the enemy through binoculars detecting course alterations, but with the ships some fifteen miles apart the only things visible above the horizon were usually masts and funnels. Radar for ranging was not yet available in Australia.

The most uncomfortable part of my first sea journey was to be with the Officer-in-Charge of the Transmitting Station where I was stationed. Nothing was ever done or said to reveal the cause of his antagonism, nor did it manifest beyond the two of us. Even over the next quarter of a century our relationship remained 'correct'. I was always conscious that if he ever said anything about me to someone higher up the line, it wouldn't be to my credit and Naval service doesn't permit the luxury of avoiding some people forever.

On the afternoon of Sunday 30 January our ship, along with the *Sydney, Waterhen* and *Swan,* were open to the public. Other ships in the fleet had been open on Friday as part of Fleet Week and the national celebrations. I watched on and smiled as other small boys emulated my own childhood actions and wondered if they would follow in my footsteps.

Also taking part in Australia's 150th Anniversary of the first penal colony established at Port Jackson were a number of foreign ships. The cruisers *Milwaukee, Trenton, Memphis* and *Louisville* came from the United States, the sloop *Flores* from the Netherlands, the training cruiser *Jeanne d'Arc* and sloop *Rigault* de *Genouilly* from France and light cruiser *Raimondo Montecuccoli* from Italy. The Italy Captain was one of the finest ship handlers I'd ever seen.

Ship handling is something that many people can do; some of them well, but very few in a manner that sets them apart from all the rest. Unfortunately some stand out because they do it so badly — and those in this category rarely admit the fact to themselves or do anything to improve their performance, even simply practice.

Sure there are fundamental principles to follow, but from watching others one can always learn more. It's not a matter of speed. Going balls out for the wharf and slamming the engines astern at full speed is not the hallmark of a good ship handler, although there are times when it may look spectacular. Knowing what to do, when to do it and with the fewest possible engine movements ensures the best defense against Murphy's and O'Brien's Law. Murphy's Law states that if something can possibly go wrong it will. O'Brien's Law states that Murphy is an optimist!

There is a surprising belief that ship handling in confined waters requires special attributes that are not called into play in open waters. It's my experience that although the penalties for poor performance close to wharves may be more obvious, the results of poor handling at sea are usually quite disastrous.

The visiting international ships arrived and departed at various times during the next two weeks, but the pomp and ceremony always took pride of place. As they passed Garden Island and us, as the Flagship, cheering and a Royal Twenty-One Gun Salute were exchanged.

The afternoon of Tuesday 1 February 1938 was spent rigging the ship for the ball to be held on board to honour the visiting warships, but at the last moment arrangements were made to relocate to the ballroom of David Jones Ltd on George Street, Sydney. The emergency organization was carried out smoothly and all present had a wonderful time.

However the rain was so heavy the following day our cricket match between the *Canberra* crew and the New Zealand crew from *Achilles* was cancelled. It was my good fortune, not good cricket I might say, to be selected to represent our ship in the many cricket matches between visiting ships and our own. At every shore opportunity matches would be organized.

On Saturday 12 February 1938 I made my first of many appearances in the competition for the I Zingari (I Z) Shield which had been presented in 1929 'for competition amongst ships of the Royal Australian Navy'. From then on until the end of my active service career in 1962 I never failed to be selected to play cricket whenever the exigencies of the Service allowed.

As a Midshipman it was traditional that one be required to keep a Journal to be presented at the Examination in Seamanship for the rank of Lieutenant. My entry for Friday 4 March 1938 in Hobart reads:

'Three members of the Australian XI, Barnett, Barnes and Fleetwood-Smith were entertained in the Gunroom on completion of the days play in the match Australia versus Tasmania.'

open scuttles told their own story. Although none of my contemporaries were destined to reach Flag rank, I'm glad that those who were able to influence me did so, and have come to the realization that it is more important to train a naval officer's mind, than to belabour his backside.

Wastage rates in officers training are bound to be high given the very nature of the standard of dedication and achievement required to be a successful leader over a long period. However a better success to failure ratio is likely from entrants aged eighteen, given that those expected to serve for forty years and reach high rank will always be very small. It's paradoxical to find the Navy prepared to take its Lower Deck ratings in at a younger age than its officers, when traditionally the reverse has been the case.

Anyway, at the end of our training period in HMAS *Canberra* we all sat for our Midshipman exams and passed. Following the established practice, those heading to executive officer careers left Australia for service with the Royal Navy in their Mediterranean Fleet ships.

Setting sail for Malta in P & O's *Cathay,* I said goodbye to my family and my grandmother for the last time. It was May 1938.

— 5 —

Malta Bound

Although P & O's *Cathay* was an ageing ship, shipboard life was still grand and an extremely comfortable form of travel in 1938, once one accepted that fresh water was limited. Even the hot baths, run with such care by the Goanese bath stewards, were drawn from seawater that had been through the ship's condensers. Meals were excellent and the drinks, once we'd cleared the Australian coast, were within our means, which were not all that lavish.

Somehow we'd all managed to do what was regarded as impossible in those days, and that was to live on a Naval Officer's pay.

Leaving Sydney the ship rolled its way to Hobart, much to the delight of one of our party who'd been smitten by a local girl he'd met during the summer cruise. (Incidentally, they later married and lived happily till their divorce many years later!)

Port calls were made in Melbourne and Adelaide before going on to Fremantle, where the family of our latest man to join entertained us all for the day. His father was the local schoolmaster at Kalamunda, then the epitome of an outback town to me, though in reality it was suburban to the locals.

Then it was off across the Indian Ocean to Colombo. Also on board were a group of young Britons, taking mid term leave from postings in India to do the round trip from Bombay. Their presence gave us a cruise ship mentality that wasn't entirely appreciated by the older element, particularly the first class passengers, but was accepted by the Ship's Officers. The Lascar seamen and the Goanese stewards took it all in their stride.

Our wildest excesses were checked by the presence of a Lieutenant of the Royal Navy returning to England after posting with the RAN. Thankfully he was preoccupied with a beautiful young lady who happened to be travelling in the wrong end of the ship, as far as he was concerned. As we spent a great deal of our time down her end and she spent a great deal of her time in our end, the balance was kept quite admirably.

I had met this girl before when she'd stayed with her sister and husband, a serving RAN Officer, and on one memorable occasion after we'd danced at the Combined Fleet Ball, she'd persuaded me to help her finish a bottle of champagne which had been given to her by a French Officer, who she didn't want to offend by leaving it untouched. As it would've been very ungallant of me to refuse, I agreed. You can imagine my surprise when the bottle turned out to be a Magnum. I floated down to Man-o-War Steps in the early hours of the morning, drifted in and out of the boat, hovered up the gangway and eventually lifted my weightless body into my hammock. Next morning I tried unsuccessfully to haul myself out of my hammock, instead hitting the iron deck with a thud that brought me quickly back to reality. Ever since I've had a healthy respect for bubbly, although having champagne tastes on a beer budget has certainly helped.

Nothing can replace that first sight and smell of the mysterious East. In the light of dawn, before the steam rises and obscures the view, and the breeze that brings the vegetation smells of the land, one can believe all the romantic rubbish that has ever been written. Once ashore the quixotic evaporates and reality exposes the tremendous gulf that divides the haves from the have-nots.

For the next two years I was to have every illusion I'd ever nurtured about the British Raj shattered completely. It's amazing that by the time the events of World War II had engulfed that part of Asia and was overrun by Japanese forces there was any goodwill left for Britain to enjoy.

Nevertheless, that day in June 1938 I spent as any pukka sahib should, haggling with the shopkeepers and buying nothing, pre-lunch drinks at GOH and a drive in the afternoon to enjoy tea at the Galle Force Hotel, before returning to use the shore to ship part of the ticket so thoughtfully provided by P & O for our stay.

In Bombay we lost our leisure hour companions who were replaced by a few who'd completed their tour in India and didn't qualify for a passage home by troop ship. Strangely we never got to know any of them, as they seemed to live completely within themselves. It wasn't until I reached England myself, that I realized how depressed they all were to be going back to Balham or Tooting and a meal at the Lyons Corner House in the Strand, a far cry from the elegance of their life in India with servants and the ability to convince one another that they really counted for something.

Aden depressed me. The sight of endless columns of wretched human beings staggering up inclined planes with baskets of coal to fuel the furnaces of grubby tramp steamers flying tattered Red Ensigns, brought home the immense difference between those like myself who could aspire to make something of life, and those for whom there would simply be no opportunity, not only for themselves, but for their children and even children's children.

The passage through the Suez Canal provided an excuse for staying up all night — a must for every traveller on their first occasion.

Port Said was an introduction to the erotic literature of the 19th Century, in which the heroes were always Naval Lieutenants called George and did things to pure young girls, the daughters of clergymen, in hansom cabs while driving through Hyde Park. And the pictures — no account of Port Said would be believable if one did not refer to postcard sellers and get dog-eared wares, all portraying plump ladies of indeterminable age and origin, run off in a job lot for the Paris Centennial Exposition 1889. They had little chance of making a sale but deserved full marks for their energy and persistence. All this was prior to the pre-drug scene, when sex was the ultimate experience for the young and we all believed that one day we'd see the lady and the donkey.

Five weeks to the day after sailing from Sydney, *Cathay* arrived in Malta. During the early hours of Thursday 30 June, I joined HMS *Malaya,* which hadn't had any Australian Midshipmen since those who entered the RANC in the year I was born.

With the threat of war ever present in Europe during 1938 and 1939 my sporting activities in the normal course of events had to take a low priority when compared with the development of my chosen career. Arriving in Malta the last day of June marked the middle of the short cricket season for which representative teams had already been chosen. There was no opportunity for any colonial to break in. Moreover the lack of cricket-playing countries bordering on the Mediterranean meant that the only venues with cricket grounds were Gibraltar, Malta and Alexandria. Opportunities for playing were few and far between.

Although British ships of the time were commissioned in a home-port and paid off after a set period, there were always a few with long memories who could recall the outstanding incidents, real or imaginary, from previous commissions. These stories were told and retold during night watches, on long boat trips, or when closed up for long periods at action stations, forming a body of folklore which inspired those who came after, to equal or outdo the feats of those who went before.

We learnt very early on that the RN Midshipmen who were serving in *Malaya* had been warned that their lives were going to change dramatically once the Australians arrived. We also learnt that only three of our eight were to stay with the ship and foolishly imagined that the possibility of a solid body of eight was too much for any RN ship to handle.

The reality of the situation was of course simply a matter of numbers a Gunroom could accommodate, especially to be able to handle a proper blend of theoretical training and on-the-job experience in order to produce officers qualified to be Lieutenants in the future.

To this end my five compatriots were first rescheduled to join HMS *Repulse*, but this ship's future in the Mediterranean fleet was in doubt. Instead they joined HMS *Sussex*, but unfortunately this would give them no different experience from that which they'd already gained in HMAS *Canberra*. Finally they were posted to HMS *Hood* and from all accounts enjoyed their time in the ship known throughout the Navy as 'Mighty'.

The training and employment of midshipmen in the Royal Navy varied immensely from ship to ship and depended to a large extent upon the officer designated by the Captain to take charge, the so-called 'Snotties Nurse'.

I was fortunate enough to have one of the most able Navigating Officers that the Royal Navy had produced. As soon as I was able to do so I became his 'Tanky', which meant that each morning and evening at sea and out of sight of land I prepared the programme for the star sights and recorded the times of the observations. I shared the responsibility for winding the chronometers and comparing their rates and for ensuring that the Wireless Office received accurate time checks. I reported every night Chronometers wound to the Sergeant Major Royal Marines who in turn reported this to the Captain at 21:00. In harbour I corrected the charts. Occasionally I was allowed to look on while the great man planned an ocean passage, an approach to anchorage, or a harbour entrance. As he was the only officer in the ship who could carry out the more difficult manoeuvres, like taking station in the line and turning in the wake of the next ahead without losing station, he was an ideal teacher of the art of ship handling. Moreover, he was a man of wonderful temperament, yet he was destined to become the most pathetic of Naval Officers, being a passed-over two and a half twice, although he continued serving right through World War II.

Service in the Mediterranean Fleet during peacetime was regarded as the best possible preparation for war. While the China Station had quite a reputation for gracious living at reasonable cost, and the Americas and West Indies Squadron was the place for those with private incomes and social aspirations, especially the possibility of marrying the daughter of a wealthy British industrialist, or a young American heiress, the Mediterranean was where tactical doctrines were tested and where the navies of Italy, France and Spain were known to be seen to challenge British supremacy.

Religiously we put to sea to refight the Battle of Jutland, with the object of achieving a tactical victory. We'd prepare to bring the enemy to a night action with the forces left after the day action, hurriedly reorganized so that every torpedo would be fired and just sufficient shells as were necessary to send all the enemy ships to the bottom would be expended.

Attacks by aircraft from our one and only carrier HMS *Glorious,* were also a feature of major exercises, but as night operations from carriers were somewhat hazardous it became fairly easy to predict when these were likely to happen.

Motor torpedo boats also figured predominantly in the scenarios for Mediterranean Fleet Exercises. As we had very few of these it was often necessary for fast picket boats from the capital ships to represent them. This sometimes gave the exercises an air of unreality, as their use was limited to calm water in the vicinity of feet anchorages. Nevertheless the objective was clear. The Mediterranean Fleet would assuredly destroy the Italian Navy if they strayed outside their own coastal waters to seek a showdown.

Exercises were only a part of life in the Mediterranean Fleet. As well as showing the flag, ships were required for all manner of purposes in support of British policy. I was fortunate to be involved in some that would not normally have come the way of an Australian leading an ordinary life in his own country. To me in my late teens, they were adventures.

My first adventure was during HMS *Malaya's* visit to Venice. Although the ship was anchored seven miles from the city I made sure that every minute I could get ashore would be spent exploring and absorbing the atmosphere. It's amazing how many hours can be spent over a plate of spaghetti and one glass of wine in St Mark's Square, the parade of people providing an ever-changing show.

The following is an extract from my Journal:

24 July 1938

Venice, famous in antiquity for its position of a wealthy and prosperous republic now pours its wealth into the coffers of Il Duce. Gone is the oldest republic the world has ever known, gone are those ships which made this proud city one of the greatest trading centres, gone are the old masters, but something remains. It is to be found, not in the people, who are modern, nor in their ways of life, but in the old buildings, standing as they stood many hundreds of yeas ago, in the paintings, all the remains of an art, not lost, but changed out of all proportion.

Along the canals one sees the sights always attributed to Venice, and Venice alone, the gondolas, identical with those used years before, plying their way under bridges, outwardly ancient, in reality a product of modern engineering and science. But the average conception of Venice lacks one thing – reality. Behind the outward glamour there are dangers, only fully realized by the inhabitants, from the water surging around and under the city, dangers from disease and decay. In time, perhaps, Venice will fade, as did the old republic.

Just walking in Venice is probably the most enjoyable experience for the visitor. Inevitably I found myself in unfamiliar surroundings with absolutely no idea how to get back to the Square in time to catch the last boat back to the ship. Fortunately my plight was recognized by a student keen to try out his command of the English language. On the way back to the landing he told me of Adolf Hitler's recent visit to Venice and how Mussolini had endeared himself to his fellow northern Italians by how he had introduced the German dictator to them. He'd used as many superlatives of which the Italian language is capable, to make Hitler look ridiculous. Hitler and his party, whose knowledge of Italian was rudimentary if anything, interpreted the applause that greeted Mussolini's performance as being positively directed towards them and the purpose of their visit. Their obvious pleasure at being insulted so subtly added to the Venetian's delight and the whole process fed upon itself. The Rome-Berlin axis at that time was in pretty poor shape.

The highlight of our stay was provided by William Gower, who gave a cocktail party at his canal side home in honour of Lady Iris Mountbatten. His daughter, then aged eighteen, and some of her friends were to be there, so it was considered appropriate to invite the Gunroom Officers. I turned up dressed in my best brown suit from Marcus Clarke, which in the 30s offered the very real advantage of payment by installments for its goods. The English midshipmen, who normally went ashore in what were known as ‘dog-robbers’ (clothes that in most English households would have been used to line the dog’s basket), were there in their impeccable grey pinstriped, double-breasted suits bought on tick from Gieves. And the girls simply had to be seen to be believed. The essence of elegance, they were dressed in the height of fashion and unbelievably blasé.

I realized then what made Australians in the company of Englishmen stand out like sore thumbs. It was the clothes we wore. The three-piece suits topped by the inevitable Akubra hat were as distinctive as if we had been stark naked, streaked with white clay and carrying a throwing stick. Indoors, with the hat parked as far as possible from the incredulous gaze of late arrivals, the short back and sides haircut did nothing to provide anonymity. I decided that attack was the only method of survival.

I approached the most unapproachable looking girl in the room and straightaway asked her who the fellow inappropriately dressed in a dinner jacket making such a fool of himself at the other end of the room might be.

“That,” she said in a voice that could only have been developed at Roedean, “is Noel Coward.”

“Oh,” I replied, “Do you know him?”

“Oh yes, we’re on the stage together.”

Now my mother had been on stage. One of our family photographs showed her at age twelve dressed in loose fitting trousers, blouse and clay pipe, taken at a time when she was doing a monologue at the Broken

Hill School of Arts. Needless to say I didn't reveal to my companion the limit of my acquaintances with thespians and the fact that I accepted her statement is such a matter of fact way, established a bond between us. I was to learn much later that when there are no naval lieutenants named George in the immediate vicinity, eighteen-year-old English girls are apt to relax and become quite friendly.

She proceeded most discreetly, to put me in the picture as to whom was who, and I was duly impressed to be in the same room as Douglas Fairbanks Senior and his wife, the former Lady Ashley, Ivor Novello and Princess Alexandrine, the sister of the Duchess of Kent.

The evening was so successful that the Gunroom invited Miss Gower and her friends on board for pre-lunch drinks the next day. Such a coup couldn't be kept a secret. Before we knew where we were, we had so many friends among the Wardroom Officers that we were in danger of being overwhelmed.

Finally the matter was resolved to everyone's satisfaction. The Gunroom was given the use of the Quarterdeck to entertain its guests; the Captain, the Commander and all the Officers who had anything remotely to do with Midshipmen were invited. The spirits consumed were not debited against the personal accounts of the Sub-Lieutenant and those Midshipmen over the age of twenty who were normally the only Gunroom Officers allowed strong drink. Noel Coward and Douglas Fairbanks Senior played their celebrity parts to perfection. Never since Trafalgar, had Midshipmen been held in such high regard.

All this only convinced me that sooner, rather than later, I must do something to pep-up my appearance in plain clothes. This took some time to do, but in the doing Gieves came to the fore.

Questioned with, "Do you require a Midshipman's suit or something more distinguished?" the answer was a double-breasted grey flannel suit with a brown pork-pie hat. This to top up a pair of brown leather hand-made shoes at a cost of four pounds which was eventually paid some years later due to the uncertainty of mails to Malta from the outside world.

However we were soon to be involved in more serious business. While *Malaya* had been in dockyard at Malta, the Midshipmen had been put ashore with the Royal Marines at the Ricasoli Rifle Range for training in the use of small arms and infantry minor tactics. The situation in Palestine had been going from bad to worse since early July 1938. In an effort to relieve the British troops stationed in the Middle East, the Royal Navy had undertaken to keep a ship in Haifa and provide assistance to the Palestinian Police, officered largely by Englishmen on contract in keeping order.

— 6 —

Palestine

On 22 August1938 HMS *Malaya* arrived at Haifa to relieve HMS *Repulse*, to take part in the military control of Palestine. The main advantage in using sailors in an aid to the civil power role is that they are traditionally here today and gone tomorrow. This made it much easier for them to be impartial, than for the soldiers who come to be identified, rightly or wrongly, more with one side or the other in local disputes. Not that it was easy for us to sort out who was against whom in these particular circumstances either.

Jews generally were not the destructive element. The main trouble appeared to be generated from outside Palestine. The rebel leader in the north, Abu Dabi, was likely to be more hostile to Paris, remote from or lukewarm to the cause than to Jews. The British administration was the main target and all terrorist actions were aimed at convincing the people that Britain was no longer capable of guaranteeing their safety.

Simply by its presence the ship demonstrated that Britannia really did rule the waves. The ships men and Royal Marines provided armed parties to cope with emergencies requiring field tactics, mortar crews, lorry drivers and guards to back up the RACS and demolition parties to assist the Royal Engineers.

My particular function was in one of the search parties looking for weapons and explosives. Provided we acted as though we meant business, our presence served to deter those who may have been persuaded to take up arms against us. Lest it should be thought that the fate of the British Empire rested in the hands of an eighteen-year-old Midshipman, I must say that a member of the Palestinian Police was at my side whenever I set up a random search activity and he always controlled the when and where of these searches.

We won some and we lost some. Haifa was the magnet that attracted the residents of the outlying villages like iron filings. Each car, bus and lorry coming into the city was crammed to capacity with humanity, produce and animals not in any particular order of preference. By setting up roadblocks and searching all vehicles and persons we made it more difficult for those who were trying to get weapons into the city. But it was from information received that we expected to get our best results.

Once I was reliably informed that two revolvers would be handed over to men required to carry out some special task and that this would be done at prayers. Setting up a surveillance operation of all the mosques throughout the day was a fairly formidable task, allowing for the fact that the devout Muslims offer up prayers on at least eight separate occasions daily. This kept me and my search party fully occupied, particularly as it achieved nothing. I have often wondered what really changed hands somewhere else while we were so busy. There is no doubt that we were set up.

During a house search in an Arab settlement to which we had been directed, a pipe bomb was thrown over the fence. Fortunately it failed to explode, but it made life very difficult for the residents who had a hard time convincing us that they weren't somehow involved.

One of the main tasks given to the ship was to establish a camp at Lydda, a railway junction about seventy miles south of Haifa, and to provide a Royal Marine detachment to defend the station and its operation there by helping to keep the Palestinian Railroad open for traffic.

As our Royal Marine detachment only had three officers it was decided that midshipmen should be added to the strength to carry out the duties of Officer-in-Charge of the Station Guard by day and Orderly Officer. Because midshipmen in tropical dress wore no distinguishing badges of rank it was impossible for the uninitiated to distinguish the OIC from the members of the guard. That's how I came to be unofficially and locally commissioned a Second Lieutenant in the Royal Australian Marine Corps (non-existent) when I arrived at Lydda on 9 September 1938, after a five hour journey in what was called an armoured trolley, essentially two Ford trucks with metal trays bolted together back-to-back and fitted with four train wheels.

Although I was wearing a steel helmet throughout the journey I kept my head close to one of the many bullet holes in the side, exercising the popularly held belief that bullets never passed through the same hole twice. Ambush usually threatened after derailment, so the main task of those in the trolley was to watch the line ahead for obstacles, or missing rails and to keep an eye on the approaching terrain for the sort of place where one could expect trouble. Although a bomb on the line on the way up had delayed the trolley, its downward journey was without incident.

During the two weeks spent at Lydda, events in Europe were rapidly reaching a crisis and the issue of the Sudeten Germans in Czechoslovakia had been brought to a head with a speech at Nuremberg on 12 September. This led to a headlong rush to Munich. With what was taking place in Czechoslovakia; it's little wonder that historians have ignored our activities at an obscure railway junction in Palestine.

Neville Chamberlain and Lord Runciman took over the world stage and with the help of Daladier, the French Premier, acted out the drama that was to have such an impact on the whole world for the remainder of the 20th Century.

On 23 September 1938 HMS *Malaya* was relieved by the light cruiser HMS *Penelope*, taking over duties in the town of Haifa. The *Malaya* sailed to join the greater part of the fleet at Alexandria. The overnight voyage was not without its own dramatic overtones.

Shortly after midnight we darkened ship, increased speed to the maximum available, about twenty-four knots, and began to zig-zag at the same time heading for a dawn rendezvous with the destroyers *Greyhound* and *Glowworm*. For me this caused the greatest inconvenience, as I was sleeping on a canvas stretcher on the quarterdeck, when rudely wakened by a shower of hot soot from the funnel landing on me. Vibrations across the deck also made further sleep impossible. I had no choice but to retreat below decks until it was time to close up to Day Action Stations.

The next few days at Alexandria were hectic. While Hitler was delivering his ultimatum to Czechoslovakia, the ships of the Fleet were preparing for war. We fused ammunition, 4 inch, 6 inch and 15 inch, and loaded the two-pounder pom-pom and the 0.5 inch magazines. We drilled the guns crews and went to sea, shooting at targets. Other ships sailed off to their war stations.

On 30 September 1938 it was all over. Chamberlain, Hitler, Daladier and Mussolini signed the agreement under which the German demands were met and the new borders of Czechoslovakia were established. While Chamberlain was proclaiming peace in our time I wrote in my journal:

'The crisis has passed, the threat of war has been removed – but how far? The Czechs have been martyred and the methods of arbitration have scored a victory over armed forces. But how long will it last? The bluff, if it was such, has succeeded and in order that it may not succeed again we must be firm or we too may be pressed.

We still have the colonies – Hitler needs colonial expansion; so the time may come when we find ourselves in a position paralleled to that of Czechoslovakia. When and if that time comes there can be no middle course.'

It's perhaps as well that Midshipmen of the Navy are not given the job of running the country.

After Munich it was a case of business as usual, with two or three days each week being spent at sea on the individual exercises which were so essential to maintaining the efficiency of the weapons systems and the group exercises by which cooperative skills were developed.

Some idea of the problems we faced can be gathered from the fact that after what was considered to be a particularly effective demonstration of the ability of our close range armament, supplemented by fire from Lewis guns, to engage aircraft pressing attacks on the ship only twenty-two hits resulted from what I then considered to be an enormous expenditure of ammunition.

It was during this time that the British began to take a serious interest in the capabilities of the Egyptian forces. HMS *Elgin*, a minesweeper was transferred on loan to the Egyptian Government and was manned largely by Egyptian Officers and men. Its Captain was one of the liveliest characters to be found in the pre-war British Mediterranean Fleet. Lieutenant Commander J E Slaughter, Royal Navy, known to all his contemporaries as 'Jacky' and never referred to as anything else by the irreverent Midshipman to whom he was to impart so much seaman-like knowledge and good commonsense about getting things done on board one of His Majesty's ships.

The Navy also provided some much-needed support for the Egyptian Artillery manning the shore batteries. I spent a day at sea in His

Majesty's tug *Roysterer* under fire as the artillerymen came to grips with the problems of trying to hit moving targets at sea from gun emplacements ashore.

But all was not work in those heady days after Munich. A colleague and I were fortunate in being able to accept the invitation of the Australian Trade Commissioner to visit Cairo for a few days. As it was Ramadan the only restrictions placed on us were not to use the driver of the car placed at our disposal after 17:00, as the fasting was likely to impair his judgment as the day progressed. Otherwise we pretty well had the run of the place.

One of the most beautiful and intelligent girls it has ever been my good fortune to meet, guided us through the Pyramids of Giza, saving us from the interminable tourist bit of Mr. Macgregor and all that which is probably still par for the course. The only fault that I could find with the hospitality of the Trade Commissioner was that they expected such a paragon to actually work in the office for the rest of the day and not stay with us for the full gamut of the Sporting Club and Shepperds. Although as an Egyptian she would merely have been a spectator to our indulgences at least until sundown.

With the easing of international tension in the Mediterranean came the need to return to Malta, the base and refitting port of the Fleet.

The population of the island had been hard-hit by the absence of the large ships for the best part of three months and as they carried all the midshipmen in the Fleet, two particular young ladies had had nothing for their confessions for quite some time. Some midshipmen to be sure, were having interesting discussions with the Principal Medical Officer and others were bemoaning the fact that Alexandria nightclub ladies, probably the youngest and prettiest in the world, had long ago decided that Midshipmen were all alike: 'All prick and no bloody money'.

But one thing was for sure — life was never dull. No sooner had we returned to Malta, than Mustafa Kemal Ataturk, President of the Turkish Republic, died. He'd done so much to restore the prestige of his country and the morale of his people after World War I. and HMS *Malaya* was to fly the flag of the Commander-in-Chief, Royal Navy in the Mediterranean, Admiral Sir Dudley Pound.

— 7 —

Ataturk

We left Malta Tuesday evening 15 November 1938, arriving at Istanbul the following Friday morning. Later that day the escorting fleet accompanying the Turkish Battleship *Yavuz* (the former German ship *Goeben* of World War I) had grown considerably. There were two other Turkish destroyers and two submarines, the *Moekba* from Russia, Greek destroyer *Hydra,* Romanian destroyer *Regina Maria,* German cruiser *Emden* and the next day the French cruiser *Emile Bertine,* which had steamed at 28 knots from Toulon. You may think that nine days was a long time to get ships to Istanbul from ports in the Mediterranean, but when you consider the political situation that brought about the Munich Agreement of 29 September 1938, now acknowledged as *'one of the more infamous acts in history'*, it shows the truth of what I wrote in my journal as an eighteen-year-old Australian midshipman at the time.

Our journey to Istanbul took us through the Dardanelles in daylight. Having been brought up on a regular diet of Anzac Day, Villers Brettoneux and the great days of the men of the 35th and 53rd, it's little wonder that I wrote in my journal some banal observations which bear little resemblance to what was in fact an ill-conceived and poorly executed military operation, which has as its only lasting result, the determination on the part of all Australian politicians, that never again would Australian soldiers be committed to military operations under the command of British officers.

Our arrival off Istanbul in the early morning, presented us with one of the world's most magnificent sights — the Mosque of San Sophia (Hagia Sophia) with its four minarets seemingly suspended in the clouds — reminiscent of the Hollywood scenery that passed for Baghdad in the extravaganzas made famous first by Douglas Fairbanks Senior and then Errol Flynn. It was many years before I was to go to Baghdad and see it as it really is, utterly flat and featureless.

I counted it a great honour to be selected as a member of the Ceremonial Party for Mustafa Kemal Ataturk's funeral. The Ceremonial Party consisted of one hundred and twenty Seamen and Stokers, sixty Royal Marines, ten Officers and the massed bands of the Royal Navy's 1st Battle Squadron from *Warspite, Barham* and *Malaya*.

The funeral was in phases. First the lying in state at the old Sultan's Palace in Istanbul, then the sea saga in which the coffin was transferred to a destroyer.

The *Yavuz* fired a salute of 101 guns and the foreign ships each 21 guns. The destroyer at slow speed passed the line of ships and transferred Ataturk's coffin to the quarterdeck of *Yavuz* that was covered in a mass of flowers.

Next was the slow eastward sea passage towards Kartal in the Gulf of Izmit in line ahead in the Sea of Marmara. On a signal from *Yavuz* the foreign ships of the escort, with *Malaya* leading, increased speed to 16 knots coming abreast the coffin to port, officers saluting, and in succession altering course 180 degrees to starboard.

Leaving the evening of Saturday 19 November, the funeral train was ahead of our Ceremonial Party train from Istanbul. It took 19 hours on the 250 odd mile journey to Ankara. We made many stops along the way as people had come to the railway line from miles around to pay their last respects.

At 08:00 on the Monday the Royal Naval Detachment left our quarters to march into the city. We joined the other units and waited for the arrival of the Turkish Artillery who would lead the procession.

Two hours later in the snow, the foreign detachments moved off in alphabetical order in Turkish. We passed the coffin marching with arms reversed coming to a halt about a mile further on.

Then after a short interval the entire cortege moved at the slow march for about three miles to the Museum. We were the only group to march with arms reversed. As the coffin, carried on a gun carriage drawn by Turkish soldiers, passed we rested on our arms reversed. This alone endeared us to the hearts of all present.

The arrangements for Ataturk's funeral in Ankara were impressive. Ankara in 1938 was rather like Canberra in 1960, not really complete or sure of its identity as a national capital. The intention to honour the founder of the modern Turkish nation by housing his remains in a mausoleum was a decision easily taken, but until the mausoleum was built an alternative resting place was found in the Museum.

The British Empire representative at the funeral was Field Marshal Lord Birdwood, who had opposed Ataturk in the Gallipoli Campaign. But he was now a frail old man unable to march. Nevertheless in paying his final tribute from a balcony opposite the Museum, he exemplified the desire of the British people to keep Turkey on side.

As Lord Birdwood was not fit enough to attend the reception held the day after the funeral, the Commander-in-Chief Mediterranean took his place. This meant another day in Ankara for us, and a chance to see something of the city.

We were billeted in the newly completed building at the Institute, which was equivalent to a modern university. It so happened that our closest neighbours were the German officers and cadets from the training ship *Emden*. It fell to me to issue an invitation for a representative party of them to meet us for drinks after dinner. During the course of the ensuing entertainment I was treated to some interesting sidelights to German philosophy. In answer to the question, "Wasn't it wonderful the way in which the Fuhrer stopped the war?" it was necessary to reply that perhaps Mr. Chamberlain also helped. It was clear that the majority of the young officers had no time for the few of their seniors who were openly members of the Nazi Party.

As the only Australian living that was part of the official mourning party, I'm welcomed to attend the Ataturk Memorial on 10 November each year to address Turkish children from Sydney.

In the months that passed I corresponded on a casual basis with one of the German cadets, until it became quite obvious that his letters were being written under control. Perhaps the best exchange was at Christmas when we talked of the social aspects of our respective lives.

— 8 —

1939

While definitely a momentous year in world history, 1939 was to also prove a rewarding one for me professionally.

Throughout December 1938 I was playing rugby three games a week for various under 21 teams, earning the approbation of my Captain who was being dragged along to the Marsa Ground by his young daughter. He was either a devotee to the game or to me; I never discovered which, although a few years later I was to meet her again. She was by then a WREN Plotter, knitting furiously well while at the same time manoeuvring enemy forces that I was trying to annihilate during a tactical exercise at HMS *Dryad*, the Navigation School at Southwick outside Portsmouth.

Needless to say she didn't give me a second glance, so it must've been the rugby after all. However, her father did give me a crash hot report when he left the ship to return to England early in 1939.

'An outstanding young officer. Keen and zealous for the Service. Physically well built. Good power of Command. Keen on games and keeps himself fit. He is good at Rugger.'

And this is something no naval officer can ever do without. No matter how many good reports are made, it only needs one bad one to blight a promising career.

Anyway apart from what I'd always considered a to be a 'brief encounter' during my short visit to Cairo to renew acquaintance with the Assistant Trade Commissioner for Australia in Egypt, love was the last thing on my mind throughout 1939 and preparations for the coming war. I had decided that there was no way in the name of good sense would I ever take seriously the prospect of marriage should I be involved in war. I'd seen enough of World War I couples who'd been devastated by the loss of a partner.

Early in January I was appointed to HMS *Cossack,* a Tribal Class Destroyer commanded by a Captain. Not only was this unusual, but the whole concept of the tribal class was unusual.

Up until this time Destroyer Flotillas in the Royal Navy had consisted of eight ships of more or less similar construction — the dissimilarities were often associated with the yards in which they happened to be built — and one slightly larger ship, the Flotilla Leader with a Captain in Command and carrying most of the Flotilla Staff Officers, specialists in Navigation, Gunnery, Torpedo, Anti-Submarine and Supply.

Command of the ships of the Flotilla was exercised largely by Lieutenant Commanders with no specialist qualifications, the salt horses. And in some cases Lieutenants who'd come to the fore in some particular way, usually by doing well at the Command Examinations held from time to time.

Many of the prewar destroyer captains were characters, who could boast that the last time they had set foot on board a ship with a wooden quarterdeck was when they were Midshipmen in the fleet, as I was then.

Some of them made a deliberate habit of not reading correspondence and their abhorrence of paperwork meant that someone, usually the most junior executive officer, the Sub-Lieutenant, with the aid of an untrained seaman writer, carried the burden of the administrative effort.

The Engineer ran his own show, with the help of a trained stoker, who usually went on to become a Warrant Officer, or in some rare cases a Sub-Lieutenant.

Although the captains were not the most elusive fellows, there was no doubt about their seamanship and ship handling. In my three and a half months destroyer time I was to hear more short blasts on the siren than in my entire Naval career, spanning nearly thirty years, which included Service at sea in all the world's oceans.

However, HMS *Cossack* was an altogether different kettle of fish-heads, as someone in the Fleet Air Arm would have put it.

As we had a Captain our ship was a Divisional Leader, with a narrow black band around the forward funnel and some of the Flotilla staff on board. I was particularly fortunate in that the officer in charge of my instruction was Lieutenant Commander V G Begg, the Gunnery Officer, who was destined to become First Sea Lord and serve with distinction as an Admiral of the Fleet. I can honestly say that there was nothing in his demeanour at that time to show that he was destined for great things beyond the fact that he shared with me a hearty dislike of the First Lieutenant, the same critical approach to the Captain's ship handling and genuine amazement at the antics of our No.2, Lieutenant G D Pound, whose father just happened to be the Commander-in-Chief Mediterranean Fleet.

I'll never forget the morning when, after a particularly exhausting set of night exercises, a signal was received from HMS *Warspite*, the Fleet Flagship, for Lieutenant Pound to 'report on board immediately'. George had just got his head down after completing the Middle Watch and was in no mood to get a harangue from his father on the presumptuous way in which he'd decided to get married as a young Lieutenant still making his way up the naval ladder, instead of waiting until he was at least a Lieutenant Commander, sure of first up promotion to Commander.

It took a direct order from the Captain to get George out of his bunk and into the boat that was waiting alongside to take him to the Flagship. Imagine the horror on the faces of those assembled to see him on his way when he turned up wearing the Gunner T's uniform jacket. As he slipped over the side he said, "If my father persists on treating me like a Warrant Officer, the least I can do is look like one."

We never did find out what George had for breakfast, but thereafter his wife was always on hand when Lady Pound and others in the social set did their thing in HMS *Aberdeen*, which doubled as the Commander-in-Chief's yacht. Those were the days in which rank certainly had its privileges.

Early in 1939 I took part in the important ritual of the Combined Fleet Exercises. This was an annual event that brought together the light grey ships of the Mediterranean and the dark grey ships of the Home Fleet. It also gave further opportunities to try out new tactical concepts, but generally resulted in a refight of the Battle of Jutland with the objective of gaining a clear cut naval victory for whichever Fleet had the good fortune to be British. Red and blue were the traditional colours of the antagonists before the days when Red Forces could not be anything but Communists.

Some important concepts were to be tested in these exercises. Two ships, HMS *Rodney,* a 16 inch gunned battleship, somewhat foreshortened as a result of the Washington Naval Agreement of 1922, and HMS *Sheffield*, a 6 inch gunned cruiser of the new Town Class, were fitted with new equipment for radio direction finding (RDF). Of course this was nothing more than a sea adaptation of the system being designed for the location of aircraft coming from the continent and bent on attacking

Britain. At the time no particular secrecy was attached to this early form of radar and I was to write in my Journal after the exercises:

'Another important factor in naval warfare is the introduction of the Type 79X RDF gear as fitted at present in Rodney and Sheffield. The range of effective reception has been proved as being in excess of 100 miles and by its use the presence of formations of aircraft can be easily detected in a way analogous to the A/S principle.'

There were other tactical gems such as the ability to act on signals from the homing beacon of *Ark Royal,* the need to use tribal class destroyers to make good the serious deficiency of small 6 inch cruisers for Fleet work, large cruisers should be employed on the trade routes for which they were built, the place for the aircraft carriers was in the line with the Capital Ships (Battleships and Battlecruisers), except when flying on and flying off aircraft, and the method of challenge and reply was ineffective by want of more frequent changes. Needless to say these lessons were well and truly assimilated by the time war broke out some six months later.

After the hectic professional activity of the exercises it was a round of port visiting. *Cossack*, with *Maori* a sister ship of the first Tribal Flotilla, was fortunate in being allocated Le Lavandou, then an undiscovered fishing village set in beautiful countryside between Toulon and Nice and connected to both by rail. The town boasted a magnificent restaurant and a Mayor with the Legion d'Honneur, who was without doubt one of the most gentlemanly gentlemen I've ever met, a fine patriot and an excellent host. Not only did I cover most of the local area by bicycle, I also managed to get away for the weekend to St Raphael, Cannes, Antibes, Nice and Monte Carlo, all for the princely sum of five pounds. I shudder to think what a trip like that would cost today. Mind you I had to be careful, but with champagne cocktails a shilling a time at the bar, well stocked with chips, nuts and so forth and sufficient Naval College French, albeit with an atrocious accent, 'Comme un Turque' as a charming Francaise once put it, it is surprising how well one could exist on the Riviera in those salad days before World War II.

While serving in HMS *Cossack* the first of my term mates from Cook Year 1934, met his death. Midshipman A J Anderson drowned at St Maxime after a boating accident on 30 March 1939. A keen sailor, he'd taken the skiff out for the afternoon with a couple of young girls, who were holidaying in the area, as crew. A sudden gust had caused the skiff to capsize. Too far from his ship, their plight was not known. After making sure that both girls were safe and stressing on them the need to stay with the upturned boat, he set off, swimming for help. Despite his ability to swim breaststroke for a long distance, he wasn't seen again. Two frightened and exhausted girls were discovered just after dusk, clinging to the boat and from them the story of the tragedy was pieced together. A thorough search of the area failed to reveal anything. The French Authorities eventually recovered his body, and he was buried at St Tropez on 18 April 1939.

Rereading my journal for use of Junior Officers Afloat, I'm surprised at the number of collisions there were between exercising ships taking one another in tow. Great store was set by the procedure by which one ship of a class would take another in tow, or be taken in tow. Cruisers towed Battleships, Destroyers towed Cruisers and ships of the same class towed one another. It was ironical that when war actually came and ships were damaged by air or submarine attack, it was necessary to sink them rather than to risk an undamaged ship in a towing operation.

Most of the collisions were brought about by a lack of appreciation as to how a disabled ship could be expected to behave when subject to the vagaries of the wind and sea.

The war was fast approaching. In February General Franco had tidied up the mess of the Spanish Civil War, freeing German and Italian volunteer forces. In March the German Army occupied Czechoslovakia, Hungary took over Ruthenia, Germany forced Romania to give up manufacturing and return to agrarian pursuits to supply Germany. In April Italy invaded Albania, in May England took a firm stance against German demands on Poland and in June the Japanese occupied Susowatow.

In the Mediterranean I was one of five Midshipmen lent to the 3rd Minesweeping Flotilla to survey parts of the Egyptian coast between Alexandria and the Libyan border. Originally the task was to have taken ten days, but I spent a total of six weeks aboard HMS *Sutton*. While an old coal-burning minesweeper of World War I vintage, to me it was the most wonderful ship in the world. I was the Navigating Officer and allowed for the first time to take charge of the watch at sea on my own.

With the survey completed and operating areas established for use by destroyers to bring gunfire to bear on the motor road from Libya to Egypt. Should Italian forces advance on Egypt through Libya, there was working a plenty for minesweepers.

In August a large scale exercise was held to see whether the British Mediterranean Fleet could effectively sever communications between Italy and Libya, and as the Fleet had to provide the enemy as well, some remarkable doubling up to be done. *Warspite* for example represented itself and another of its class on the British side, while *Barham* and *Malaya* each represented two Italian battleships. The exercise area was bounded by Crete, Palestine and Egypt, each of which represented in order Italy, Libya and Malta. If the reader thinks this is confusing, it's nothing compared with the box in which the warhead of the 21 inch Mark IX torpedo was stored. This bore the enigmatic inscription, 'Top marked Bottom' to avoid confusion.

Who won, you may well ask? That question was never really answered because the day the series of exercises ended was the day the Germans began invading Poland.

On Sunday morning 3 September 1939 the Commander-in-Chief, Admiral A B Cunningham, came aboard HMS *Malaya* to which I'd returned just a fortnight earlier and gave a brief rundown of the preparations the Fleet had made for war. In his opinion we were ready for any eventuality. As he was about to leave the Quarterdeck he turned and said to the Officers who'd been listening to his address, "By the way gentlemen, we will be at war with Germany from noon tomorrow, but I wouldn't let that interrupt your plans for the afternoon."

Colin Maud, Captain of HMS *Icarus,* was one whose plans were interrupted most seriously. On patrol outside the Great Pass he had the misfortune to be run into by a Greek merchant ship that was behaving erratically and thus became perhaps the first casualty of the war. With the forward boiler room flooded he brought his ship into harbour to enter dock just as the cinema performance on *Malaya's* quarterdeck was ending. What a way to start a war. Later, Kenneth Moore made Maud famous when he characterized him as the Naval Beachmaster, complete with dog and walking stick at Normandy in *'The Longest Day'*.

The only effect war had on the larger units of the Fleet was we spent less time getting ready for it. Until now we'd been at sea at least three or four days each week, now we stayed in Alexandria's harbour. This was useful for me as I prepared for my Seamanship examinations for the rank of Lieutenant. I expected this to be my last chance for promotion that would be decided entirely upon by my professional ability.

Only once during the war's early days did the Mediterranean Fleet proceed to sea on an enterprise remotely like those we'd been practising throughout the last two years. We spent the second week of war covering two large convoys and acting as a deterrent to any Italian thoughts of falling on such a prize. It was not long however before activities in other seas started to have an effect on our disposition.

However war did bring an end to organized sport throughout ships of the Royal Navy and the Royal Australian Navy.

Early in October the two 8 inch cruisers *Shropshire* and *Sussex* were the first to go. *Malaya*, the aircraft carrier *Glorious* and three destroyers *Dainty, Daring* and *Bulldog* soon followed, forming a special squadron off Aden to hunt for the *Von Scheer*, believed to be heading for the South Atlantic to join up with supply ships located on the East African coast before descending on the trade routes in the vicinity of Socotra.

There are many accounts of World War II as seen from the top; this, without a doubt, is the only position to see a war. There are also a variety of worthy accounts of war from the private soldier's point of view. No two people experience the same war. I always marvelled at those who were rescued from one sinking ship only to be promptly sunk again. Also the large numbers who spent a greater part of the war in transit camps waiting to join a ship or regiment that no longer existed, or waiting until some accident of paperwork should throw up their name and location, setting them in motion again.

My own war I regarded as an extremely personal one. Given that my father had survived World War I, I took it as a basic assumption that I would survive World War II. At peace or war, a regular Naval Officer was required to serve eight years in the rank of Lieutenant. Therefore it was extremely unlikely I'd do anything significantly individual. Service in submarines and aircraft was not an alternative as the RAN had abandoned its submarine force in 1928 and its air arm in the 30s. I was to meet a number of Australian Naval Officers whose career prospects had gone down the drain with these activities and a sorry lot they were too. To me the best I could hope for was to become a Lieutenant as quickly as possible and see how long the war would really last.

The British Admiralty amply supported my views. It didn't take long to decide that Acting Sub-Lieutenant's could work longer hours during the week and on Saturday mornings to complete the courses for the rank of Lieutenant in Gunnery, Torpedo, Navigation and Signals. Anti-submarine, as a fairly recent discipline, was a field principally for the Reserve Officers who would be employed in the smaller escorts then being built in large numbers in yards around Britain. Accordingly, course lengths were drastically reduced, but nothing was taken out of the syllabus and the scope of the examination was unaltered. The standards to be attained to achieve first and second-class passes were maintained. War, or no war, the training of Midshipmen had to go on and accommodation at sea was a premium.

Early in November Captain I B B Tower threatened two midshipmen with being sent to the trenches, after failing in Seamanship. The rest of us he sent to England from Aden in the first passenger ship that could take us. This act alone concentrated the minds of those two young gentlemen brilliantly. While joining the programme of the courses somewhat belatedly, they were spared the Western Front.

The approach to the British Isles in the first few months of the war was made somewhat hazardous by the German penchant for dropping magnetic mines from aircraft and the unfamiliarity of Merchant Service Officers with the new requirements of war at sea.

For many years Merchant Service Officers were encouraged to join the Naval Reserve and spend prolonged periods in HM ships to obtain a Naval Watchkeeping Certificate and gain an insight into the workings of the Kings Regulations and Admiralty Instructions. The Reserve Officers who I'd associated with during the two years prior to war, fell into two main categories, those from small companies who could see the war coming and wished to prepare themselves for naval command; and those from large companies, particularly those carrying passengers, which had decided for one reason or another, that a spell of naval discipline wouldn't do their hot-blooded, amorously inclined Second and Third Mates any harm. Without exception those I'd met were all first-class seamen, but of course there were not enough of them to go around. British ships that could boast a Naval Reserve Officer in command and a proportion of their officers in the Chain Gang were permitted to fly the Blue Ensign. But red, white or blue, all were the same to the magnetic mine in those days.

RMS *Strathallan* put into Plymouth and we boarded the train bound for London. Once there we reported to Australia House. It was early December 1939.

— 9 —

An Intellectual Renaissance

Our first night in London became a turning point in my life. One of our group had been to England some years earlier with his parents and knew all there was to know. We booked into the Strand Palace Hotel, the closest to Australia House. Its Edwardian, or may be Victorian, I'm no expert, but its grandeur and opulence overawed us.

We didn't realize that in those days one simply didn't stay in such places. Englishmen, if they had to spend the night in town, stayed in their Club, with a relative or friend, or at Brown's, or with some other Englishman's wife somewhere or other, but never at the Strand Palace or the Regent Palace. Moreover, Englishmen never took taxis unless they had luggage, or were in the company of a lady of 'that sort'. I clearly had so much to learn.

During the night there were some explosions that felt extremely close. However no one appeared to be taking any notice, brushing it aside with the off-handed quip, 'It's the IRA up to their usual game'.

Next morning the Naval Liaison Officer at Australia House wasn't pleased to see us. Two Paymaster Captains had rotated between Australia House as NLO and Navy Office Melbourne as Director of Officer Appointments for as long as anyone cared to remember and the annual visitation of Australian Midshipmen, or Acting Sub-Lieutenants, preparatory to their courses in Portsmouth was something they could well do without. Not only that, they actually had nothing for us to do until January 1940.

Promptly despatched on leave, we were told to keep in touch and directed to see a Miss Celia MacDonald of the Isles. During World War I she'd instituted a programme for young Colonial Officers to stay for three days with English families who had offered to have them, thus keeping them out of the temptations of the low-life in London. Her office near Sloane Square was once again looking after those who had no friends or family in England. As a fifth-generation Australian on one side and fourth-generation on the other I had no relatives in England that I knew of. Certainly none had ever been spoken of.

The interview with Miss MacDonald of the Isles was far more daunting and probing than any I'd ever experienced, including my entrance to RANC at 13, or since for that matter. It concluded with Miss MacDonald's firm words, "Be here tomorrow at two o'clock in the afternoon with your suitcase and I will tell you what to do."

No order from a Senior Officer had been more specific. With the words of my Term Officer at the RANC in 1934 ringing in my ears, "It is better to be ten minutes early than ten seconds late", I duly arrived back the next afternoon with some trepidation and presented myself before the commanding presence of the Grand Dame.

"You will leave here and go directly to Waterloo Station and take the train to Dorchester in Dorset where you will be met by Mrs. Turner. You will stay for three days."

I barely had time to thank her and get to the train, let alone think. Having been provided with a warrant for a railway pass, I endured the cold winter English evening in the Southern Railways 1st Class compartment all alone, until suddenly assailed with a loud voice from outside yelling, "Dargester."

In the pitch black of a December night I opened the carriage door to be greeted by the words, "My god — you're tiny."

This to someone who although under six foot had always been able to pass for five foot eleven at least, I was slightly taken aback. Apparently my hostess's idea of Australians was that they were tall, suntanned and slow of speech, and from whom she might have had to struggle to keep her virtue.

The car trip from the station to her home, the Manor House, Piddletrenthide, a village some seven miles from Dorchester and slightly more from Yeovil, provided for a brief get-to-know you time followed by a tete-a-tete during dinner. From then on began a process of education and re-education that was to have a profound influence on my life.

Piddletrenthide village had a church, a pub and an identity, General Sir Henry Jackson, who'd recently retired from the position of General Officer Commanding Southern Command. Before going to bed on the first night I was told I'd be going hunting with South Dorset the next day. Apparently the look on my face was enough. Mrs. Turner queried, "You do ride don't you?"

"Ride what?" I replied dumbfounded.

"Horses of course."

When I answered that I'd never seen a horse except pulling a milk or bread cart by our front door, let alone ridden one, her air of disbelief was quite genuine. "But all Australians ride horses, don't they?"

"Not all, but I'm only here for three days anyway."

"That's ridiculous. You will stay till after Christmas. And tomorrow you will go to the field opposite with Cyril Nicholson, the groom, and he will teach you to ride with hounds."

Next morning under Cyril's expert tutelage, I was taught to ride and to fall off without doing myself irreparable harm. After all we had a war to win and I couldn't go about killing myself in a hunting accident.

Then it was back to London to get kitted out accordingly. For a modest sum I bought breeches and string gloves from Moss Bros. For even a more modest sum, a plus four suit from Montague Burton, the jacket of which doubled for riding. I was then ready for the South Dorset, having also learnt how to open and close the gate without having to dismount.

In the next few weeks I was to frequently indulge in what Oscar Wilde once regarded as 'the pursuit of the uneatable by the unspeakable'. Having no wish to alienate one side or the other I will offer no judgment on blood sports as such, beyond to say that I never actually saw a fox, let alone see a kill. There was a lot of tooting and yelling, baying of hounds, sweating horses, flowing women and some of the most unprintable language from the most delicate of female mouths, but nothing to which any naturalist could possibly take exception.

Hunting as a pastime, seemed to me, an admirable way for the English to keep in trim. After nothing more substantial than a boiled egg, a cup of tea and occasionally a cherry brandy by courtesy of the Master if the hunt happened to be meeting that morning at his place, the assembled throng simply rode back and forth, sometimes at a trot, sometimes a gallop and sometimes a walk from early morning to late afternoon. Then it was home at a trot and walk, curry comb, rubdown and brush the horses and put them in the stables for a well earned meal, clean the tack and retire indoors to tea in front of the fire.

During the early days of war, tea consisted of those impossibly thin cucumber sandwiches that only the English hostess can provide, along with watercress, of course. Later, the ultimate was toast and beef dripping, well salted and provided in the most wonderful of ways, the food parcel from abroad. It was not until 1946 and 1947 that I was to experience real hunger in England. And by that time the black market was totally organized, so if you knew where to go and had the money to buy, almost anything was procurable.

One afternoon Mrs. Turner announced, "Tiny, I shall call you that at home as I intend to treat you as one of my family. I have three children, Jennifer who is 13, Christopher 11 and Michael 9. Both boys are at school in Winchester and Jennifer is at Sherborne, a school for girls about 13 miles further on from here. In England their long break is in the summer so over Christmas and New Year they will be here. I also want you to meet my father who is in London before he comes down here on Friday for the weekend."

"Where in London is he?" I enquired.

"The House of Lords," came the quick reply, as she continued. "We will travel 3rd class in the train. Only snobs and undesirables travel 1st class. And in London we'll get around by tube or bus. We only travel in taxis when we have luggage."

"My husband, Theodore, wants to meet you too. He is in Wandsworth Prison."

From the startled look on my face she instantly added, "Not as an inmate, but as one of Britain's leading barristers. He is ensuring that arrested German spies have a fair trial. Now do you have any questions?"

My head was spinning from all this newfound information, but I had one important question, "This is so much to take in, and so unexpected. What shall I call you? I have a mother not much older than you, but so far in my life Mrs. has been bestowed on the wives of naval officers with whom I've served, or mothers of daughters who've come to see me play rugby."

Her reply was most unexpected, "Of course you must call me Betty in this house, and I am sure you will work out when it is, or isn't appropriate elsewhere. Now I have a question — can you drive a car?"

On receiving the answer, no, she promptly added, "I will teach you. We will get you a learner's permit in Sherborne tomorrow."

So I was duly taken to Westminster to meet Sir Claud Schuster GCB CVO QC, who was then the Private Secretary to the Lord Chancellor, and then to the famous prison to meet Mr. Theodore F Turner.

And so it was. An only child suddenly had responsibility for siblings.

I noticed when the three children where at home, they spoke among themselves using quotations. Upon asking their grandfather what books could I read to broaden my knowledge in this area, Sir Claud Schuster pointed out, "I couldn't possibly tell you that. It is something that you will have to learn in the years to come."

This had a profound effect on me, so much so that I'm now in the process of getting together a library of classics to leave behind when I go. Each carries the following inscription:

This book is a gift from the library
compiled by
Captain W. Graham Wright RAN (Retired)
in his 90th year and beyond.
It is one of many that he considers to be
required reading for one to obtain a
rounded education.

It was fortunate that Piddletrenthide Manor lawn tennis court hadn't yet been dug up to grow potatoes, so I was able to prove some of my sporting prowess. I was also a better than average Bridge player, albeit in the two and a half quick tricks and Culbertson answer to the four no-trump bid from a partner looking for a slam. At threepence-a-hundred I was quite happy to lose three shillings and sixpence any night. As a Chief Cadet Captain at the RANC, where I'd originally learnt how to play, that represented my weekly pay.

That first Christmas of the war was everything a Christmas should be in England. Snow fell in Dorset on Christmas Eve. Carol singers were out. The church was full on Christmas Day. Even the local lake froze over so we could partake in some ice-skating — some better than others. Suitable gifts were given and received. To this day I sit at my dining table in Yarralumla and use a collection of tablemats and coasters depicting hunting scenes from England, a memento of that Christmas. Another that I still treasure is *Shakespeare's Complete Works from Oxford University Press 1894*, a gift from Mrs. Pass's sister, Beatrice Gaynor, whose son was in the RAF and the same age as me. The inscription reads, '*There's Rosemary, that's for Remembrance and Pansies that's for thoughts. Walter from Bee.*'

Somehow it seemed that meeting me, made her son's participation in the war easier to endure. In May 1945, I was to meet her son while I was serving in HMS *Anson*. He'd become a Group Captain and I was a Lieutenant.

Even our Christmas dinner was a revelation. Up until then I'd always been subjected to the midday feasts in Australia with temperatures hovering on or about the old Fahrenheit century. The pudding had been cooked for hours in the copper, seemingly stuffed full of three-penny bits and sixpences saved from last year and religiously boiled. The family rule required an announcement as to who would get the next piece, so should a coin be cut that person became entitled to it. Of course no one actually spent the money. It was the ritual that counted.

In England I experienced the real thing. Size of family and social scale position usually decided the question of turkey, duck, or chicken. Midday or evening was simply a matter of class. But it was the pudding that was the real surprise. It was black with a sprig of real holly and was served with a hard brandy sauce and lashings of cream. I'd never tasted its equal before, or since for that matter.

With the approach of 1940 the weather continued to be seasonal, but there was fuel for the fires even though it meant wielding the axe and using the wedge oneself. Conscription had seen to it that there were no idle hands.

Not only did Christmas 1939 bring a whole new family experience, I was introduced by Elizabeth Turner to another family in Dorset, with whom I renewed acquaintances in 1944 whilst serving in HMS *Anson*, whilst it was being fitted-out in Devonport Dockyard for participation in the Pacific War with Japan. Douglas Pass, his wife and five daughters, together with Larcombe the butler, all accepted me, particularly Douglas, who was happy to have me ride his hunter to hounds.

Douglas's comment was, "Each of my daughters has married a man to whom horse-riding is something quite foreign to his nature. I own five farms and not one of my sons-in-law is attracted in any way to country life. As a former Prisoner of War in Turkey in World War I, I can no longer enjoy the thrill of the hunt, but to see you, Graham, when you come in from the Tavistock, brings it all back to me."

Theodore and Elizabeth Turner, although not separated were virtually living apart, and like the Garden of Eden, there was a snake-in-the-grass. Living in the Manor House was a former old school friend of Elizabeth's, with an unmistakable interest in Theo. However, he had the hots for Totts, the wife of the Master-of-Hounds of Tavistock, and much younger than her husband. (Much later, after World War II was over, and death and divorce had made it possible Theo and Totts married, settling happily in New York.)

I was never really accepted by Theo, and I never knew why. But in 1944 when I returned to Greenwich to become the RAN's 14th Qualified Navigator and developed the burgeoning connection with his daughter Jennifer, he discouraged the relationship, making it quite clear I was Australian, not British. Nevertheless both Elizabeth and Jennifer came to my first wedding in 1946.

The final scene in Act I took place on 1 April 1940, while visiting the seaside at Lulworth Cove in South Dorset. After walking across the pebbly beach to the waters edge, I plunged head first into the English Channel and froze in that position, arms and legs outstretched for what seemed ages. Nothing could've been more unlike Coogee Beach where I'd taught myself to swim out to the shark enclosure and back some ten years before.

'Oh, to be in England, now that April's there.' Certainly Robert Browning (1812-1889) hadn't done what I'd done then!

— 10 —

1940

As with all good things, they must come to an end and I rejoined my colleagues for what were called Subs Courses — Navigation at HMS *Dryad,* then in the grounds of Portsmouth Dockyard, Torpedo at HMS *Vernon* just along from the Hard, Signals at the Royal Naval Barracks and finally Gunnery at HMS *Excellent* at Whale Island.

Our Course RAN and RN Sub-Lieutenants (me centre front) at HMS Dryad Navigation School Portsmouth Dockyard January 1940

It was during this course that a minor disaster struck, in the form of German measles. To me this was the first hostile act from the enemy. It meant that I was unable to complete the course unit with the rest of the Australians and had to start a completely revised course with what were described euphemistically, as a bunch of stragglers.

As it turned out, this course was much more realistic than my previous one. Because we didn't have the numbers for a 13 inch Turret Drill which figured prominently in group activities we were able to devote more time to the Night Action teachings and master the intricacies of the Spotting Rules. To those familiar with the capabilities of Precision Guided Missiles and the modern curtain of fire through which an attack must pass to obtain a hit nowadays, our techniques may seem incomprehensible.

Having used the best available information regarding the course and speed of the enemy ship and its range the first salvo was fired to fall to the left of the targets, the second salvo to the right of the target and the third in line with the target. This was known as spreading the line. With any luck one of the three salvos would fall in such a way as to show whether it was short of or beyond the target. The next three salvos could then be fired in up ladder or down ladder separated in range by about four hundred yards. Hopefully one of these salvos would fall in such a way that the target would be crossed. Once this had happened zig-zag groups could be fired. This consisted of three salvos, the first two hundred yards short of target range, the second two hundred yards over target range and the third at target range. If one of these actually happened to hit the enemy, rapid salvos could then be fired until the target either escaped or sank. The expenditure of ammunition was considerable. It's little wonder that later in the war the Japanese were to develop a much less elaborate method of putting enemy ships out of action.

With my courses successfully completed, gaining firsts all round, it was time to get back to sea and qualify for my Watchkeeping Certificate. During peacetime this used to take a minimum of six months, but with ships spending so much more time at sea in war the Admiralty had decided to reduce the minimum period to three months. The RAN hadn't yet expanded beyond the ships it had acquired under the 1936 expansion programme and there was a limit to the number of Sub-Lieutenants a ship could carry. A pre-war destroyer for example could accommodate, besides the captain and engineer officer, a First Lieutenant, another Lieutenant (the No.2), a Sub-Lieutenant and a Gunner T. As all the billets in our ships outside the Australia Station had been filled I was to return to Australia to join HMAS *Adelaide*.

Across the Channel the war was really getting into its stride and plans were being changed on a daily basis. After joining RMS *Orontes* at Southampton on 18 April 1940, we sailed off, only to find that we wouldn't be going through the Mediterranean after all, but around the Cape of Good Hope.

On arrival in Cape Town we were directed to Bombay to carry out the original schedule. We were probably the last passenger ship to run the regular route as if nothing had changed, continuing onto Colombo before Australia and the usual round of Fremantle, Adelaide, Melbourne and Sydney.

Throughout the six-week voyage with the aid of press reports and a map Mr. Roberts, the Chief Officer, followed the events in Europe, which were becoming more and more gloomy as each day passed. As a Naval Reserve Officer he and I shared the same view at the time — what on earth were we doing on a cruise when there was so much happening where we'd just been? Little did we know there would be plenty of action for both of us before it was all over.

The number of First Class passengers had also been reduced to a total of eighteen and besides myself there was one other RAN Officer returning home after service and training in Britain. An elderly Warrant Officer, he kept to himself except when befriending a lady of his vintage and nature took its course.

An exceptional traveller was the playwright of the thriller, *'Who Killed the Count'*, which later enjoyed a successful season for the best part of a year in Australian theatres. He was besotted by a lady who joined the ship with her two young children just before sailing time. However by the time we'd reached Cape Town her threat to leave the ship and settle in South Africa instead of Australia killed off whatever he might have had in mind.

Two more interesting passengers were a mother and daughter, returning to Australia to obtain a divorce from the daughter's grazier husband who was having an affair with a Tivoli showgirl. The mother, Mrs. Gray, was a keen Bridge player. Along with the aunt of a young Australian girl of my own age, playing Bridge occupied most of the afternoons. I was thankful that I'd been brought up in the hard school of Piddletrenthide, where Sir Claud Schuster had been such a stickler for conversations and I'd learnt how to really play Bridge through the only way possible — to lose money playing it. The strange thing is that if you play regularly with these same people, as one is apt to do on a sea voyage, the winnings and losses inevitably cancel each other out. Nevertheless, a small slam doubled and re-doubled with an over trick when vulnerable, can bring in a tidy sum at five cents a hundred.

It was perhaps inevitable that on such a prolonged voyage in the company of Jane, the attractive Australian girl of my own age, that romance should occupy a large part of the available time. After dinner each night the band played. Jane, who'd had her 20th birthday at the end of April, became my dance partner. The two of us also helped the mother with her two youngsters, a boy and a girl, by assisting with bathing before bedtime.

Jane insisted on calling me Billy. Apparently I reminded her of her pet kangaroo on their New South Wales property where she'd grown up. Her aunt and chaperone was my bridge partner and it wasn't long before she sanctioned our after-dancing walks on deck.

As a natural navigator, it was inevitable that I'd also show her how to find south by extending the long arm of the Southern Cross to meet the perpendicular bisector of the pointers and dropping this to the horizon.

This copy of 'Star Gazing in the Tropics and its Mysterious Influence' from Captain Lecky's 'Wrinkles in Practical Navigation' 19th Edition 1918 p. 348 shows inevitably how ship-board romances begin

Once back in Australia it was a quick reunion with my parents and a once over inspection by Jane's parents and sister. It's often said that 'love conquers all', but in the matrimonial stakes of that time I was an impossible lightweight. Moreover, girls were starting to realize that there was more to life than being left alone in a small flat with perhaps a baby to look after while some fool of a husband went off around the world fighting a war. The trouble with wartime Australia of course, was that girls kept leaving School with the firm conviction that if they weren't married by the time they were twenty-two, they'd be left on the shelf, so in the two years prior to that time there was a whirlwind round in which as many swains as possible had to be assessed. Parents of Depression children had acquired the outlook often attributed only to the French, that marriage should be guided more by economic considerations rather than by passion.

On reporting to Navy Office, Captain Parker who'd been in charge of Officer Appointments since year dot, informed me, "Wright, your next job is in England."

"But, I've just come from there."

"Well you'll just have to go back, won't you?"

Fate, however, was to take a hand.

Having been overseas since June 1938 there was Foreign Service Leave to be taken. Also time at sea was essential to obtain my Watchkeeping Certificate and promotion to Lieutenant. Then Germany came to my aid by dropping a bomb on Thornycroft's Woolston shipyard, causing a delay in launching the ship to which I'd been posted.

At 09:00 on the morning after attending my first and last ever Chamber Music Recital at Hopewood House, a Finishing School for young ladies, attended by Jane's younger sister Judy, I fronted up to the Captain of HMAS *Adelaide*, Harry Showers, to get back to sea. Showers had been the Commander of the RANC when I'd joined in 1934. However, twelve hours later I was on the operating table of the private hospital in Darlinghurst, where Dr. George Bell, one of Australia's finest surgeons, relieved me of my appendix.

The *Adelaide* sailed from Sydney without me. Steaming north at high speed against the southbound traffic it struck a merchant ship. Fortunately only a glancing blow which didn't interfere with the progress of the mission, which was to bring the administration in New Caledonia over to the Free French persuasion.

While the *Adelaide* was busy off Nouméa, I was convalescing by making myself useful to the Hydrographic Office on Garden Island. I didn't know then how valuable this experience was to be later on.

This interlude also gave me an opportunity to press my suit in the vain attempt to show that the young lady and myself were not simply victims of the traditional shipboard romance. In the course of a day under sail on Sydney Harbour I managed to get my skiff sandwiched between the *Queen Mary* and the *Empress of Australia*, then in Australia on trooping duties. The tacking back and forth between the two ships taxed my one girl crew severely, but I think it was the cheers and whistles from those on board that really upset Jane the most. My sailing skill went unnoticed and completely unappreciated.

As I was living on board HMAS *Platypus*, then moored at Garden Island, I was able to entertain in a modest way, but to people living in the country districts of New South Wales, the whole idea of the Navy and navy life was an alien concept. I might as well have been a creature from outer space for all the good it did me.

Finally, HMAS *Adelaide* and I joined forces and we set about protecting the east coast of Australia from its enemies. For the most part this meant patrolling fifteen miles out to sea by day and five miles out at night between Broken Bay and Botany Bay. Occasionally we would dash down to Bass Strait to check on reports from the lightkeeper at Gabo Island Lighthouse. As part of these activities we indulged in gunnery practice. My particular duty was that of High Angle Control Officer, requiring me to sit in the Director perched high on the foremast, locate the target, a sleeve towed by an aircraft, follow it through my binoculars attached to the Director which was moved in one plane by the Trainer and in the other plane by the Layer. I controlled an arrow that then aligned with the target, gave the input to the calculator that had to predict where the shells would burst. The better all this was done, provided the height and speed of the aircraft were assessed correctly, the more nearly the fuse setting was likely to cause a burst in the vicinity of the target. In a clear blue sky the colour of the sleeve target was white. On a cloudy day the colour preferred was red.

Invariably I would be trying to track a white sleeve against white clouds, or a red sleeve against a hazy blue sky. Quite often the Captain on the Bridge would spot the sleeve and be quite mystified as to why I couldn't see what he could see quite clearly. It was a case of all heads being better than one.

On some occasions in the Director I would be spot on and ready, but prevented from opening fire because the Captain couldn't see the target and wasn't sure that we were firing in the right direction. It's little wonder that our antiquated methods of fire control seemed at variance with the problems we would face if we actually came into combat with enemy aircraft, particularly those that didn't oblige by flying on a steady course, at a steady speed, or at a steady height. Even under ideal conditions I would report, "Ready to open fire" to the Gunnery Officer on the Bridge.

He in turn would report to the Captain, "Request permission to open fire, Sir."

The Captain would then order, "Open fire." By the time this order was relayed back to me there was usually only scope for firing three or four rounds before the target was out of the area in which firing was useful. More often than not the Cease Fire bell would be ringing just as I was about to fire the first shot. Fortunately we were soon to discard this ritual in the face of German and Italian air attacks on ships escorting convoys of merchantmen.

Once more HMAS *Adelaide* was sent to New Caledonia to bolster the authority of the Free French Governor, Monsieur Sautot. Apart from his support for de Gaulle and the Cross of Lorraine, the most notable attribute of this extraordinary man was that on arrival to take over the administration he'd brought both his wife and her twin sister. When asked how he could possibly tell them apart he answered, "Ce n'es'pas difficile. One has a, how-you-say, mole here." Pointing to the inside of his leg well above the knee. He never did say whether it was his wife or her sister who had the mole — very French.

On New Year's Eve the Governor gave a Ball to which we were invited. As the clock ticked 1940 away, the word went around that we were to make our way, as unobtrusively as possible, to the boat which was waiting to take us back to the ship – we'd been ordered to sea in a hurry. On departure I made a resolution that one day I would return to finish the dance.

— 11 —

1941

Gaining my Watchkeeping Certificate, my promotion to the rank of Lieutenant arrived almost instantaneously. This promotion also came with seniority adjusted to take into account my results on graduation from RANC and the Sub's Courses. At the same time I was appointed to HMAS *Norman* (G49), an N Class Destroyer then being built by Thornycroft's at Southampton. So once again I was heading back to where the action was.

Prior to leaving and also our 21st birthdays, Jane announced, "Don't ask me to marry you before you leave. I don't want to be left alone in Sydney with a baby to look after in a flat by myself."

Her family were clearly on her side too, intercepting the Hardy Brothers present I'd ordered and giving it to her themselves. In a letter I received after the event, she gave a detailed description of the great present she'd received from the family. Although I still held hope, love just wasn't meant to be yet.

Boarding the Blue Star Freighter *Africa Star*, I was in the company of a group of young RANVR Officers who'd just received their Commissions as Sub-Lieutenants and were being lent for service in Royal Navy ships. When I found out that their only instructions were to present themselves on arrival in England to the Admiralty appointing authority I suggested that we use the voyage for some theoretical and practical instruction in Navigation. On leaving the ship in Liverpool they could all use the sextant and complete a day's work, consisting of morning stars, observations of the sun in the forenoon, at noon and in the afternoon, and evening stars. Moreover, they all knew the theory behind what they were doing, which meant that any mistakes they made were readily apparent and easily corrected.

It was a far different England to which I returned. We made the North Western approaches through a North Atlantic gale and proceeded up the Mersey during an air raid on the night of Monday 10 March 1941. It was my 21st birthday and the bar of the Blue Star Line ship was shut.

The train to London was stopped while unexploded bombs were removed from the tracks and London looked as though it had been hit by a bomb, which of course it had, many times.

Australia House had bad news for me. Thornycroft's shipyard had been bombed and although *Norman* had not been hit, production in the yard had been interrupted and work on the ship was behind schedule. In the meantime, I was to go to the Royal Naval Barracks Portsmouth, where crews for the Australian destroyers were being assembled.

As all the urgency seemed to have been taken out of what was being done I gladly accepted the offer of some leave and once again Mrs. Turner was delighted to see me. South Dorset and the pursuit of the fox over ground was becoming rather familiar to me, so much so that I graduated to the group who jumped rather than waited to go through the gates. On one occasion I found myself neck and neck with a young girl heading for a hole in the hedge through which I'm sure only one horse would pass at a time, but the hole was not really a hole but a wall with a ditch beyond. My horse knew all about this particular place and so did the other horse and its rider. I just went along with it all and somehow we all finished up in proper order on the other side. My reputation as a horseman was made.

One afternoon will always stand out in memory. Broadway performer, Mary Newcombe, was playing in a travelling show of *'Gaslight'*. People for miles around were invited to attend the performance in the village hall at Cerne Abbas. I sat on a rough wooden bench in my riding breeches, absolutely transfixed by her brilliance. Much later I saw Ingrid Bergman in the film version, but it didn't grip me as did that totally unpredictable performance in a Dorset village. Full credit must be given to the rest of the cast and those back stage, typifying to me the spirit of England at the time. People were prepared to do what they did best provided it added to the war effort in some way.

Shortly after this I fell ill. The English climate was never kind to me and sooner or later I'd get a cold that couldn't be shaken, always threatening to turn into something worse. As the Royal Navy had set up an auxiliary hospital in the vicinity I was able to present myself for treatment and before long was fit enough to be discharged. In view of the rather unusual nature of my admission the doctor-in-charge said he'd get in touch with Australia House, but in the meantime I should go back on leave until I heard from them. A week passed. Nothing. I sent a telegram and to my astonishment received a rocket in reply that read, "Report to Royal Naval Barracks Portsmouth forthwith and forward your reasons in writing for not doing so immediately on discharge from hospital."

Needless to say 'reasons in writing' meant much the same as 'report on board immediately', which meant in the pre-war Navy wearing a frock coat and sword. Nevertheless, I submitted my reasons in writing and heard nothing more. When next at Australia House I mentioned the matter to the Assistant Naval Liaison Officer who said, "You know if you hadn't sent us the telegram we would never have known where you were – we might even have lost you altogether."

I wonder how many people during World War II were simply lost in similar ways...

Portsmouth was under nightly bombardment from the air at that time. The docks area the main target. But the Germans realized that greater disruption to the repair and supply of ships could be achieved by attacking the workmen in the homes. After a few sleepless nights and mornings spent cleaning up debris from the raid the night before it was too much to expect 100% effort on the job the next day. Yet most people were giving that and more.

The Royal Naval Barracks continued to act as a clearing-house. Most of the teaching establishments had been moved into country houses, the Navigation School to Southwick House over Portsdown Hill, the Signal School to Haslemere, but *Vernon* and *Excellent* continued to operate. Many afternoons were spent in funeral parties at the Gosport cemetery, where chipped gravestones were mute evidence of the German predilection to strafe such bodies paying homage to those killed in previous raids.

Unexploded bombs probably caused the most disruption to our daily lives at that time. One of these crashed through a wing of the Wardroom, ceremoniously ending its journey in a bed and looking like some fat slob in a drunken stupour. It was such an obscene sight that we all had to look at it. The bomb disposal experts soon put an end to our amusement, shunting us as faraway as possible until they had disarmed the bomb, removing it by lorry for disposal elsewhere.

As a result of this episode approval was given to living out on the nights we weren't required for defensive duties within the Barracks. I obtained lodgings with a young couple in the suburbs over Portsdown Hill and close to the bus route. As I arrived late, left early and was away at weekends the arrangement didn't distract them unduly and they felt that they were contributing to the war effort.

The inaction soon came to an end and those of us with a job were moved to Woolston and an office in a house outside the Thornycroft yard.

Two main tasks were to be performed. One was to stand by the ship being built and the other to protect it while it was being built. To carry out the first task was to ensure that those building the ship installed the equipment correctly, which in some cases meant not necessarily in accordance with the plans. On the bridge for instance it was essential for some people to see some instruments from the position in which they would normally be standing. The Ship Foreman was particularly pleased to have both the First Lieutenant and the No. 2 available. The Engineering Officer had arrived first and was totally occupied below decks where, as a fact of life, no two ships of the same class had identical main steam runs. When it came to auxiliaries then each installation was practically custom built.

The second task was the brainchild of the new Captain of *Norman,* Commander Henry Burrell, who'd arrived from the United States. With the German invasion of the Soviet Union in June and Norman alongside the yard with a Bofors Gun in place, Henry, with great enthusiasm, decided that a crew should man it in the dark hours and an officer should be on hand to take charge. By some process of logic that has always escaped me, the main danger was seen to be from low flying enemy aircraft following the course of the river. Needless to say we were not called upon to fire a single shot in anger.

I did this duty on a couple of occasions, but the logistical effort required became intolerable and Thornycroft's staff weren't enthusiastic either.

Standing by a ship under construction during the cricket season had a plus. As the shipyard work progressed the number of ships company gradually grew. Thankfully I had responsibility for two other projects due prior to the ship's commissioning — the arrival of a set of Admiralty Charts to cover the Home Station and an issue of appropriate sporting gear. The delivery of cricket equipment came early, so with the help of Able Seaman Archer, a namesake and not a relative of the two Australian cricketers of the 1950's, we formed a team and with the Woolston Oval as a home ground and I duly entered our team in the Twilight Competition in Southampton. With double summertime and perfect English weather these games were played over two evenings beginning at 18:00 and stumps just before 21:30, allowing time to get to the pub before closing. Teams from all walks of life took part, and years later I realized that the Southampton Police Team had John Arlott playing for them. He went on to become a world-renowned Test commentator and writer of cricket books.

German air activity was always a possibility but Portsmouth Dockyard and its surroundings proved a better opportunity than a few flannelled fools on open ground remote from any worthwhile targets, especially after Hitler decided to take the war into Russia. Of the standard of cricket there is not much to be said beyond the fact that there were some very good players whose only opportunity to perform on the field of play was in these twilight games. In spite of the devastating loss to England at the Oval in August 1938 Australia retained the Ashes throughout World War II and every team we played in Southampton tried to win them back for England from us.

Although Henry Burrell had played cricket as far back as 1924 with the Hampshire Wanderers and had done well with 50 odd at Woolwich in 1938 while on Staff Course at the Royal Naval College, Greenwich, I couldn't wean him off tennis, particularly doubles in which he excelled.

One day Henry mentioned his failed marriage, into which he'd entered as a newly promoted Lieutenant Commander in 1934. It had recently been terminated, but he maintained he was always looking over his shoulder for the King's Proctor who had the power to cancel his decree nisi and prevent it becoming decree-absolute.

Feeling his pain, I invited him to a weekend at Piddletrenthide for dinner and Bridge with Mrs. Turner's father, Sir Claud Schuster. But truthfully I had a deeper motive, for him to meet Elizabeth Turner, now aged 37. Her marriage was definitely on the rocks. We drove over in Henry's ancient and not very sporty sports car. While a most pleasant weekend, there wasn't a flicker of romance. Or tennis for that matter, as the lawn court had been converted for growing potatoes! The consequence however, was Sir Claud was invited to the mid-September commissioning of *Norman*.

While Henry, Neville and John stayed at Botley Grange Hotel, I'd found suitable accommodation through one of the Thornycroft executives, with a charming family at Botley. The mother of two young children had recently been widowed. Her husband had been a Naval Reservist. Her mother-in-law was living with her too, and while a great comfort, it was also something of a mixed blessing, but financially my contribution was rather opportune. Most weekends I spent at Dorset with Mrs. Turner and my adoptive family, enjoying their special friendship.

Romance was still in the air for me, kept alive by virtue of long letters sent at great expense via Air Mail through the United States. Mine to her were full of long discourses on the depth of feelings, strength of devotion and so on, and hers to me of the wonderful times with the boys in Anti-Aircraft, who of course weren't being sent overseas because of the need for home defence.

As the summer of 41 developed, I became aware of a very attractive girl in the Thornycroft Main Office. It wasn't long before we were strolling around Woolston at lunchtime and going dancing at the Southampton Town Hall on Saturday nights. This was real Palais de D stuff, with a giant mirrored ball spinning slowly in the middle of the ceiling and couples slithering and sliding to the big band sound. Eventually I managed to convince Eunice that there was more to dancing than athletics, so she agreed to come with me to the Dinner Dances at Southampton's best hotel at that time. Here the dancing could be punctuated by food, drink and talk. Best of all though were the Sunday evening excursions to the Swan Inn at Bursledon. The way lay through a typical English woodlands and with double Summer time it was still daylight by the time the evening was over. The food at the Mucky Duck, as the pub was called, was well worth the walk too. It's probably just as well that I loved another at that time, or I may have easily been influenced by the peace and tranquility of it all.

Commissioning Day came at last. On 15 September 1941, the highlight of the occasion for me was when, in the moderate-sized Wardroom, the Australian High Commissioner, Stanley M Bruce, came face-to-face with his colleague Sir Claud. "What are you doing here?" he questioned incredulously.

Sir Claud smugly replied, "I'm the Captain's weekend guest."

The occasion was made.

A day later we raised steam for sea trials. Sure enough the first time we put the wheel to Starboard the indicator on the Bridge showed that it had gone to Port. This was easily fixed by connecting the wires in reverse order. Once out into the Channel we put the ship through its paces and I think we were all surprised when we went from Full Ahead to Full Astern and then back to Full Ahead again in an alarming swift pace. The sensation was not unlike the one you used to get in lifts before buildings became as advanced as they are today. Although the machinery behaved perfectly on this occasion, we were warned not to repeat the performance too often if we expected it to last out the war. Therefore the Captain was meticulous in the manner in which he increased and reduced speed, so much so, that on one occasion I was forced to ask him to stop the ship until I could find out exactly where we were. We had very few aids for position finding in those days and in tidal waters there were enough unknowns without adding one's own speed to them.

After a hasty dash down the Channel to Plymouth where we dropped off the Thornycroft people who'd come to sea with us to finish off the inevitable last minute jobs and to satisfy themselves that they'd built yet another fine ship, we took on our first real job — to rendezvous with an R Class battleship and escort it to Scapa Flow.

— 12 —

Archangel

Most of the crew had previously served in HMAS *Kanimbla,* commissioned early in the war as an Armed Merchant Cruiser. Neville McGuire, Engineer Officer, had been an HMAS *Tingira* boy and subsequently entered the RAN College in 1922. The First Lieutenant, John Dowson was an old school destroyer man and had just come from the same position in HMS *Tenedos* based in Singapore. I was Second Lieutenant (No.2) and in addition to being the Navigator was also Signals Officer, Torpedo Control Officer, Radio Direction Finding (later Radar) Officer and Watchkeeper, and for good measure the Sports Officer. The Gunner T was also an old schoolman, but our Captain, Henry Burrell, thought he was too old to keep watch by night. The Sub-Lieutenant, Neil Macdonald, had no Watchkeeping Certificate, so I took the First and Morning Watches and the First Lieutenant did the Middle, training the Sub-Lieutenant.

The relationship between Henry Burrell and his three principal officers in HMAS *Norman* needs some careful consideration. One can accept Burrell's vision of himself as 'having a lot to learn' after all he'd been behind a desk for the previous two years of the war. And also the relative ranks and various age differences of the Officers. The Engineer was 33 years of age to Burrell's 37, John Dowson was 28 and I, 22. But when Henry dashed around the Bridge like some blue-arsed fly from telephone to voice pipe to torpedo sight, from port wing to starboard wing and then back again like a one-man band trying to play the right tune, it didn't help any of us on the Bridge to do our jobs properly.

Since 1938 I'd been at sea in a succession of ships as the Assistant to the Navigator, colloquially known as 'Tanky'. Plus in 1940 I'd succeeded where Burrell had failed; I'd gained five firsts in my examinations for the rank of Lieutenant. This was also at a time when the cut off had been raised from 75% to 85%. But no matter how well I'd done in theory or practice, working with anyone else, I was soon to learn how just one person can successfully damn another's career and there was little one could do to salvage it afterwards.

In 1986 I was to read on page 115 of Vice Admiral Sir Henry Burrell's autobiography, *Mermaids Do Exist:*

'On the way an incident occurred which taught a lesson to my inexperienced navigator. The shipping tracks through Spithead and Southampton waters were marked by buoys of distinctive shape and colour and at night by lights of differing characteristics. As we passed a buoy on the starboard hand I noted a distance from the chart and, knowing our speed, calculated that it would be nine minutes before the next major alteration of course. After about five minutes, as we came abreast of a buoy, the navigator requested permission to make the big alteration. I said no. We both looked at the chart and he realised that the buoy in the channel had tricked him. He had taken no precaution by calculating time, by taking a check bearing from a land object near the beam, or by noting the markings of the buoy. However, he was to become an efficient navigator as the commission progressed.'

This is the first of three incidents quoted in his book that are pure invention. What really happened in this particular incident was that after the full power ahead and then full power astern trial in the English Channel in broad daylight *Norman* returned to Southampton via the Needles, the western end of the Isle of Wight. I drew the Captain's attention to the fact that the Admiralty Chart positioned a buoy on the port hand that was no longer there. As this was a rarely used passage, the normal approach being through Spithead on the eastern side of the island, I said I would go through the normal process of informing the necessary authorities. Some weeks later a Notice to Mariners to amend the chart was published.

Later on page 221, Burrell quotes that this first of three incidents in my career *'which could have jeopardised ... chances of reaching flag rank.'*

Off Liverpool we ran into some German aircraft that were leisurely laying mines in the Mersey estuary. I pressed the alarm rattlers and all hit Action Stations. We must've given them a fright as we blazed away with every gun that could be brought to bear and I suspect others that just fired anyway not to be outdone.

After picking up the battleship we took station, proceeding on our way north. I turned over the Watch at midnight and went down to the Chart House below the Bridge. I'd just dropped off to sleep when I was awakened by the most fearful commotion from the Wheelhouse nearby. The Revolution Telegraph was furiously being wound up to several hundred revolutions, while at the same time the ship heeled violently as we turned under full rudder.

Dashing back to the Bridge I eyeballed a white faced Sub-Lieutenant, staring in disbelief at a dark shape now rapidly disappearing astern in a pall of funnel smoke. At the same time a small white light blinked away the message, *'Knock off larking about and take up your appointed station.'*

What had happened was of course a classic case. The signal had been made to take station so that when course is altered to the new course you will be in the same position relative to the guide that you now occupy. The Sub-Lieutenant, fresh from courses, made the fundamental error of altering course towards the battleship from a position before the beam and found himself bearing down on it at an alarming rate. Fortunately he had the good sense to turn away and increase speed; the first number that'd come into his head was 286, which was the pattern number of the radar set we happened to be fitted with, and although the Engine Room hadn't a hope in hell of getting to that speed, it did the trick as they tried to get as close to it as they could in the shortest possible time.

I'm pleased to say that the Sub-Lieutenant eventually served with distinction as an Admiral in the RAN. I never found out why he'd been left in charge, but he certainly learnt fast.

'Working up', as it was called in Scapa Flow, was really a process of shaking down. The autumn gales that swept the area caused disruption to our programme and one afternoon while trying to do a sub calibre shoot on 6 October, fog closed it down.

The Captain then received a signal from the Admiral in the Depot ship *Tyne*, which simply said, *'Close the Flagship.'*

We crept back to the buoy and secured. Setting off in the Jolly Boat down the flow the Captain eventually found the Flagship to be met by the Admiral who said, "Where's your ship?"

"Secured to the buoy."

"Well bring it here."

Back he came in fog even thicker than before and we finally got down to the vicinity of the Flagship. This took more than four hours before we were in spitting distance from the flagship. Off he set once more. On returning he looked directly at me, querying, "Pilot, have you got charts to get to Archangel?"

Saying I did, he beamed, "Good. Set course for Seydisfjord at full speed." Then proceeded to wind up the revolutions before we'd even closed the boom gate.

Only those who've navigated in tidal waters around the British coasts will realize that there are a number of calculations that have to be made before a reasonable estimate of the tidal streams to be encountered can be made. Added to this as it was wartime, were a number of checks to be made on the location and extent of minefields before setting a course that would not lead to disaster, such as had befallen the British A class destroyer we were off to replace.

After taking on fuel, off the coast of Iceland they'd run into a mine that had blown their bow off. That it was a British mine was of course no consolation.

Thanks to my navigation our results were more successful. Although I had some difficulty in convincing the Captain, himself a navigator, that the land he could see quite plainly, was in fact some 80 miles away and far outside the range of our radar. What we had at that time was an adaptation of the very early radar equipment fitted in aircraft and its performance close to the surface of the sea was much less effective than it was in the air. As we continued to steam towards the land at 30 knots and it didn't get any closer, the Captain gradually came to the realization that I was right.

At Prime Minister Churchill's instigation, a delegation headed by Sir Walter Citrine and consisting of leading members of the British Trade Union movement was being sent to Russia for a meeting with Stalin in Moscow. They were to ascertain whether Russia had any hope of holding out against the German invaders, then practically at the gates of Moscow. As soon as we'd fuelled and embarked Sir Walter and his party we set off for Russia, passing north of Bear Island and making best speed.

In the intense cold of the Arctic Circle, even wearing the special fur lined coats and foul weather gear we'd been given as a parting gift by the Flagship *Tyne* in Scapa Flow, we weren't able to continue keeping four-hour watches, especially in exposed positions.

I solved my problem of bodily warmth by putting my flannel pajamas on under everything else. Sir Walter later referred to this in a book he wrote of his journey to Russia, inferring I'd donned the one pair on leaving Iceland and left them on unchanged until we returned to Scapa Flow some two months later. I didn't sue him for defamation though. He really was a decent chap.

With only three qualified Watchkeepers in our officer complement, John Dowson the No.1, Gunner T. Mitchell on loan from the RN, and myself, it was clear that four-hour watches were no longer advisable given the conditions. And particularly as the captain had decided that Tom Mitchell was too old to keep watch at night.

Fortunately as one of the 7th Destroyer Flotilla ships *(Napier, Nizam, Nestor, Norman, Nepal)* we had some supernumeraries onboard. With Neil Macdonald, our Sub Lieutenant, our RANVR Asdic specialist Whitehead, and Warrant Officer Gunnery Specialist George Glossop who was onboard for the working-up it was possible to have two officers on the Bridge for two-hour watches throughout the dark periods.

At the speed we maintained two factors affected ship safety: the fuel used and the seawater and spray that turned to ice on the upper deck, guardrails, and superstructure. The RN had not yet adopted the standard practice of the United States Navy of pressing up the fuel tanks. As a consequence *Norman* faced a real possibility of bringing the centre of gravity and the centre of buoyancy dangerously close.

Neville McGuire the Engineer Officer and John, the First Lieutenant set up a veritable 'Heath Robinson' arrangement of steam hoses to cope with the worst of the icing problem.

One fall-out from this was that I was virtually confined to the Bridge during the hours of darkness, but this had many advantages because the time during which observations could be made was greatly increased. However there was no way of coping with using the sextant without exposing ones fingers. It's impossible to make the adjustments necessary to take accurate sights wearing gloves. While the true horizon would often unexpectedly be visible together with a range of heavenly bodies, sufficiently divergent in bearing to produce a reliable fix, the light would often then fade just as suddenly. Many a time I returned to the Chart House to work out my observations quite incapable of moving my fingers, and in agony as feeling began to return to them. I soon learned that putting them in a glass of water sped up the recovery process.

We left Scapa Flow at 21:30 on Day One arriving at Seydisfjord at 14:30 on Day Two. After fuelling and embarking our passengers who arrived by flying boat we sailed at 17:00. Had it been possible to go from Seydisfjord to Archangel as a crow, the distance covered would have been some 1370 nautical miles. Our passage north of Bear Island involved some 2470 nautical miles mostly inside the Arctic Circle and as far north as 75 degrees N latitude.

Sir Walter Citrine, as befitted his status, was given the Captain's Day Cabin aft. At 30 knots he found the vibration unbearable, so being interested in what was going on he decided to spend as much time as he could with me in the Chart House below the Bridge. He realized that the

Captain had so much on his mind that he couldn't expect to be entertained, plus I had a heater and was doing interesting things like taking the altitude of Polaris to check latitude and the Moon's Upper Limb to check longitude whenever Aurora Borealis disclosed the sea horizon.

Sir Walter Citrine was a far cry from the stereotype of a Pommy shop steward, and in fact vastly different from the four other influential leaders in the British Trade Union Movement who were accompanying him. He'd been an old opponent of Churchill during the General Strike of 1936 and in 1940 had been part of a Labour mission of inquiry and encouragement to Finland in its war with the USSR. He supported Labour in the events of 10 May 1940, when Churchill supplanted Chamberlain, but didn't wish to be in Government, preferring to remain as General Secretary of the Trades Union Congress.

Britain's strategic situation at the time was:

- an almost desperate Russian position
- Britain's economy was fully mobilized for war — by end of November 1941 it was almost as precarious as it had been a year earlier
- the entire coastline from North Cape to the Spanish frontier was in German hands
- an Italian fleet operated under shore-based air cover from an impregnable central position in the Mediterranean, and
- there was a latent threat from the powerful neutral navies of France and Japan.

Among the plusses:

- Churchill and his relationship with Roosevelt, an inconclusive offensive against the German and Italian forces in Libya
- Pearl Harbour was yet to come on 7 December 1941, followed on 10 December by the sinking of *Prince of Wales* and *Repulse*.

At 23:00 on Day Three north of Bear Island we altered course and made a landfall off the Kola Inlet at midnight on Day Four. We were off the entrance to the White Sea.

The Russian authorities had agreed to operate the lighthouse for about five minutes on the hour. Sure enough, through a clearing in the snowstorm there it was, exactly where it should have been. Despite what the Captain may have thought about me, I think my reputation as a Navigator was made there and then.

I'm sure some of you will remember the classic exchange of signals that occurred in the USN during a fleet exercise. A light was sighted dead ahead and the flagship sent: 'Alter your course 20 degrees to Port I am an Admiral.' The reply came back: 'I strongly advise you to alter your course 20 degrees to Port. I am a lighthouse.'

Day Five was spent circumventing a declared minefield in the White Sea, arriving at the mouth of the North Dvina River at 14:30 on schedule.

The passage up river was unbelievable and memorable in more ways than ever imaginable.

The British Admiralty Chart which I had to use had been produced from information provided in the late 19th Century and had not been corrected since just after World War I.

The navigable channel was marked on the ground by leads and a pilot who spoke no English had been provided. He and I soon established a communicable working relationship. He would say, "Starboard" and I would put the rudder over to start the turn. Then would come, "More Starboard" and I'd increase the rudder angle. Then without warning he'd say, "Steady", meaning that he was on the leads. I'd then have to use full opposite rudder to stop the ship overshooting the new course. It was all right for me, but the poor Coxswain in the wheelhouse finished up stripped to the waist and dripping with sweat.

Before leaving for Moscow Sir Walter confided in me. Imagine, if you will, the state of mind of a man without military training, or experience, faced with the uncertainty of flying from Archangel to Moscow, hedge-hopping all the way and practically in sight of the deadly enemy. No wonder he wanted someone to know why he was doing it.

Stafford Cripps, British Ambassador in Moscow, was in London when the Germans attacked the Russians. He didn't think the Russians could hold out for more than a few weeks, in organized resistance to the Germans. This was, at that time, official British military opinion.

Churchill was sending Citrine and his mission to have first hand discussions with Stalin as to whether the Russians could hold out. If not, the British Trades Unions were to be called out by Christmas and a deal would be done with Hitler. This was for my information only, never to be revealed.

Our berth up river was alongside a timber yard. We said goodbye to our supercargo as they headed to Moscow, some 400 miles away. Hedge-hopping all the way, the official party arrived only to find that the people they'd come to see had moved to Kuybyshev, a further 500 miles to the east, just beyond the River Volga.

Now once again the next version of events differs markedly from that in Henry Burrell's version in his autobiography. His book states the *Norman* was ordered to *'carry out an anti submarine patrol off the entrance to the North Dvina River.'*

However it was Burrell's decision alone to continue our working up practices as if nothing had happened. So free of responsibility for delivering Citrine and party we headed out into the White Sea to hunt German submarines.

The local Naval Commander, while visibly shaking his head, said he had no authority to approve what was being proposed and would in no way cooperate by providing any personnel under his command, so we had to go it alone. Even the locals couldn't comprehend it. German forces were 20 miles from Moscow, German tanks were at Petsamo, and fishermen we'd talked to, had said they'd come upon submarines on the surface at night charging batteries and were sure they were German.

The Captain set on having his way ordered we steam off down the river and into the White Sea, without a pilot this time and with a lot less work for the Coxswain at the wheel.

After the Captain managed to get a signal through to the Admiralty telling them in London what we were doing, I cannot swear to it, but I think the Prime Minister practically had apoplexy, and we were told in no uncertain terms to get back to Archangel and wait for Sir Walter Citrine and his party to return.

One result of this little excursion was that I acquired a shadow, a Lieutenant from the Russian Navy. Rightly or wrongly, he wanted a track chart of where we'd been and what we'd done while we were away. He indicated that he would stay put until he got it.

He was a pleasant fellow, so we gave him a berth in the Chart House and fed him until the document he wanted so badly was finished.

Lest it be thought that all Russian military officers were stooges for their political bosses, I can assure you that my shadow's offer of a trip to Moscow to see the ballet was genuine – he wouldn't have done the commercial if it wasn't. He had the authority to call on a military aircraft for a flight to Moscow and back. I would go along for the ride, ostensibly to answer any questions that might arise from the examination of my track chart. I knew the Captain wouldn't wear that one, but it was a tempting offer.

The next offer I got was from another Russian Navy Lieutenant, and one I could accept. This Lieutenant had come to Archangel in the former Czar's Royal Yacht with the Commissar of North Russia to offer hospitality to Sir Walter and his party before they left Russia.

The Russian Naval Officer in question was a female interpreter. While waiting for the party to return she was forced to make many visits to the *Norman* to receive the latest updates. I was able to convince her that as I was also the Signals Officer (true) and as such I'd be the first to know when they'd be back on board (untrue). Moreover, I was the only one who had the exact shade of lipstick to suit her.

It just so happened that one of my functions was to arrange for any attractive females to be invited to the Wardroom for appropriate entertainment, morning coffee, afternoon tea, meals and drinks. For such occasions I kept a drawer in my desk stocked with a few things in short supply that would appeal to ladies denied little luxuries because of wartime restrictions.

Those of you who follow women's tennis will be aware of Anna Kournikova, who although she's not number one when it comes to tournaments, she certainly wins the admiration of male fans. Looking back on it I would say this Naval Officer could've been Anna Kournikova's grandmother. Fortunately I didn't know that my Dear John letter awaited my return to Scapa Flow, and after all there was a war on.

Finally the delegation returned to Archangel. In return for the favours she invited me to the function onboard their yacht. What a party. The comrades really turned it on. The vodka flowed, the Commissar danced on the table, and at a very late hour I was involved in a conversation on the relative merits of the socialist and capitalist systems that revolved around the felling of timber in North Russia, shipping it to England to have it made into a door, and then shipping it back to Russia for use in a house. One of the British Trade Unionists, in a loud voice, espoused his thoughts on the subject for at least an hour, finally silencing all opposition. One of the Russians who'd been following the argument intently turned to me and with an appealing gesture said, "Please. What is a door?" So much for communications.

Ice had closed in on the river by the time we were ready for the return journey. With the assistance of a Russian icebreaker we made passage downstream. The trick was not to let the icebreaker get too far ahead, or to try to follow it too closely. At the same time we had to be sure that in looking for a passage through the ice we were still in water deep enough to stop us going aground.

Clear of the river we topped up with fuel from a county class cruiser that had come to make arrangements for the reception of the supply convoys that were to make the run to Murmansk and then to return in the shortest possible time. By then I had discovered that the minefield we had been so careful to avoid on the way in to the White Sea didn't really exist. This meant we could take a short cut on the way out.

Again, if one is to read Burrell's autobiography he reports difficulties in getting to sea on leaving Archangel. However, these are exaggerations of minor incidents mentioned above, as we followed the icebreaker down river. Incidentally, it's interesting to note that he made no mention of his own poor ship handling on casting off from the cruiser sent to refuel us and how he caused the ship's motor boat to be wrecked in the collision with the county class cruiser's port side. This incidentally was my 'abandon ship' station.

The fact is war history is invariably written by the victors. Churchill has documented the period I've been talking about in what he claimed to be only a contribution to the history of the Second World War from the standpoint of the British Prime Minister, with special responsibility as Minister of Defence for military affairs. It was published in 1950. On 4 November 1941 Churchill offered to send Generals Wavell, Commander in Chief India, and Paget, Commander in Chief Designate for the Far East, to meet Stalin anywhere in Russia. Stalin replied 'it would be very difficult for him to find time for the conversations'. On 23 November 1941 Stalin agreed that an early visit to Moscow by the British Foreign Secretary, Anthony Eden to formalize a written treaty of alliance would be welcome. Throughout this record no mention is made of the Citrine mission. I rest my case.

Over succeeding years Henry Burrell and I had many disagreements but considering that as a junior Commander he incurred the wrath of an Admiral, the incredulity of a Prime Minister, both of Britain, a country which in due course rewarded him with two high honours, he was wise to write what he wrote about taking Citrine to Russia.

Burrell being a smoker and Citrine not, I'd also put money on the proposition that the memento Sir Walter gave Henry was the one he'd received from the Commissar of North Russia.

Anyway, apart from the weather, which was appalling, the return to Scapa Flow was quite uneventful. It was clear however, that we'd have to go back to Thornycroft's for a final check before we became operational, as the entire upper works were leaking. The high speed, vibration and intense contraction had worked the plates so that it was necessary for them to be crimped together at the edges.

In the first mail to be delivered I received my Dear John letter from Jane telling of her forthcoming marriage to a famous polo-player a few years younger than my father and never likely to go any further in war with RAAF than Bradfield Park, it was no great surprise In six months she'd be 22. I was also not a boy from the Anti-Aircraft.

Anyway the champagne was on me that day as I learned that there was more to life than love. I suddenly realized I was surrounded by men in bondage — the Captain was avoiding the King's Proctor, the Engineer Officer never went ashore, the First Lieutenant was devoted to his wife back home and the Doctor couldn't trust himself to visit any hospital we happened to be near in case he should see someone who reminded him of his wife. War was no pastime for the married. Once I'd made up my mind not to get married until the war was over, life took on a much rosier hue. I was free!

The trip to Thornycroft's was fortunately short and Eunice Coxon was on holiday. There was no need to put the new me to the test, nor to test the proposition that I had in some way been a disappointment to her. Eunice was a very pretty girl, but I suspected that I'd been tried and found wanting. I often wonder whether she ever met and married the man of her dreams and whether in fact she ever got to London. When I met her she'd not been further afield than Torquay where the family went for a holiday each year. Her cultural excursions had never taken her beyond Bournemouth. But as I said, she was a very pretty girl.

— 13 —

1942

Generally regarded as the year in which we started to win the war, 1942 for me held little optimism. HMAS *Norman* was to join the other ships of the 7th Destroyer Flotilla around the Mediterranean Sea where the first ships to be completed had relieved those of the Scrap Iron Flotilla. HMAS *Napier*, the leader, was under the command of an RN Officer Captain S H T Arliss. HMAS *Nizam* was commanded by Commander M J Clark RAN who'd spent many years in destroyers. HMAS *Nestor* had experienced some troubles during the work-up period at Scapa Flow, resulting in a change in command. Commander A S Rosenthal, who was originally scheduled to take command of HMAS *Norman* was slotted in, together with an RN Officer as his Second-in-Command. Thus leaving Burrell in charge of *Norman*.

Rosenthal was an officer of immense ability with a reputation for demanding only the best from his subordinates. Despite his obvious talents it appeared his career in pre-war RAN hadn't prospered, so much so that he'd transferred before war broke out to the Auxiliary Services.

It's difficult to think of a present day parallel to this, but it's a bit like turning Phar Lap over to pull a milk cart. It's not enough to say that clashes of personality will always occur, or to admit that luck plays a large part in who should rise to the top in any particular Service. There has been, and I'm sure there will continue to be, a total lack of appreciation that the mechanistic methods of selection coupled with an almost complete absence of career planning produces a situation in which there are more good officers than there are good jobs for them to carry out.

Most senior service officers counter this contention with the aphorism that there are no good or bad jobs, only good or bad officers and to add credence to their belief often manipulate the postings and promotion system to this end. What they fail to see is that the favourite sons who are used in this way have already been predestined for promotion by the process of the monkey-chain principle that is so prevalent particularly in small Services.

The Armed Services are not alone in this. The various Departments that make up the Commonwealth and States Public Services and private enterprises of comparable size are all prone to exactly the same methods of operation. The difference is that the individual expects this sort of treatment there. One doesn't expect it in the Services.

If the Mediterranean were to be our theatre of operations, we certainly went the long way round. Firstly, *Norman* was dispatched to Milford Haven to pick up passengers bound for an unknown destination somewhere in Africa.

In view of our success with the British Trade Union mission, our expectations were for more high-flyers to come aboard. It was something of a let down to find that we'd been saddled with a couple of very ordinary, very junior, non-fighting members of the British Army whose contribution to the war effort was likely to be marginal to say the least. Nevertheless we made them welcome and I gave up my aft cabin for the convenience of the Bridge and moved to a bunk in the Chart House.

The only thing I can remember about my guest, apart from the smell he left behind in my cabin, was that he shaved in the morning without removing the cigarette from his mouth. He just scraped away the whiskers, soap, ash and all.

Before leaving Milford Haven one important ritual had to be performed. In my capacity as Wardroom ponce, it fell to me to entice the local WREN officers onboard for a farewell drink. This proved a totally delightful interlude and yet sad in a way as the girls were always saying goodbye to people they'd often never meet again, more for the reason that they'd finish up at the bottom of the Atlantic or Mediterranean. Nevertheless we became something special for them as more often than not the hospitality for them was entirely one sided. They'd be descended upon in their quarters, and as one bright blonde Second Officer confided to me, the Norwegians were the worst. Their English expression was apparently limited to the phrase, "Lock the door. It will only take five minutes."

This was the first occasion that they'd been invited on board and as it involved a trip by the ship's boat from the jetty to our anchorage, it was also an adventure for them.

In a destroyer sailing alone, it was surprising how the war seemed to be passing us by. Throughout January 1942 the most significant events were taking place in the waters north of Australia, while we seemed to be at the mercy of every whim of some staff officer at the Admiralty.

First we put in to Ponta Delgada in the Azores. As Officer-of-the-Guard I boarded the Portuguese destroyer stationed there and was interrogated most skillfully by its Captain, an officer who'd distinguished himself in the Portuguese Navy by writing a definitive work on the life of Horatio Nelson. As my own efforts to that time had been limited to a thumbnail sketch of James Cook delivered to the assembled Cadet Midshipmen as an Anniversary to celebrate the birth of the navigator and explorer, I was duly impressed.

I had enormous difficulty in convincing him that there was not some great battle going on in the near vicinity from which we'd been momentarily detached. It was his firm desire to sail with us and join in, and to hell with neutrality. He must have carried this theme much further with the Captain when he paid his call, because we were to be subjected to a few weeks of planning in which G49, which was the pendant number we carried, was to win the war at sea single-handed.

Our next assignment was to escort a convoy of ships carrying military equipment and stores, but few personnel, bound for goodness knew where. We picked it up at Freetown and headed south at what for us was slow speed, but for some of the ships was practically flat out at nine knots or thereabouts. Thankfully this didn't last long. In response to an urgent signal we increased speed to just under 30 knots and made for Cape Town. Once there no one had any idea what to do with us, so we waited.

The euphoria of going ashore in a city where the lights were on at night and there were no restrictions on what could be eaten in the restaurants and cafés was uplifting. Just how this affected our sailors can be judged from the experience of one group who went ashore to do what sailors do, but decided to eat first. The initial order was steak and an egg, followed by steak and two eggs, and the final order not to be outdone was steak and eight eggs.

Finally orders to proceed to Durban were received and we rounded the Cape of Good Hope. This was to become very familiar to us over the ensuing months, although we didn't know it then.

On arrival at the Durban roadstead we were greeted by the convoy we'd left on the other side of Africa, to which it seemed we were doomed to return. But fate again was to play a hand and we were off on our own at best speed to Colombo, arriving the day Singapore fell. Dinner that night at the Galle Face Hotel was a very sad occasion. The band played as it had done every evening up to then and when it came my time to request a number I asked for *Valse Triste*, which summed up everybody's feelings. Colombo would never be the same again.

There's been a great deal of criticism about the standard of staff work and operational planning that led to the defeat in detail of the British forces stationed in the Far East. The loss of *Prince of Wales* and *Repulse* that had been left without the support of the accompanying carrier *Indomitable*, coming so soon after the paralyzing effect on the United States Navy of the Japanese attack on Pearl Harbour, left planners with minimal scope for initiative. Yet it was evident that the mad dogs and Englishmen syndrome still persisted.

After arriving at Colombo I made the customary visit to the Naval Staff Office and mentioned that we'd not received any communication from the shore during the passage from Addu Atoll. Nonchalantly the Staff Officer Signals handed me a bunch of messages. One referred to the existence of a minefield off Colombo and the location of a swept channel through it. I was aghast, telling him this was the first information we'd seen of such a hazard. Casually he informed me that had the ship blown up it would've been his responsibility. Surprise swept his face when I angrily replied, "Yes, but it would've been my ship!"

I got the distinct impression that our arrival was an unwarranted intrusion on what would otherwise have been a perfectly normal day with drinks at the GOH, home for lunch and a zizz, followed by tea and tennis at the Club.

When the Captain paid his formal call, he was chipped about the militancy of one of his officers. To his credit he defended my attitude and honestly, I think he was as appalled as I was at the state of affairs. Matters weren't improved by the arrival of more ships carrying Australian soldiers from the Middle East either. The soldiers were left in limbo, not knowing whether they were to be thrown into the land battle for

Burma currently underway, or repatriated to Australia where they were needed to bolster up the rapidly expanded units of the militia recruited for home defence. We could only assume that we'd be required to escort them to whatever their ultimate destination was.

Again we were quite wrong. Our role was to form part of the First Eleven of the Eastern Fleet then being formed.

The Eastern Fleet was a masterpiece. Just as that minefield off Colombo and the swept channel were figments of some staff officer's imagination, the fighting power of the Eastern Fleet was more apparent than real.

Ships capable of a Fleet speed of 20 to 25 knots automatically qualified for the First Eleven. The rest that could perhaps sustain 15 knots made up the Seconds. Relying on the doctrine made famous by the pre war Commander-in-Chief Mediterranean, that in a Fleet action the slower fleet would dictate the tactics, we set about denying the Indian Ocean to the Japanese Navy.

There were two factors in our favour. First the Commander-in-Chief Eastern Fleet, flying his flag in HMS *Warspite*, was Admiral Sir James Somerville. His Second-in-Command, Vice Admiral Sir Algernon Willis was perhaps the finest trainer of ships for their role in combat in any Navy. Under their leadership we achieved a state of readiness and a thirst for action that was quite remarkable in the circumstances. Not that there was much to be complacent about in the months that followed the fall of Singapore. We lost the old aircraft carrier *Hermes*, the destroyers *Vampire* and *Tenedos*, a personal blow to our First Lieutenant who'd served in that ship in peace, and on 9 April 1942 the 8-inch cruisers *Dorsetshire* and *Cornwall*.

While a Japanese task force rampaged around the Bay of Bengal we found ourselves forced to retire to our base in the Maldives to refuel.

Anxious to be off, the First Eleven sailed in the middle of the night leaving the remainder to follow on as best they could. We raced around the ocean at high speed but never made contact with the enemy. Whether the enemy was trying to make contact with us was never clear. As a sea battle it wasn't destined to make the history books, but a brief reference to it has been made in *The Navy Day by Day: Historic Naval Events in Australia and Abroad*.

Once it'd become clear that Japanese naval activity would not extend far into the Indian Ocean for some time to come, it was decided to use the escorts for the Eastern Fleet where they could be of greater use against our enemies. We were off northward for a particular mission in the Mediterranean. It was business as usual in the Suez Canal, though as a single warship we didn't have to form part of a convoy, merely to conform to the general principle that northbound and southbound ships didn't meet in the canal proper.

On arrival at Alexandria it was soon apparent that we were to be part of something big with a code-name *Operation Vigorous* and a cover story involving Turkey. Large crates of goodness knows what labelled 'Winter Clothing' were dumped on the upper deck in full view of the fellucca men who plied their trade around the ships in the harbour. Boxes stencilled with ISTANBUL were sent from shore to ship, much to the amusement of the locals who without prompting shouted, "Johnny, you go Malta."

How wrong they were. We never made it.

For four days and four nights we steamed back and forth between Benghazi and Crete, the notorious Bomb Alley. By day we were subjected to high level bombing, dive-bombing and torpedo bombing, and harassment from E Boats and submarines by night. Our sister ship HMAS *Nestor* was damaged by a near miss from a bomb during *Opera-*

tion Vigorous and had to be sunk by one of our own ships, HMS *Javelin* to avoid it falling into enemy hands while in tow.

Relations between the Captain and myself, had been becoming more and more strained, particularly as tension built up between the Captain and the First Lieutenant. This reached an all-time low during a torpedo bombing attack, pressed home with courage and vigour by units of the Italian Air Force.

Unable to penetrate the barrage fire from ships screening the merchant ships in convoy the Italians turned their attack on the screening ships. In such a situation there are three courses of action; turn towards the attacker and present the minimum target, turn away and increase speed to outrun the torpedo, do nothing and hope the torpedo will miss. Whichever course chosen requires an instant decision to be made at the moment the pilot released the weapon. There was no time for debate. In the event I made the decision to turn away and increase speed. We weren't hit, but from that moment on my naval days were numbered. I know this for sure now, especially after reading in Burrell's autobiography *Mermaids Do Exist* on pages 138 and 139 the description of the aerial torpedo attack on Norman during *Operation Vigorous* in June 1942:

> *'On one occasion I turned away on a course parallel to the tracks, moving out of the screen. I then had to decide when it would be safe to turn back and regain station.'*

In fact Burrell was at the after end of the Bridge watching the 4 inch high angle gun and the Oerlikon guns firing at the attacking aircraft approaching from the starboard quarter. I, as Action Officer-of-the Watch immediately ordered Hard-a-Port, Revolutions for 25 knots, raised the Asdic Dome before the Captain could turn around and see what was going on at the compass platform. It was this quick reaction that saved the ship to return to Alexandria.

The sinking of HMAS *Nestor* led to some profound effects for us in *Norman*. Suddenly more officers were available. But when our First Lieutenant met with an accident in somewhat mysterious circumstances ashore in Alexandria and was to spend some months in hospital before returning to Australia, my hopes of stepping into his shoes were dashed when he was relieved by the First Lieutenant of *Nestor*, a bustling super-efficient RN Officer who quickly made life onboard, on what had been a mostly happy ship until then, into something of an ego trip.

It's become fashionable to extol the virtues of the Australian fighting man to the extent that war couldn't be won without his unique display of talent and resourcefulness. When he's winning there's probably no better fellow. When things aren't going so well there is a tendency for him to act irresponsibly. In these situations officers have to be particularly careful that they exercise firm leadership and show that they're in complete control of the situation, even though they may have doubts. It's almost the same as an Australian team attitude in sporting events. Winning is done extremely well; losing is quite a different matter.

The First Lieutenant John Dowson's accident weighed heavily on me, and not merely because I missed out on promotion. Dowson had gone ashore to recover from the angst. As Officer-of-the-Day I saw the return of the libertymen in the midnight boat and retired to my cabin in the aft part of the ship. For some inexplicable reason the signal to *Norman* to leave harbour and anchor off the Great Pass at 07:30 next morning was never received. Sub Lieutenant Neil Macdonald, the Officer-of-the Day, woke me at 06:30 with the news that the First Lieutenant hadn't returned on board, and that both Watches were preparing to get underway and steam was being raised to enable the ship to proceed as soon as practicable. The Captain wasn't pleased; and guess who was the one to blame? The next in command, yours truly.

Later that day when things had calmed down we learnt that the First Lieutenant had been assaulted on his way back to catch the midnight boat. Badly injured and in hospital, he was unlikely to be able to return. There was now a direct line to me for Burrell's wrath.

For some months a separate staff had been planning what was to become a masterpiece of strategy — *Operation Stream-Line Jane*, to take over the occupation of the island of Madagascar from the Vichy French in September 1942.

The presence of an anything but friendly regime in Madagascar threatened British control of the Western Indian Ocean. Little was known of the relationship between the Japanese and the Vichy French in Indo-China, but that facilities might become available in Madagascar to support the operations of a Japanese fleet was thought to be a possibility.

The decision to forestall any attempt by the Japanese to take Madagascar by occupying it ourselves was not easy to do. With Dakar in 1940 still fresh in mind and plans for a joint American/British operation in North Africa, success depended on French cooperation.

HMAS *Norman* was to figure prominently in the actual invasion. Our task was to break away from the invasion convoy heading for Majunga and proceed under cover of darkness to a position close to the reefs and act as a marker beacon to ensure that the ships carrying the assault force didn't run aground.

The success of the operation depended upon navigational skill. We were chosen for the job because the Captain had been a navigation specialist in earlier times and could be expected to understand the problems associated with accurate position finding. You can imagine my chagrin when it was decided that a qualified navigator of the planning staff, another RN Officer, was to join the ship temporarily to take over the navigating duties.

In the event we anchored in the right place at the right time, the assault landing took place on schedule and the mobile column proceeded overland to link up with the main assault on Tamatave, which was to force the capitulation of the Vichy French Government. Such was the economy of scale of the operation that we were required to up anchor and proceed at high speed round the north of the island to join up with the main assault force.

Before leaving the reef the Gunner T reported that a test of the two-pound charges was long overdue. The test explosion resulted in a 27-foot whaler full of fish and a welcome relief from the tinned tongue and onions that had become staple fare for lunch for as long as anyone cared to remember.

The operation at Tamatave went smoothly, but once again the Captain and I found ourselves at loggerheads. The arrival of the armada had caused great excitement among the local population. Dressed in their Sunday best they flocked to the shoreline to see the spectacle. Some sense told them not to venture beyond the line of trees flanking the beach, which was dotted with dugouts and log revetments and completely unmanned. In the uneasy period between the call to surrender and the acceptance of that surrender a shot was fired. It's never been established whether it was the result of some itchy fingered young sailor frightening himself half to death, or whether it was some earnest patriot committing an act of defiance for la belle France. Whatever it was, the effect was dramatic. From the Flagship of the operation came the signal, *'Open Fire.'*

Then we questioned, "On what?" Over which the Captain and I disagreed. He was all for peppering the beach. I argued that shots in the air would suffice. As all the people were at the shoreline there wouldn't be anyone left inland to be threatened by overs. As the first rounds were fired the spectators disappeared and long after each ship ceased firing the order, *'Cease Fire'* came from the Flagship. So much for the doctrine of minimum force. What do you do when people, especially children, get mixed up in your battle?

All's well that ends well, and to this end the operation was mighty successful. So successful in fact that it was repeated later in the war with the landings in France and Henry Burrell was awarded a Mention-in-Despatches, acknowledging the good work of all onboard.

After Madagascar we returned to the apparently aimless task of patrolling between Durban and Cape Town. On one of these patrols we sighted a ships lifeboat under sail making for Table Bay. It was dusk, and in the stiff breeze then blowing and allowing for a change in direction with the dawn, the occupants would surely have made the safety of Cape Town next day. We took them aboard and proceeded on our patrol, taking the precaution of sinking their boat first.

They were to be with us for another five days exposed to the dangers of the sea and the violence of the enemy. Having been sunk once by a U Boat, they were anything but reassured that they wouldn't be subjected to the experience yet again. They had absolutely no faith whatsoever in our ability. Fortunately the issue wasn't put to the test. Undoubtedly we obeyed the first principles of seamanship in picking them up, but given the circumstances I believe we should've offered them the choice of continuing on under sail. I was beginning to realize that the decisions facing a Captain weren't to be found in books, certainly not those I'd read up until then.

It was during the 32 days of constant steaming that fuel ran so low there was an ever-present chance that the ship might stop and have to be taken in tow to some point to be fuelled. In one of the alarms and excursions I unfortunately barked my shin on the teak support of the gyro compass. This broke the skin and it developed into a tropical ulcer which defied all the treatment that could be given by the Sick Bay on board and the training and medical experience of the good doctor, Surgeon Lieutenant Symons, who later became an eye-specialist of some note.

After three months the oval shaped wound five inches long and four inches wide showed no sign of healing so near the end of 1942 I was bundled off to hospital in Cape Town.

During our sporadic visits to Durban we were known to trip the light fantastic in a nightclub euphemistically called 'Stardust'. Through one young woman I began an affair with one of her friends. While it had become serious, my accident and short hospital stay in Cape Town soon doused the flames, and also my time in destroyers was coming to end.

I was relieved onboard *Norman* and to take passage back to Australia on the Blue Funnel Line ship *Themistocles* for an unaccompanied voyage across the Southern Ocean during which we sighted absolutely nothing as we travelled via Port Elizabeth, Durban, Fremantle, Adelaide and Melbourne to Sydney.

The dear old ship was a coal burner with a top speed of about nine knots. Most times the cruising speed was nearer six knots and probably independent routeing was the only sensible way to operate such a ship. It was as well that we had a few young people among the passengers otherwise the days at sea would've dragged interminably.

I played Bridge with the Captain and two of his officers regularly every night and held such poor cards that I scarcely bid a hand for the whole voyage.

On the return voyage was another officer who'd been in my year at RANC and was also returning to Australia for a shore appointment. A young woman, engaged to be married to an RAN sailor, was travelling alone, and was being eyed-off by one of the younger ship's officers, who was in the habit of going off watch at midnight and coming into her cabin.

Enlisting the help of a third Australian Naval Reserve Officer the three of us set about putting an end to this threat to the dignity and reputation of the young woman, embarking upon the adventure of a lifetime. This involved swapping cabins from time to time to confuse and confront the offender without the necessity of making a great fuss among the ships officers. To keep up our image as bon viveurs and partygoers each of us took turns at hosting a cabin party. These started when everything else in the ship closed down, soon after 21:00 at night as the card game folded. The cabins in *Themistocles* were anything but spacious and by the time six or seven people had arrived there was no room to breathe. In a darkened ship with primitive ventilation it was soon uncomfortably warm. Nevertheless, it was a party and everyone was determined to enjoy it.

Our high jinks worked like a charm, until one morning after my party the cabin steward came to me at breakfast, which all the passengers seemed to be able to have together, and with some solemnity he announced that while making my bed he'd found my cuff links which he proceeded to place in the palm of my hand. They were in fact earrings belonging to the young lady who couldn't for the life of her remember when she'd seen them last.

My cabin steward was one of the old school who probably dreamt of the days when he could look after the rich and famous on the cross Atlantic run in the real passenger ships. He was the most tactful man I have ever met.

Anyway that is the way reputations are won and lost. No doubt some members of the crew were well aware of the situation and approved of what we Australian Navy men were doing to protect our own.

Unfortunately while I'd been in hospital in Cape Town someone else had packed all my gear from my cabin in *Norman*, except for my Work Books and Notebooks. These remained in the Chart House and are probably now lying in some long-forgotten repository somewhere along with the Log Books of *Norman*. Unless by some stroke of fate these should ever see the light of day, we've the two versions of *Norman's* epic voyage from Scapa Flow to Archangel which are dealt with in this book, the true version and the one concocted between the two Knights of the Realm, Hamilton and Burrell.

It's also interesting to note that although 1942 didn't end particularly well for me, early 1943 finally took its toll on Neville McGuire in *Norman*, just a few months before Henry himself was relieved on 24 June 1943. Neville had fallen from a hatch at upper deck level to the level below. Burrell wrote:

'He was returned to Australia and recovered, although it took a long time. Always calm and efficient, he was one of my few seasoned officers and one whom I could ill-afford to lose.'

Apparently it never occurred to the Captain that in some respects the premature departure of his three principal subordinates may have had some relevance to his demonstrated account which attributes every happening on the bridge when under way, as being as a result of his personal effort. *Mermaids Do Exist* p 150.

Also the account of *Norman's* activity at sea during the last months of Henry's captaining. Obviously he took a much more hands-on activity with regard to navigation and there appeared to be some incidents of uncertainty concerning where the ship actually was. The Sub-Lieutenant had taken on the job of navigator, and was later to qualify as a Navigator who went on to Fleet Commander in 1977-78. He acknowledged after retirement that he learnt more about his craft from me than he ever did from Burrell.

It is particularly significant that when Henry Burrell was promoted to Captain on 30 June 1946 he followed the practice that was in vogue then and became the Deputy Chief of the Naval Staff. The Chief at that time was none other than Vice Admiral Sir Louis Hamilton KCB DSO RN. Funny that!

However the world is a small place and the RAN even smaller. It wasn't the last I was to see of Burrell, or to feel the effects he could have on my career.

— 14 —

1943

Sydney in 1943 was transformed. The foyer of the Hotel Australia was no longer the place in which one arranged to meet the love of one's life. The only way to get a taxi was to go with the girl friend's girl friend whose friend was an American Serviceman.

However, I soon remembered the habits of my childhood and discovered that it really was possible to get around Sydney in trams and that there were still girls who thought that the end of a perfect evening at Princes was to be taken home in the all night tram. The key to success was to judge the leave taking to a nicety so as to pick up the tram on its way back to the city. The girls from Double Bay and Edgecliff did far better than those from Vaucluse who had to be satisfied with a quick peck before Romeo was off like a rabbit to the tram stop.

But there was still a war on. I was appointed First Lieutenant of HMAS *Shepparton* a Bathurst class minesweeper that had been allocated to surveying duties in New Guinea waters.

These ships were really the most amazing craft ever devised. The basic design was British, but any semblance of ship building principles had given way to expediency. As long as it fitted it was secured in place. The early ships of the class had out-turning screws driven by fairly simple reciprocating steam engines. To get the maximum power while driving the ship ahead one engine had to be installed back to front, which meant some nifty placing of the controls to enable the one operator to control the engines.

The method of estimating the speed at which the engine was turning the shaft was ingenious. The throttle operator put his hand on a small crank feeding into a revolution counter and in the manner of a nurse taking a patient's pulse counted the number of revolutions per minute. If these were not what the Bridge had ordered he then put in a bit more, or less steam, until it was more or less right.

Somewhere along the building process the engines got themselves turned around and the later ships of the class also had in-turning screws. This was more efficient when going ahead some said. It made less wake and so cut down on the chances of being spotted from the air others said.

I don't think anyone really knew the full story, but the end result was some appalling ship handling from those who got their ships in irons and tried to turn at rest using the engines. At sea they were something else. Used as escorts to merchant ships they were flat out at 13 knots and in a seaway they rolled, pitched and corkscrewed, but somehow hung together. I can well imagine the crews of the new Fremantle Class saying, "What's new."

My time in *Shepparton* was all too short. Having worked the ship up into fighting trim I transferred to HMAS *Whyalla* to carry out the surveys necessary to occupy the Trobriand Islands and to prepare for the assault on Lae and Salamaua. Then it was to HMAS *Benalla* for more surveying until I was relieved by one of my Cook Year contemporaries who wished to make a career as a Hydrographer.

There was something very satisfying about surveying under the enemy's nose. By day we sounded from the ship and at night we anchored as close to the shore as possible without being in range of the malaria carrying mosquitoes.

I frequently went off for the day in a skiff fitted with a Chapman pup engine armed with a 45 service revolver and carrying a sextant and notebook to do what was known as coast-lining. This involved fixing several points on the shore-line and recording the nature of the terrain between them, more often than not mangrove swamps, but occasionally a sandy beach fringed with coconut palms. I always expected to meet the enemy around the next headland, but never did. Nor did I ever see any natives.

One day I was so thirsty I just had to have a coconut. I'd seen the way the experts tied their ankles together and shinned up the tree, but didn't fancy my chances. Being a hot shot with a pistol I decided to bring one down with my 45. The first shot hit all right, but nothing happened. The second produced the same result. With the third I got results, but not what I'd expected. I've often wondered what would've happened if anyone had seen me flat on my back under the palm tree with my mouth open catching the drips from the three holes which I'd pierced so neatly in the nut some fifty feet above me. My admiration for Daniel Defoe went up after that.

During my surveying days I grew a beard. Every man grows a beard once in his life. Some of course fancy themselves so much that they keep their facial adornment long past the time that it could be considered even moderately attractive to women. Most men succeed in looking like rats peeping out through lavatory brushes. But there is something about the first beard, particularly if it's grown in competition with others.

We worked it out very carefully with the amount of steaming we did on the survey ground it meant that we'd have to do a boiler clean in Cairns about every six weeks. That was just long enough to develop a good growth which wouldn't be too unsightly on the next visit and which would, if necessary, disguise one sufficiently in case there happened to be a new girl in town who was better looking than the one you happened to have landed last time.

Sporting my beard during one of our visits back to Cairns 1943

What we didn't know was that it wasn't us the girls were after, but the petrol we brought with us. Every time we came down for a boiler clean we'd bring a 44 -gallon drum, picked up from the beach up north. It was Japanese petrol that'd come from the transports sunk in the Battle of the Coral Sea some months before. As it was colourless it baffled the snoopers who were on the lookout for illegally acquired petrol and it provided the wherewithal for picnic trips to the beach and to the Barron Falls. What we didn't realize then, was that the real winners were the Yanks who went to ground when we were there, but came out in their jeeps once we'd gone.

For females, particularly in North Queensland, the war was a supreme opportunity to fulfill their girlish dreams that had been fuelled by Hollywood throughout the years of the depression. Just as the next generation, the development of Canberra opened up the prospects of a good job away from home and the chance to meet an eligible fellow with better prospects than those of the boy next door at home, the presence of so many servicemen, particularly those from the United States gave true love a chance to flourish. That so many of these wartime marriages turned out so well is a tribute to the triumph of the human spirit over adversity.

For career naval officers, marriage during a war was possibly the last thing to be contemplated. Far more important was the problem of whether or not to specialize, and if so, in what. Engineers had already embarked on a long course of training immediately after completing their initial sea time as Cadet Midshipmen. The rest of us had to decide whether gunnery, navigation, torpedo, signals or salt horse offered the best prospects for the future. There was no chance of the RAN career officer getting into submarines or the Fleet Air Arm, and anti-submarine was an occupation exclusively for Reserve Officers. Radar offered possibilities, but it soon became obvious that it was not possible to combine in the one specialization the technical aspects and the operational aspects. Since the earliest days I'd been determined to become a navigator and finally my persistence had paid off. I was nominated for the Specialist N Course in the United Kingdom that was due to start in the second half of 1944.

— 15 —

1944

Once again I was faced with the prospect of waiting for the next event to happen. I was appointed to HMAS *Assault,* a land establishment on Nelson Bay in Port Stephens just north of Newcastle, New South Wales. This was a training set-up for crews of the landing craft operating from the assault ships *Manoora* and *Westralia* that had been coastal passenger ships before the war. As the allied advance in New Guinea prospered, the base for these ships was moved further north and *Assault* was left as an anachronism.

When I took up my appointment morale was at an extremely low ebb. There were too many people with not enough to do and the entire purpose for the existence of the base no longer existed. With the aid of some pamphlets lent to me by an enthusiastic member of the Volunteer Defence Corps and some real support from the Gunner and the cooks I was able to organize some effective training in infantry minor tactics, which captured the imagination of the ship's company and gave them something to look forward to, other than how quickly they could get a draft out of the place.

To maintain morale I instituted a routine of weekly battalion drill on the parade ground and a series of light infantry attacks and defence across the peninsula to the ocean beach as well as weekly talks on the progress of the war in general. The incidence of minor punishments for petty infractions of the Standing Orders all but disappeared.

From September 1941 until January 1944 cricket for me had been non-existent. But now once again land based I was able to take part in the Newcastle District Cricket Competition, which gave me an opportunity to play against Grade level competition

There wasn't much else to do in Newcastle and despite being born there I'd left at age three. Therefore I went to Sydney whenever I could, but the competition for female attention was pretty fierce, particularly as the Anti-Aircraft boys were still around.

Renewing the friendship with the family of my erstwhile, now married old flame, I spent several weekends up the North West Line, mostly polishing off a sugar bag of fresh oysters and firing the cut-down 303 rifle at tin targets all in the name of emulating minor infantry tactics. Incidentally there was no hint of romance with the younger sister either.

One romance was beginning to flourish in Sydney when I received a posting to the Staff of the Army Staff School that was then attached to the Royal Military College Duntroon. After an interminable train journey from Sydney to Canberra I arrived at the Officers Mess, Duntroon House. My quarters were shared with an Army Officer on the staff. During our conversations I happened to mention that I'd just received a letter from the young lady with whom I was somewhat attracted at the time. Funnily, he'd also recently received a letter from the same person. After showing me his and I showed him mine, with the exception of the soubriquets they were identical. She married someone else soon after that, but neither of us ever let on how in fact she lost two suitors at the same time.

My position was the Naval Adviser on Amphibious Warfare. I was a Lieutenant with three and a half years seniority and a further four and a half years to serve before promotion to major equivalent. My fellow staff members were a couple of years older than me. They were half-colonels with service in the Middle East. The only old man was a full Colonel, (surname of Leonard), who was a loading expert whose claim to fame was to load last what you needed first on the beach. He had great difficulty persuading artillerymen not to put all the guns in one landing craft and all the ammunition in another.

I'd always been strongly attracted to the idea of inter-service cooperation. At Naval College I'd played cricket and rugby against the Air Force Cadets at Point Cook, but we were always too poor to do anything with Duntroon. My contact with the Royal Marines and through my father and one of my cousins, both members of the 30th Battalion NSW Scottish Regiment before the war, had given me some insight into the rationale of army life.

At Duntroon I found the introduction to staff work quite fascinating, particularly as we were involved in preparations for amphibious landings using the lessons learnt from Dieppe and other small-scale operations in occupied Europe. The duties also left me sufficient time to follow other pastimes.

The Duntroon stables were still in full operation, the only difference being Cadets were no longer trained in cavalry tactics, but in mechanized warfare. However there was a shortage of staff to exercise the horses. When the Corporal of Horse discovered that there was a naval officer prepared to go riding, the temptation was irresistible.

The first morning I turned up in my best English riding breeches from Moss Bros and string gloves. The entire stable staff watched on as the horse was paraded for my inspection. It was truly magnificent. As I mounted and adjusted the stirrups to the English style, somewhat modified by my experiences with the broken down racehorses that were always to be found on properties up the North West line, the Corporal, a master of subterfuge, had assured me that my mount was quite knowledgeable concerning what was expected. His parting words went something like this, "Just take him slowly down the track (which became the original Badge Gates and in the vicinity of the now main entrance to RMC), then turn right for about a mile to another track on the left. Go down that, across the road, and he will do the rest. Good luck, Sir."

I trotted off down the road leading to the Molongolo River. Sure enough at the end we turned right and soon broke into a canter until we came to the flat. From then on it was a full gallop, across the causeway that really was a causeway then, up over the Cooma Road and through the bush with me holding on for dear life and wondering if this mad dash would ever end. Finally, forelegs in the air, with much snorting and puffing, we came to a grinding halt at a high wire fence surrounding the tennis court at the Canberra Church of England Girls Grammar School.

From that moment on my social life in Canberra took on a rosy hue. Daily rides to the School soon led to cozy dinners for two at the Hotel Canberra under the eyes of anybody who was anybody in running the war. This was not so bad, but the real problem was the questioning from the little, and not so little girls, who attended every going out and coming in of their beloved mistress who, incidentally, was – hush, shudder – a MARRIED woman.

So sadly had the Americans corrupted our young girls that it was impossible for them to imagine that some of us still lived by the code that another fellow's wife was off limits in certain things. There must've been something there however, because it wasn't long before I was being fed the line, "When you go to Sydney you must meet my younger sister."

By the time I next saw Sydney much had happened and her younger sister had taken the plunge herself.

It shouldn't be thought that much of the war was simply a long series of poodle-faking episodes. The serious side of Staff College involved many hours of making up and revising the loading tables to ensure that the right units hit the beach with the right equipment so the effect of the inevitable losses would still enable its objectives to be captured and defended.

At last all was ready and we were to go to Moruya to put the plan into action. Engrossed in the many problems facing a Beach Master while conducting a landing exercise (TEWT: a tactical exercise without troops), something happened to me that you only read about in books.

Along the waters edge came a female, dressed in regulation khaki, vaguely reminiscent of one of those exquisite people who used to grace the social pages of our prewar newspapers every Sunday. She was a member of the AWAS (Australian Women's Army Service) — a squattocracy and she was after me. Her mission was to drive me back to Duntroon to collect my things and then on to Goulburn where I was to board the night train to Melbourne, then report to Navy Office at Victoria Barracks and be ready to embark in a ship to get me to England by 1st June. All this, she assured me, was of the utmost importance. It was early May 1944.

Strangely, the Director of Plans at Navy Office was Commander Henry Burrell, my Captain from *Norman*. He was keener to have my views on what should be done about *Assault*, than to provide the details of my next appointment. Many years were to pass before I learnt of what seemed to me my death knell. When he became Chief of Navy he let it be known that there were only two RAN officers who he deemed to be capable of original thought. Surprisingly I was one.

The next day I set sail in HMS *Ranee*, joining this wondrous ship of British improvisation at Williamstown, about thirty minutes prior to sailing time. The *Ranee* was fundamentally a merchant ship with a lid made of wooden plates bolted to a metal surround on it, servicing as the flight deck. Officially classed as an Escort Carrier, the ship had been designed to protect convoys crossing the North Atlantic. As there was no aircraft embarked the ship had some cabin space that the RAN took up.

The ship was on its way to England across the Pacific, first stop Victoria British Colombia, and no orders after that. As a passenger I had no status whatsoever. The majority of officers were T124X, agreement drawn from a variety of seafaring pursuits around the British Isles, fishermen, coastal freighters, you name it you have it.

I can honestly say I was the only one in that Wardroom who spoke the same language as King George VI. No one spoke to me; I never met the Captain, an RNR officer who never left the Bridge area. I was the only one in the ship with straight stripes.

The whole purpose was a shakedown cruise in relatively safe waters to get the crew working together for what might be the ships ultimate purpose of providing air cover for slow moving convoys mainly in the North Atlantic.

By common consent Saturday night at sea seemed to be Punch-up Night in the Wardroom, when individual differences of opinion were settled in a manner in which officers and gentlemen of Royal Navies were not encouraged to indulge. I made sure I was otherwise engaged on such occasions.

I'm a great believer in not spoiling a good story by an obsession with historical fact, a belief espoused by the late Professor Manning Clark who I was acquainted with some 40 odd years ago, but I have had some difficulty in reconstructing the details of what turned out to be an extraordinary journey. In simple terms Melbourne to Victoria, British Columbia a distance of about 7000 nautical miles at a cruising speed of 16 knots meant that *Ranee* arrived late on Sunday 14 May. As a navigator it was obvious to me that the ship was unlikely to get to England in time for me to meet the deadline I had been given. Although no one was prepared to discuss the future with me, I believed that the ship would probably have to pick up its nine aircraft somewhere in the United States, together with the complement necessary to fly and maintain them, and then join a slow convoy across the Atlantic. No way.

As soon as I could I nipped ashore to the magnificent hotel, the name of which I can never remember, commandeered a phone and called the Australian Embassy in Washington D C collect. I spoke directly with the Naval Attaché Commander A S Rosenthal, who by then had won a couple of DSO's, and was to have been my Captain in HMAS *Norman,* but took over *Nestor* in May 1941. He was a man of few words. His instructions to me were simple and went something like this, "Stay where you are. Leave the ship. Tell the hotel to send the bill to us. Decide whether you want to go CNR or CPR across Canada."

I'd always wanted to see Mount Robson in the spring. Two days later I left Vancouver by CNR, saw the snow-covered peak in daylight and arrived in Montreal at 11:30 on Sunday 21 May.

Leaving the train I called at a hospitality booth at the station, asking the young lady, who seemed about to close down, what Montreal people usually did on Sunday? The answer came, "They usually go to New York."

To which I replied, "I'm in Canada to see Canada and anyway I'd probably get an opportunity to see the United States some other time, but Canada never again."

As it's turned out I haven't been to the United States, but certainly got back to Canada again.

Anyway within the hour I was practically a member of a Canadian family with my feet under the mahogany enjoying lunch at home with her mother and a sightseeing programme that ensured I was to see all that was to be seen before dropping me back at my hotel, the Mount Royal. An Australian Naval Lieutenant in uniform was obviously someone that Canadians were not accustomed to seeing. I had a great time. And all this because I reacted in a totally unpredictable way.

Next day I was like a real tourist and was able to shop to augment my meagre wardrobe and buy a casual jacket and a wristwatch. On returning to my hotel I dressed for dinner and while walking through the lobby, coming towards me was a young woman who smiled and greeted me in the most friendly manner possible. "Hello. It is so good to see you again."

Quick as a flash I became Richard Hannay in *The Thirty-Nine Steps*, my welcoming performance would have won me an Oscar. Now if what I am going to tell you sounds like fiction I can only assure you in the words of Captain Queeg, 'I kid you not.'

The performance started with drinks in the full view of the public, including residents of the leading hotel in Montreal and those intending to have dinner. Conversation came easily and my invitation to join me for dinner was eagerly accepted. There was one condition, however. A call had to be made on another resident to inform him that the lady had changed her plan. It was accepted that I would accompany her as this was done.

I'd chosen to dine on the top floor so naturally we took the lift, stopping at one of the intermediate floors to knock on a door, which was then opened partly. The occupant wasn't revealed to me, but it was clearly a man. She had a brief conversation in a foreign language, which I knew wasn't French, having studied that language since age ten, and having used it extensively during my two years in the Mediterranean before the outbreak of the war.

Dinner followed, during the course of which my companion continued to indulge in what appeared to be her favourite tipple – gin and tonic. The conversation always tended towards an answer to this question, "What was an Australian naval officer doing in Montreal, how long would I be there, and where was I going?"

I managed to field all these queries quite truthfully, because at that time I hadn't received my onward instructions from Washington.

At this point in my narrative I can see what some of you may be thinking, but I can assure you that was not what I had in mind.

As the evening developed there was no interruption to the flow of gin and tonic and then came the moment for the next logical step – dancing. It was not to be. The lady was paralytic.

With the help of a friendly waiter I managed to take advantage of the position of our table next to a curtain behind which there was an opening onto the outdoor fire escape. A call to the front desk brought the night manager with the key to meet me at the entrance to the fire escape on the appropriate floor and the incident ended with the clear understanding that now she was safely in her room I was off to my room. There was no funny business at all.

Next morning I contacted the Royal Mounted Police with a request for an interview with the appropriate authorities and at the same time received my orders for onward trip by train to Halifax and passage across the Atlantic in a fast troop ship. In the afternoon I gave a factual account to a couple of intensely interested, and to me obvious 'spooks', to whom I stressed that I was not able to ascertain whether the woman was deliberately trying to pump me for vital information regarding the apparent increase in volume of personnel movement from Canada to Britain, when the air was full of rumours concerning the opening of a second front, or whether she was simply 'on the make', or trying to prove a point to a man with whom she was involved romantically. My suspicion of the foreign language incident seemed to be the key.

The 'spooks' were grateful and said that they were aware of efforts to obtain information by people not entitled to it. That night, my last in Montreal, I received a call on the phone in my room from the mysterious Lady X, obviously to establish if I was still in Montreal and hadn't yet gone anywhere.

Although the Battle of the Atlantic had been virtually won by then, there was still the possibility that U Boats would make attacks on transports leaving Halifax, particularly if they had prior information of the sailing times and the units being carried. To this end there was an extensive network of agents supplying bits and pieces of information, particularly picked up in bars frequented by officers in uniform. During my time in Alexandria I'd often been subjected to the 'Darling buy me a drink' routine, but what had happened in Montreal was a real first for me.

On arrival in Halifax I joined the *Empress of Japan* for an unescorted dash across the Atlantic. Unlike the trip in *Ranee* the first action on leaving harbour was an exercise in 'Abandon Ship'. To give you some idea of the scale of such an operation in this instance the following account that I received second-hand will set the scene.

At one lifeboat station a young female Canadian Air Force other rank confided to her girl friend in the following terms, "Do you realize Claire that there are 5000 men on board this ship? That means there's about half-a-mile of dick waiting to be satisfied and I can't get a measly six inches for myself. Honestly, I could climb into one of these boats and screw my way across the Atlantic."

The conduct of trooping for the four-day voyage had become standard. Units were under the control of their own officers and NCO's. Males and females were segregated. Those officers like myself who were spare numbers had superior accommodation, such as it was, and the key to enjoyment was to establish a group of eight like-minded bridge players. Four at a time playing, with the other four at a time occupying the seating space waiting their turn to play. With two meals a day and sleep on a hot-bunk system with ones uniform ready to don in the case of an emergency, a similar group of eight would share the playing space. Night and day became just expressions, and unlike peace-time ocean voyages the walk 'nine times round the deck equals one mile' a dim memory of what sea travel used to be like. If there was a horizon none of us saw it.

There was no doubt about what was to happen in the near future with the war in Europe. An Allied invasion of Europe was at last about to take place. On board we had a contingent of the Canadian Army – The Rocky Mountain Rangers. The officer who commanded this outfit was impossible to miss. On each hip in elaborately decorated holsters he wore pearl-handled revolvers, and one could be forgiven for thinking that he was really the US General George S Patton. I asked one of the Canucks in my group if this was a Commando Unit to be part of the initial assault in the prospective invasion only to be informed, "God no! The Colonel is a real estate agent from Saskatoon, Saskatchewan and the Rangers are going to England to clean up the camps that the fighting units are about to leave."

On Wednesday 31 May I arrived in Liverpool for the second time in World War II. I'd imagined that England on the eve of the invasion would be a huge armed camp. To my surprise the port was practically deserted and the train trip to London was thoroughly civilized. Travelling overnight by train, I reported to Australia House in London next morning at 09:00.

Having made it by the 1 June, the anniversary of that famous naval battle called *Glorious*, I was about to learn exactly what the future had in store for me.

"You've been appointed to HMS *Dryad*. When you were here last it was in the Portsmouth Dockyard, but since then has moved outside the city to Southwick House. You won't be going there as it's been taken over as the Headquarters for General Dwight D Eisenhower for *Overlord*. Go down to the Royal Naval College at Greenwich. You are expected. Settle in and let us have your completed Travelling Expenses Form remembering that taxis must be only with luggage and if they are under five bob you don't need receipts. And by the way we would like you to play cricket for us whenever you can get away during the weekend."

Fortunately I managed to join my fellow would-be navigators at Herstmonceux Castle in Sussex just in time to start the course.

As is well known now D-Day was to have been at an appropriate time during the no moon period covering the first weekend of June 1944. Early morning of Tuesday 6 June I was awakened in Herstmonceux Castle by the sound of aircraft. Peering out, the entire sky was clouded by the airborne invasion from towed gliders on their way to Normandy.

While these momentous events were unfolding I'd spent the day studying the effect on the magnetic compass of heating the funnels of battleships and the correcting effect of the Flinders Bar. This is not a drinking bar, but an actual upright metal pole named after Matthew Flinders, that counteracts the effect of iron in a ship's funnel when heated, thus providing correct compass bearings.

And why battleships you may well ask? Because I'm being trained for what may be my next appointment – in a battleship.

Later we experienced the first of the V-2 flying bombs passing directly overhead. The V-2 pilotless planes from Peenemunde passed overhead at 51 degrees 30 minutes N and 0 degrees E and W, to be followed by the V ones, euphemistically reported as gas mains explosions.

The Royal Naval College Greenwich became home for the five-month duration of the Long N Course. The long hot summer passed pleasantly enough. By day we tackled the intricacies of heavenly bodies and by night, when not on the roof doing a stint of fire watching, we grappled with equally intricate earthly bodies at Ciros and the Coconut Grove nightclubs.

I also renewed acquaintance with the Turner family. Jennifer was then 18 and working at the Admiralty in Whitehall as a Temporary Clerk Class 3 and living with her grandfather Claud in his South Kensington apartment. Meeting her on her way home late one afternoon the pleasure was mutual. In no time at all the two of us were frequenting Ciros nightclub, especially when I didn't have to do night watch on the roof of Greenwich.

There was another Australian on course, together with three Canadians and seven Brits, one of whom had been selected specially to top the course and go on to a particular appointment as part of the work being done at HMS *Dryad* on Action Information.

David Stevenson, the Australian who'd been two years ahead of me at RANC, had only been married a few weeks before coming to England and was very keen to get back as soon as possible. This didn't stop him from persuading me to do his stint on the roof one night while he took Jennifer to dinner at the Savoy, a fact he never mentioned.

The summer of 1944 was marked by exceptional weather in London and it was not long before one of Jennifer's girl friends and another of the unattached and very English members of the course joined to make a four at tennis on the weekends at Greenwich, when flying bombs that had survived the Spitfires tipping large numbers over to crash harmlessly in the English Channel lifted high over the Observatory before coming down anywhere but the centre of town.

There was definitely romance in the air, but opposition from Jennifer's father made it clear that nothing serious was to come of it.

I played tennis at Wimbledon, not I might say in the all England Championships, but in a mixed foursome on an outside court one Sunday afternoon. I was also invited to play cricket with members of Australia House whenever I could. With matches between the Royal Navy and the other two services coming up at Lords I found that my name had been pencilled in for the first game. Unfortunately the match was scheduled for the week in which I had to be at sea off Milford Haven being examined for proficiency in ship handling and other professional activities. My replacement in the team was Writer P H B May RN, who later starred for England against Australia in the mid 50's through to the early 60's.

Finally the course ended. David Stevenson and I both qualified as Navigators in September 1944. He came fifth and went back to Australia. I came first.

Normally the new qualifiers could expect an appointment as Flotilla N Destroyers if he'd done well, something smaller if he'd finished down the list. The *Dryad* appointments officer was the same Gerald Cobb who'd been Navigator when I was a Midshipman in *Malaya*.

HMS *Anson*, then in Devonport Dockyard being prepared to join the British Pacific Fleet in what was to be the final defeat of the Japanese, the new Navigator position had been promised to the top qualifier of the 1944 Specialist Course, as they'd expected it to be the prize Englishman, Tony Griffin. But I'd pipped him by one mark in topping the course.

However my special appointment was to repeat the performance in HMS *Anson*. As Second N, I was the ghost for the Navigator. It was with a somewhat leaden feeling that I joined the ship that was then in Plymouth and set to pacing the teak as Officer of the Watch. In the chill of that winter I often consoled myself with Milton's words from Samson Agonistes:

All is best, though we oft doubt,
What th' unsearchable dispose
Of highest wisdom brings about,
And ever best found in the close.

When the Captain informed me that I'd made the grade and was to join his specially selected Ships Company I was actually pleased. Captain A G C (Alec) Madden had been Naval Assistant to the Second Sea Lord and hadn't only selected his own command, but every officer to sail with him. In such elite company I was to enjoy the best year of my Naval Service. Then when the Reserve Officers, who were junior to me as Lieutenants by some years, were suddenly elevated to the rank of Lieutenant Commander by reason of being over 30 years of age, I took this in my stride.

A girl in the Dockyard Drawing Office had a lot to do with my attitude. I'd originally met Anne when she'd come to Malta to be with her parents for Christmas in 1938. Her father was the Rear Admiral who commanded the Second Battle Squadron of the Mediterranean Fleet. In those days there was an unwritten rule that naval officers attended the Opera House on Wednesday evenings in uniform. Also membership of the Union Club was restricted to officers of the rank of Lieutenant, but for some reason that'd been lost in antiquity, Midshipmen from the Dominions were made Honorary Members. It was expected that they'd not embarrass the Club by making the fact of their privileged status too obvious.

In a dilemma I decided to dine at the Union Club in dinner jacket and then go on to *Madam Butterfly* where my presence would surely pass unnoticed, or so I thought. In a box the Admiral and his family were enjoying the performance by the touring Italian company. The daughter grabbed me at interval and insisted on taking me up to meet daddy. The whole incident passed off without so much as a, 'Young man don't you know what day it is?' The daughter was practically killing herself knowing what agonies I was going through.

One night I was called to the telephone with an invitation to make up the numbers at dinner that evening at Admiralty House. Lord and Lady Astor were being entertained together with Mrs. Gott, whose husband had been one of the British Generals of great promise but had been killed in an air accident on the eve of his appointment, to what would've been one of the decisive commands of the war. With this thumbnail sketch I had to be content.

I arrived on time. I was duly attentive to the conversation at dinner, which centred on ideas for reshaping Europe once the war had finally been won. When the ladies withdrew and the Admiral passed the port I was asked how I saw the post war scene. I gave what I thought was a well-considered argument concerning the need to reduce the overcrowding in Britain by large-scale migration to Canada and Australia, only to be told by Lord Astor that my ideas were absolute rubbish.

"You can't move people all over the place that way," he said.

I responded that all through dinner he'd been moving people from one place to another across Europe without much thought for the principles he was now espousing. He smiled indulgently at me and replied, "Ah yes. But they are not British, you know."

When we rejoined the ladies the impression I gained was that mother and daughter had come to a better understanding. I was no longer a threat to the arrangements planned for the future, besides I'd soon be off to sea.

I think she'd missed too many good films, because until I appeared on the scene they'd been inseparable.

But it was this girl who started me thinking that being smart and efficient was not nearly enough if getting on in life was what one desired. Apparently the worst thing that could be said of anyone was that he didn't suffer fools gladly. From then on I really tried, but there were times when I found the suffering almost unbearable.

Taking a week's leave in London before joining the *Anson*, I booked into the Club set up specifically for young officers, and accompanied one of them to a theatre performance on a Saturday night in Soho. After this we went to a club that the other chap had been to before and out of the blue were joined by Thora Hird and one of her theatrical friends who had to stay until the early morning Underground started on Sunday.

There was naturally much talk of the theatre, film and life in wartime, after which we decided to go to a Tea Dance at Grosvenor House because Harry Roy's Band was scheduled to play. What we didn't know was that Harry Roy had a number of bands playing in various places and that he himself might not be one of the musicians. It was quite a well-attended affair and at one stage a Progressive Barn Dance had me on the floor.

My mate had had enough, there was no Harry Roy, so he was going back to the digs to make up for the sleep lost the night before. I stayed on to have one more dance with the little girl that I'd met in the progressive.

Looking back I admit that this was one decision that proved to be wrong. It was to colour the next nine years of my life in which my first career was always in jeopardy and the conflict between my profession and domesticity was ever present.

The one dance continued until the programme ended at 17:30 by which time Jean Mackenzie had told me that she was going to hospital next day to have her ears moved closer to her head and her mother wouldn't be coming until Thursday from Carlisle, where the family lived, to pick her up.

Jean Mackenzie 1944

Full of sympathy for a barely seventeen year old, I accompanied her to Baker Street where she spent the night. The early autumn evening was pleasant for the walk, taking us past a professional photographer's studio where a recent portrait of her was displayed. I still have a copy of this. On arrival at her destination I promised to visit her in hospital and true to form spent Tuesday and Wednesday in her company. On Thursday there was a light-hearted conversation on the subject of her prospects of marriage given that her career was heading towards continuing with ballet, pantomime and learning to sing. I said the first words that came into my head, "Well you could always marry me."

To my amazement Jean took this to be a serious proposal and said, "Then we could always be secretly engaged."

Thankfully her mother arrived and the subject was not discussed any further.

I headed back to HMS *Anson* in Devonport Dockyard. In a cold November evening the Commander, Second in Command, told me that the Captain had decided I should stay.

With the certainty that I'd be with the ship until the end of the year I'd suggested to the Mackenzie family that Jean might like to join the wives of some of the ships officers where they were staying to farewell their husbands. Captain J S Mackenzie of the Home Guard approved of this proposal, but only if an official engagement notice were to appear in the Times of London.

Jean's arrival in Devonport as an official fiancée proved a great success with the wives, so much so that the daughter of one of them was a flower girl at our wedding 18 months later.

HMS *Anson* was truly a great ship. It was being prepared for the first assault on the Japanese homeland. My role in the great battles that were expected was to run the Combat Information Centre, and it was for this that *Dryad* had marked me down.

Those familiar with modern ships and their weapons systems will probably give a shrug and say, big deal, but in 1944 this was the ultimate in information gathering, sorting and interpretation. There was one flaw in the system. My position was down in the bowels of the ship below armour. My task was to present the simplified picture through an action plot one deck down from the open bridge where command was exercised. It was soon evident that the Captain and his principal staff officers wanted the very latest situation and proposals concerning the next moves based on all the evidence there was. I then became the key responder to queries from the Bridge and the adviser on tactics. The war I started in a British Battleship I was to finish in a British Battleship.

— 16 —

1945

All through the early months in 1945 *Anson* exercised with other ships and aircraft, first in home waters and then in the Mediterranean.

VE Day, 8 May 1945, found us in Malta. To me the most wondrous thing about the end of the war in Europe was seeing everything illuminated again, not just the lights in cities and houses, but also the ships at sea. Earth was alive again.

The Mess Committee decided that we should celebrate the occasion and at the same time thank those who'd helped us. They suggested I should accompany our United States Navy Liaison Officer to Naples and see if we could get some supplements to our rations, which at that stage were anything but suitable for festivities. As the Wardroom Mess Secretary I wasn't about to refute them.

Armed with the contents of the cash box the two of us got ourselves out to Kalafrana. I knew the RAF Commanding Officer's mother, so it was no trouble to get a flight to Sicily. From here my US colleague, using the most impressive set of orders I've ever seen, had us on a plane to Naples in double quick time.

Jeeps appeared wherever we went. Admirals and Generals bent over backwards to meet our wishes and we arrived back onboard in time to enjoy a lavish party with fresh seafood, strawberries and ice cream that had been flown in by a VIP aircraft. The Captain was both astounded and delighted. The guests astonished. And some members of the mess had the audacity to grumble at the extra cost per head. But as a morale booster it was absolutely worth it. The Digger had done it again.

As an old hand at passages through the Suez Canal I was stationed in the wheelhouse as we moved through. With the aid of the latest diagrams of the state of the banks, the presence of wrecks and anything else, it assisted in forecasting how such a large ship with such a deep draught would behave in the restricted sections.

Probably the most unexpected result was that we needed a speed of eight knots to keep the ship moving at four knots which was the slowest to ensure steerage way and at the same time not produce a wash of such proportions as to damage the canal banks any more than had already occurred as a result of wartime neglect of maintenance and enemy activity. Thankfully the passage was successful and I pocketed my share of the pilotage allowance with the feeling that I hadn't really earned it.

The highlight of the passage to Australia was a visit to Trincomalee and the arrival onboard of the Supreme Allied Commander South East Asia Command, Vice Admiral Lord Louis Mountbatten, a lifelong friend of the Captain. Addressing the Ships Company assembled on the quarterdeck he made, what I thought, was an unnecessarily cruel remark to the effect that he wasn't one of your pot bellied Admirals in the presence of one of his principal Staff Officers who was. It got a laugh from the sailors, but from one who was able to cast a spell over his audience it seemed to me to be in poor taste.

A lot of crap has been written and spoken about how wonderful Lord Louis was, to have stepped down from high rank to pursue his naval career, to rise in the normal way to top position in his Service and then go on to serve with distinction as an Admiral of the Fleet in Britain's top defence job. There is never any thought as to how fortunate he was in the matter of his birth and royal connections to be offered the position to develop his undoubted capabilities in the first instance. It's a far different exercise in humility to drop from Acting Admiral to Rear Admiral with an assured future, than to take the chances that most Captains in the Navy took. There are very few who fall into the category of a Commander about whom an Admiral wrote, *'This officer has far to go. Who are we to place an obstacle in his path on this occasion.'*

If I could write a book on how to guarantee nice things are said in official reports I'd surely make a fortune. However my advice to those who aspire to high rank in the Services would be quite meaningless. From my viewpoint you need to be virtually born again and do just about everything that one had done to the age of 30 quite differently. For as surely as in one report the requirement will be for you to be more self assertive, the very next criticism will be that you're inclined to be too self assertive.

Crawlers are despised in the Services and yet those who say, 'Yes sir, no sir, three bags full sir' are regarded as properly respectful. They know their place and give due deference to their superiors, no matter how fatuous they may be as the fountainheads of all wisdom and knowledge. The official report must never damn with faint praise, 'He performed admirably as Executive Officer. Unfortunately the ship failed to win the Gloucester Cup for overall efficiency' would be an example of what I mean.

The qualities needed to score highly and those needed to rate the lowest mark are so nearly expressed in the same words that for want of better knowledge most officers end up in the average bracket. Moreover the various traits under which ratings are awarded all amount to the same thing, 'Do I like this officer or don't I?'

Probably the most difficult task facing any officer who was to report on another is to write an honest report about someone you don't like. All too often the task is simply not done well and as a chore that is necessary to meet the deadline of a handover in command, or to meet some timetable in promotions.

Before those who may happen to read this wish to deny that what I've said is in fact true, let them consider the myth that he who reports incorrectly on another officer is himself judged in turn. There is a great deal of truth in the statement that was prevalent in the Royal Navy that you certainly didn't waste a brass hat on a digger. With each Flag Officer compiling his own list of promotees in order of merit how indeed could anyone compare the number ones, twos, and threes on different lists and arrive at any semblance of real worth?

As Henry Kissinger found to his amazement when writing fitness reports for his military aides, to hint that they were anything less than exceptionally outstanding in every way was to condemn them to military obscurity. But the problems facing the military officers who find themselves in a political environment I'll leave till later.

Lord Louis wasn't giving away any military secrets, but he made it absolutely clear that HMS *Anson* together with HMS *Duke of York* and the light Fleet Carriers HMS *Venerable* and HMS *Vengeance* and an assortment of cruisers and destroyers would be employed in the final assault on Japan, whether the United States liked it or not.

To this end we had to prepare ourselves, but in the meantime proceeded to Australia completing our preparation. So it was that we came to Jervis Bay, so near and yet so far away from the goal that everyone really had in mind – Sydney.

I suggested to the Captain that as the war had been going on for quite a while and Sydney had just about had its fill of entertaining visiting firemen, we should try to take the city by storm. Instead of waiting for the people to entertain us, why not as a first gesture, entertain them. The idea took hold.

As there was an airstrip at Jervis Bay the US Liaison Officer and myself were dispatched with instructions to get to Sydney and fix a party for the next Sunday evening.

What transpired during the next three days must go down in some record somewhere as a triumph of organization. None of it would've been possible without my experience with Mrs. Nancy Jobson and the School for Young Ladies she ran with such competence at Hopewood House.

In the early days of the war I'd been a regular caller for tea at four and a chat afterwards about the evils of vested interests before being permitted to escort one or other of the pupils to dinner and dancing. The first of these young ladies on my list was not only happy to come to the proposed party, but was prepared to put her father's office and telephone at our disposal and act as social secretary. With a three pronged attack we set about assailing the Sydney Social Register inviting mothers with daughters, wives with or without husbands, people known to have goodwill towards British sailors, and a good sprinkling of those who it's better to have onside if a ship's visit is to run smoothly.

HMS *Anson* did its stuff too. The ship berthed at the Dolphins, off Kirribilli Point. The local authorities provided catamarans covered with coconut matting to enable visitors in their finery to move with ease from boat to ship, ensuring it was the party to end all parties. And friendships were also made that have endured all the years between.

The hospitality given by the officers was repaid many times over, and particularly pleasing was the way in which the people of Sydney responded to the young sailors, who too often were left to fend for themselves with very little money and nothing but Kings Cross and the waterfront pubs to occupy their time. As one of my young Reserve Officers with sophisticated tastes was heard to remark as we descended the last few steps of Prince's Restaurant to be greeted by Pierre, "Ah! Civilization, at last!"

Everywhere we went there were rumours that the war was about to end. Even the boys from the Anti-Aircraft were lying low.

Suddenly, for no apparent reason we found ourselves dancing around a bonfire in the street in secluded Bellevue Hill outside the home of a beautiful lady whose husband was always busy but knew that the homburg hat on the hallstand was not his. I was later to work with a young man who was also a frequent visitor there, timing his entrances and exits as well as any modern day Henry Irving would do.

'Hooligans prematurely celebrate War's end', read the *Sun's* headline next afternoon. But it really was all over.

Early August when the bomb was dropped on Hiroshima, *Anson* was alongside at Wooloomooloo, Sydney Harbour. Just over a week later on 15 August 1945 we were celebrating V J Day with a tot of rum all around, then we were off down Sydney Harbour.

From many a window fluttered a sign of farewell. Had we had a Kamal then, I'm sure his song would have been in keeping with the mood. Many were married, some engaged to be married, but all knew what the *'Bounty'* sailors must have experienced when they set sail from Tahiti.

Our Captain was no Bligh however and had his orders from the top. We were soon up to 24 knots racing north to Manus Island for fuel, then on to Hong Kong to re-establish the British presence and take control from the Japanese.

Some Australian minesweepers had done a rush job sweeping the approaches, but we steamed in with all guns manned and all eyes scanning the shore for signs of activity which would show that some fixed defence might be exploded under us in spite of the Japanese acceptance of the unconditional surrender terms. I remember looking through high-powered binoculars at a Japanese looking at me through his binoculars and being pleased to be where I was and not where he was.

Hong Kong had been neglected. Japanese boats crossing the harbour at night used to run into mooring buoys that had been laid to provide unloading berths in mid-stream. So the Japanese sank the buoys. No maintenance had been carried out on the civic and municipal services. The dockyard was a mess. Now was the time for the Royal Navy to take the lead.

The appointed Governor was Admiral Sir Cecil Harcourt and the Hong Kong Commodore was a crash hot fix-it type, espousing, "Any Officer who cannot employ himself for eighteen hours a day report to me." I was given the job of berthing officer. In fact, I became the Harbour Master.

Ships streamed in from everywhere. Within an hour of the first British personnel arriving, the local Chinese had dug up their long buried possessions and proceeded in setting up businesses again.

The priority task for the British was to locate, interview and repatriate those who'd been Prisoners of War. Ships bringing in troops to replace the Japanese garrison were back loaded to destinations in Canada, India and Britain.

During my early days there I'd assisted Captain Anthony Kimmins, Royal Navy, with recording messages from these POW's to be broadcast by the BBC. Although their physical condition was poor, their spirits were remarkably good, though naturally enough we couldn't get them on their way home fast enough. By this time I'd transferred to HMS *Montclare,* flagship of the Flag Officer Western Area, I was working well in excess of the darg set by Commodore (they will have to make me a Rear Admiral after this) Everett.

When the number of ships in the harbour reached 105, I was forced to tell the Admiral that unless some were to leave port there'd soon be no room for any more. As the 120 mark neared the break came and from then on the jigsaw puzzle was easier to put together.

I only had one real problem in all that time. The Hong Kong power station was practically out of coal. With only a few hours supply left the *Atlas*, with a cargo of coal, announced its impending arrival. Immediately I signalled it to berth alongside the power station, giving them the position to take up via the range and bearing from the most prominent mark that would be common to all charts no matter where they originated, or how old they might be.

Imagine my consternation when the *Atlas* entered harbour and dropped anchor in the first available space to be found. Nothing would induce the ship to respond to any signals, so I jumped into a boat and went alongside. Talk about the *Marie Celeste,* it had nothing on the *Atlas*.

Eventually I found an officer who could speak English. The Fourth Engineer, an Australian, guaranteed that he could coax some life into the boilers and get up a head of steam. The Chief Officer, a Russian, was happy for me to take the ship down the harbour, after all I was the Pilot. The Captain, having plotted the position given to him and finding that it was alongside had said, "We never go alongside. *Atlas* is always far away. There has been a mistake. Let go the anchor."

With that he had, as was his wont, retired to his cabin locked the door and proceeded to drink himself into insensibility. All attempts to acquaint him of the need to unload his cargo into the power station merely resulted in a torrent of abuse in Norwegian. There was nothing to be done except for me to take charge.

The Chief Officer weighed anchor and I stood on the Bridge with the helmsman to whom I gave instructions by placing my fingers on the spot to which I needed the rudder indicator to reach. The ship had a single screw, but no one was able to tell me whether it was right handed or left handed, so it was problematical how the stern would behave when the engine was reversed.

As luck would have it the tide was on the turn and the first approach to the power station made it clear that I wasn't going to be able to berth starboard side to. Just as I was negotiating my way through the many ships that were in the process of swinging, some one way and some the other, who should appear on the Bridge but the Captain, drunk as a lord, and completely bewildered. Thankfully no one paid any attention to him and I came alongside with no trouble, the hatch covers were removed and the coal carted in baskets by hand, straight into the furnaces.

The lights stayed on in Hong Kong that night and as far as I can say, for every night thereafter. But it was a near catastrophe.

When I returned to *Montclare* and reported to the Chief of Staff what I'd done, his only comment was to turn white as a sheet and say that he hoped Lloyds of London never found out. Peace had returned with a vengeance.

With the approach of the typhoon season I was relieved of my duties by no less than a Commander and four other officers. In the meantime a start had been made on rehabilitating the mooring buoys and tidying up the typhoon anchorage so it'd be available for its proper purpose.

I then had a stroke of luck. The navigator of HMS *Venerable* went sick. The Captain asked the Captain of *Anson*, with whom he was friendly, if he knew of anyone who could do the job. In no time flat I found myself on the Bridge, but with two great disadvantages. I knew nothing about sea birds and nothing about railways, both subjects in which the Captain and his previous navigator had an abiding mutual interest.

The main task given to HMS *Venerable* was to locate and repatriate Indian prisoners thought to be somewhere in the north of French Indo-China. This meant getting as close to Haiphong as possible without running any unnecessary risks. The unknown factor was always how many mines laid by US aircraft were still active.

Naturally I avoided the Hainan Strait and approached Haiphong from the south in the deepest water there was, finding an anchorage to balance the risk with the distance boats would have to travel.

To accommodate as many troops as possible we'd landed all our aircraft, but certainly could've made use of a helicopter or a light reconnaissance plane, had any been available. Without them we simply had to rely on an advance party going up river by boat and see what they could find out.

The Vietnamese authorities were suspicious. The Japanese surrender had left a confusing political picture, particularly in the north where a Chinese Army of Occupation and Free French elements vied with the local communists for de facto control. The Indians were really not significant to the future hopes and intentions of the rival groups. To be honest, it was something of a relief for them to be rid of unproductive people who'd merely be an added administrative burden if they remained.

Transport had to be found, but it made the whole operation more complicated. Negotiations were slow, but eventually we had a full complement and the hanger deck was filled to capacity with camp beds. However a major problem existed with most of our involuntary passengers. They wanted to use their own cooking stoves and the hanger deck of an aircraft carrier, even when it is not housing aircraft, is no place for any sort of naked flame.

From Haiphong we proceeded to Singapore at best speed. Finding somewhere to anchor in the harbour was an interesting experience and called for much more skill and ingenuity than the courses at *Dryad* had ever provided. I finally managed to drop the pick by eye in a vacant space and then went down to the quarterdeck when the ship had got its cable, to see by what margin I'd missed the green wreck buoy, to which the other ships in the anchorage had given such a wide berth. It was clear to me that the berthing organization, or lack of it, in Singapore compared unfavourably with what I'd been recently setting up in Hong Kong.

After a quick consultation with the staff at the Commander-in-Chief's Headquarters, we sailed for Madras to disembark our charges and then back to Singapore, this time to the Naval Dockyard on the north side of the island where my association with *Venerable* ended with the return of the navigator who I'd relieved.

Having received a station appointment to HMS *Argonaut* that was expected to call at Singapore very soon, I waited around.

A totally different atmosphere prevailed in Singapore to that in somewhat similar conditions in Hong Kong. The Allied Military Government was composed of ex-planters and businessmen, whose primary interest was to get back to the positions they'd held before the Japanese occupation. Local political groups had absolutely no intention of allowing any form of domination over the lives of the people to replace what the Japanese had exercised. There was no way any one group could be seen to be leading.

The planning for a military re-occupation of Malaya and Singapore was so far advanced that it was followed through much as would've been the case had the Japanese not accepted the terms of unconditional surrender. As a consequence the reality of the peacetime problems were not being faced with new thought. Moreover, the assumptions that the French would return to Indo-China and the Dutch to the Netherlands East Indies and all would be as it was before were completely unwarranted.

After spending eighteen days dividing my time between Naval Headquarters, the Royal Hotel and the Tanglin Club, *Argonaut* finally arrived enabling me to take up my appointment. I was very much the 'Johnny come lately' in this ship. It had the distinction of having a new bow and a new stern built in a United States dockyard after being struck by two torpedoes from the same salvo. Once again I found myself pounding the teak in harbour as Officer of the Watch.

In a peacetime cruiser employed mainly on representational tasks, ceremonial and observance of protocol were the principal responsibilities and conflict with the Executive Officer who was trying to run the ship efficiently was all too prevalent. I was frequently at odds with the Commander who was reaching the upper limit of the zone for promotion and was anxious to ingratiate himself with the Captain, the only one who could possibly further his career.

The Captain was something of a rarity too. As one of the few Officers in the Royal Navy to have reached that rank from the Lower Deck, a phenomenon known as coming up through the hawse pipe. He was a protégée of my previous Captain in HMS *Anson* and I have no doubt that it was this association that resulted in me being in the ship.

In some ways I was better placed than some other officers to deal with the situation created by the Captain's wont to take the senior ratings into his confidence, to the possible exclusion of his Executive Officer. In Australian ships the social gulf between the officers and the men was not nearly as marked as it then was in British ships, and not even the wartime dilution had bridged that. All that had happened was it had been proved, if ever proof had been needed, that far more men were capable of showing good officer like qualities than Dartmouth, the Public Schools, Pangbourne and Keyham ever could produce. Moreover the professionalism that being the Navigator implied meant that at sea on the Bridge, the Captain was forced to rely on my expertise. This of course carries the seeds of disaster, for quite often a Navigator has to take positive action without the nicety associated with discussion.

— 17 —

Sea Service After World War II

The transition from war to peace wasn't smooth. Christmas 1945 was spent in Hong Kong, followed by service in Japan where we relieved HMAS *Hobart*, also a victim of torpedo damage, as part of the British Commonwealth Occupation Force.

Tokyo Bay wasn't exactly the haven for our operations. The Japanese Naval Base at Yokosuka was crammed with US ships of all classes. If it hadn't been for the presence of the British amenities ship HMS *Menestheus*, albeit somewhat emasculated from its original concept because of the end of war and the return to the Musical Hall circuit of the members of its ENSA Concert Parties, our men would've had a pretty thin time. We did, however, manage to get them on organized sightseeing parties. One of these provided an insight into the American tendency to drink, with full intention of getting drunk.

An advance party consisting of the Chaplain and two Officers had gone to Nikko to arrange for the reception and sightseeing for a party of sailors that I was to bring up by train the following day. Japanese railways had been badly damaged by US bombing raids and weren't being run with the efficiency now associated with them. We waited hours for the scheduled train to arrive, only for it to proceed at not much more than walking pace.

Although we were together as a group, it wasn't long before a lone US Officer attached his overly friendly self to us. At that time I hadn't really experienced West Australians either, who try desperately to live up to their image of the friendliest people in the world. Aggressively approaching you and sticking their faces close to yours they say, "We are the friendliest people in Australia."

"Yes," you reply, "but they're pretty friendly in Queensland."

"Listen," they say moving their faces even closer, "we are the friendliest people in the world." Finally gritting their teeth and clenching the right or left fist, they ask, "Aren't we friendly?" By this time you'd better be convinced, believe me.

Anyway this American Officer, to prove how friendly he was, offered to share his bottle of Suntory. I'd already discovered that a liking for Scotch whisky wasn't just very expensive, but could be a positive barrier to a successful naval career. For better or for worse, I'd decided that whisky was one drink I could well do without.

Naturally the American was affronted that I wouldn't drink with him. What had we been fighting the goddam war for if it wasn't to be able to have a drink together? If I wouldn't drink with him he was sure the Limey sailors wouldn't be so chicken livered.

Fearing an international incident I agreed to have one drink with him to celebrate the end of the war. Then we had to have a drink to the health of President Truman, Prime Minister Ben Chifley, King George VI, General MacArthur, and so it went on and on.

Finally I had to go and call god on the great white phone. While I was in the telephone booth my drinking companion had decided that it was time to get the train moving more quickly. So taking his Suntory, now his third or fourth bottle by this time, he headed up to the engine driver.

The train arrived at Nikko Station with the American perched on the cowcatcher. My party of RN sailors massed together with me in the middle, somewhat a folk hero, and a startled Chaplain quick to size up the situation.

For the next three days as I gradually sobered up I was propelled about Nikko like a zombie steadied at each elbow by a brother officer, while the man of God hovered around directing my path away from the American who insisted that he must catch up on some drinking with his great Aussie mate from the train.

Not all the Americans I met in Japan were there for the booze and broads. The American Red Cross really organized the rest and recreation centres with expert skill and can be credited with doing so much in bringing the local Japanese and the men of the Occupation Force to a state of better understanding.

Baseball, however, did more to establish democracy as an ideal pastime to be pursued by the Japanese people than any actions of MacArthur and his team of experts. Just as the British founded an Empire on cricket, so the Americans civilized the Japanese with baseball. It's a pity that soccer mostly only leads to violence; there may be some hope yet for a truly international aura of goodwill through a sport yet to be evolved. If only the French had played cricket instead of l'amour wherever they went, we might've had a more unified world by now, with both the Russians and Chinese maybe anxious to take it up to show how civilized they really are. What a World Series that would've been for *Benson and Hedges*.

I can trace my present affection for the sport of skiing to my time in Japan. With the enthusiasm usually associated with activities organized at holiday camps or in cruise ships, the American Red Cross girls had us sliding down the slopes of Mount Fuji simply because they were there. I'd always looked upon skiing as something reserved for the seriously wealthy and powerful, who crowded a platform at Sydney's Central

Railway Station attended by flashlight photographers and those bright young things who wrote bits for the Sunday papers. Australia's Mount Kosciusko was a bit like Palm Beach to me, a place where the really idle rich went to behave like the idle poor. To me, Austrians in the Alps, or the English upper classes who went to Switzerland, did the only real serious skiing.

Perhaps the most memorable event was the visit to Kure in the Inland Sea. It was still necessary to make the passage closely astern of an American minesweeper. I had the devil's own job convincing the Captain that in order to pass through water already swept it was essential to maintain a compass bearing on the sweeper and not merely try to follow in its wake.

The tidal streams in the Inland Sea were something beyond his comprehension and the thought that a buoy might be in a place other than where it ought to be, was a fact he simply couldn't accept. Once we'd established the fact that the shortest distance between two points for a ship at sea was not necessarily a straight line, the Captain and I got on reasonably well.

The visit I paid to Hiroshima was a salutary experience. Although I was to serve in the Permanent Naval Forces for another seventeen years I think the sight of the Japanese people trying to go about their normal business of living and having their being in an endless sea of rubble, made me realize that there was something basically wrong with all the underpinning of the theory of war. *Si vis pacem para bellum* and *Clausewitz* were at once discredited in my mind. When you reach the position in human affairs where the living envy the dead, war becomes the first irrelevance.

It was with some relief that I greeted the news that *Argonaut* was to return to Hong Kong to embark the Governor, Vice Admiral Sir Cecil

Harcourt, who was to return to England on completion of his tour of duty. As soon as this task was completed the ship would be placed in Reserve until the future of the other ships of the class had been decided. This would mean that not only could I marry the girl to whom I'd been engaged for some time, but I could also do the Big Ship N Course. This would qualify me for the top professional appointments in the Royal Australian Navy.

My recent contact with the officers of HMAS *Hobart* had shown that the next few years would see some cut-throat competition for plum jobs in Australia and I had no intention to be less qualified than anyone else when it came to making the selection.

When we arrived back in England I found that there was a conflict of ideas between those at *Dryad* and the appointing authorities in Australia. *Dryad* wanted me to join the first of a new series of courses designed to train Navigating Officers in both Navigation and Aircraft Direction. This activity had previously been undertaken mainly by Reserve Officers, who were now leaving the Service to resume their normal occupations, or grounded fliers from the Fleet Air Arm who weren't very good at it anyway. The appointing authorities in Australia thought I should take my turn and wait, goodness knows how many years, to do the Advanced Navigation Course. Although there were plans to acquire an aircraft carrier and to establish a Fleet Air Arm in Australia the assumption had been made in the past that the Royal Navy would provide the specialist officers if these weren't available from the RAN.

I had other ideas. I did both.

On Monday 8 July 1946 I married, Jean Mackenzie, at St Marks Church, London and joined the specially selected group of Royal Navy Navigators on ND Dagger 1. As it transpired, I was the only one who did this course that ever served as Direction Officer of an aircraft carrier. But this wasn't known at the time.

My first wedding with Jean Mackenzie in London 1946

While my career and study flourished, the marriage wasn't to fare quite so well. Being engaged, but separated for 18 months with only sporadic letters in between, then having only two weeks before being married was hardly an auspicious beginning for any marriage. After a night in London and six days honeymoon in Windsor, I then went to Portsmouth to continue with the first Advanced Course in Navigation/Direction. My new wife Jean continued her career in London.

The intensity of training navigators to absorb the new work of directing aircraft operating with the Fleet meant there were very few occasions for Jean and I to be together.

My experience with AC11, short though my time in *Venerable* had been, and the tactical work I'd done in *Anson*, in company with these ships had given me a practical background that was in fact ahead of the teaching of *Dryad* and *Kete*. This didn't endear me to the instructors in what became a classical case of the pupil teaching Anna.

Naturally I was keen to stay on with the Royal Navy and one of the RN Officers was keen to do an exchange service in the RAN. This arrangement found agreement with the Australian Commonwealth Naval Board, particularly as the Fleet Air Arm was not planned to start operating in the RAN until 1948/49. As I'd topped the ND Dagger Course a prize professional appointment could be expected. And so it was.

My reward was the appointment that no RN Officer wanted to take, to HMS *Boxer* under the command of one of the finest RN Officers never to make Flag rank — his reputation as a difficult man to serve, was probably only equalled by my reputation as a difficult man to have serving.

We certainly had our moments, but in the year we spent together we progressed the development of radar and the techniques associated with it to such a level that the post war Fleet could employ tactical doctrines that utilized the full extent of equipment capability. We both saw that there was an essential stage between what the scientists thought was technically possible and what the operator in the ship could actually achieve and we were where the pudding was eaten.

Boxer was originally built as a Headquarters Ship for amphibious landings, but was converted to an experimental radar ship with four masts and no less than six futuristic radars. Day after day, night after night, we ploughed up and down the English Channel operating with ships and aircraft until the performance characteristics of the various radars and the limits of their capabilities were beyond doubt. But the Monday to Friday work schedule allowed sufficient time in London with Jean, convincing her that she'd be able to go with me to Australia and make a life there when the time came.

Although the Captain eventually received an over-the-zone promotion, it came too late to do him any good. One thing naval administrators never understand is that late promotion for the officer whose expectations for promotion at the normal time are not fulfilled is not the answer to a previous inability to promote the best men.

Those who are promoted are inclined to attribute their success more to luck, than to any particular merit that they may possess, or to any positive contribution they may have made. Those who are not promoted usually console themselves with the thought that failure to ingratiate oneself with one particular superior made the difference. In truth neither of these attitudes is completely real. We are what we are and we are men of our time. Too often we look for those to promote too early or too late. In the Defence Force the myth must prevail that war is an ever-present reality and if it comes we must be ready. Yet the qualities required of the wartime commander and those of the peacetime commander are quite dissimilar.

I'd venture to say that we have seen the last of the Public Servant Generals, the Schoolmaster Generals and the Business Corporation Generals. The rotation system and the depth of talent in the Australian Defence Force officer corps will ensure that if World War III ever comes about we'll have the mechanism to ensure that operational commands are not given to buffoons. Admirals and Air Marshals have always come from a more professional background, that's not to say that some Admirals and some Air Marshals may not be buffoons. At any given time they are in sufficient numbers to ensure that the buffoons are not appointed where they could do any harm. If battles are lost Admirals, Generals and Air Marshals will be sacked, just as they've always been, until a team is put together than can win, or at least not lose too badly. This was certainly not the situation in Australia when I finally returned early in 1948.

Australia wanted me back in a hurry to relieve David Stevenson at HMAS *Watson* and to prepare the Navigation School to train the Radar Plot ratings required to join the aircraft carrier *Sydney*. Stevenson was to go to England to do the Advanced ND Dagger Course, particularly as his wife was a ballerina who wanted to perform in London at the time.

I had the usual battle with the bureaucracy about whether I should be permitted to return to Australia with my wife, or whether I should go by air leaving her to follow later by sea. In those days there was no concern for Conditions of Service. Officers were expected to do as their superiors had done for years. Air travel was to be involved but good fortune intervened and travel by P&O was decided.

I kept Jean close by on the way to join the ship in case there should be any last minute decision to go back to the family where crises were normal occurrences. Jean's brother and eldest son was now in the French Foreign Legion to get away from a forced marriage that had become intolerable; the number three son was facing a motor accident in which a girl had been killed; and her older sister, the number two of the four, was still inconsolable from being unmarried.

Casting off began the next testing time of our marriage. After the experience of the luxury of a First Class passage in an ocean liner, the town of Molong and having to live with my father and mother for a month while I found suitable accommodation in Sydney, was a disastrous experience for Jean.

Having to settle in and start work right away, there was no time to do the hunting needed in a market in which there was very little available anyway. When temporary rooming in a Kings Cross guesthouse became available Jean joined me and set about the daily grind of house hunting.

Fortunately during the voyage to Sydney she'd made friends with a young brother and sister who'd joined the ship in Fremantle. They in turn introduced her to the brother of a man who was later to become one of my closest friends, Bill Douglass. Between them they found an apartment in Kingsley Hall at the top of the Cross, adequately furnished into which we moved until two things happened at the same time. A sixth floor apartment that was unfurnished became vacant and my War Gratuity of 450 pounds was paid. Beard Watsons converted the money into furniture and the world looked somewhat rosier.

Although an allowance was paid to married personnel, the only increase in pay since pre-war times had been the general shilling a day increase all round and of course the wartime exemption from the payment of income tax. Given that there were standards of dress to keep up and the inescapable expenses associated with mess life, there wasn't a great deal to play with at the end of each pay period. Making ends meet for many was a struggle.

I'd previously discussed with Jean's mother the subject of having a family, but there were to be no children until Jean reached the age of 22.

I'd also promised that I'd continue with her singing tuition – this was being conducted by Nino Murotta, a bass baritone of some prominence, living nearby in Potts Point.

Another good thing to come from Jean's friendship with the brother and sister from the ship, was her acquiring a network of young Sydney people in her own age group. One of this group had an older brother who was secretary to the cricket club which he had been invited to join in 1946. When he realized that I could play I was invited one Saturday to Concord Oval for a game. My shore posting enabled me to be available on Saturdays on a regular basis.

There came a particular Saturday when I was to go to Mosman Oval to join another of his club teams then captained by Keith Storey. I was asked where I would like to bat and predictably I said, "At No. 3."

We won the toss, batted, and I was out with 46 to my name. What I didn't know was that this was the final hurdle I had to clear before being invited to join I Zingari (Australia). Bill Douglass the then secretary said on the Saturday following, "By the way, there was a meeting on Thursday and you have been invited to join the Club."

I was overjoyed. I was now to become a member of a club founded first in England as I Zingari in 1845 and then in Sydney as I Zingari (Australia) in 1888. I don't intend to give a history of these two great ornaments to the game of cricket in our world. Both have been dealt with in detail in the following books: *I Zingari Australia 75 Years of Cricket 1888 – 1963,* by W B Douglass (Deaton and Spencer Pty Ltd), *The History of I Zingari* by R L Arrowsmith and B J W Hill (Stanley Paul and Co Ltd 1982) and *I Zingari in Australia 1888 – 1988* by J M Eldershaw (Allen and Unwin Australia Pty Ltd).

So in 1948 I became a member of the club for which Bradman had played once in 1932. (He was run out for 15 in a game that I Z lost.) It is with some humility that I am mentioned in these publications not necessarily for any outstanding performance with bat, ball or in the field.

From my first and only full season of I Z cricket I was never to be in Sydney to play regularly for an I Z team. When I joined there were three teams playing regularly, the A's, B's and the Veterans. Eric Siddeley, eleven years my senior was captain of the B's. He was happy to have me in the team as in many ways I was able to bridge the age gap between him and the younger members who had recently completed schooling.

In general, batsmen batted and bowlers bowled. Games were played on Saturday starting at 13:00 with a change of innings at 15:30. The wickets were such that an individual score of 30 was considered pretty good. Nevertheless most seasons produced one or two century makers in the club, often with a not-out credit. Captains of teams would decide with their opponents on the conditions under which games would be played, such as equal times or equal overs for each innings.

Three much older cricketers now at Sydney Cricket Ground – myself, Bill Douglass, Quentin Stanham

As a member of the Sydney City and Suburban Cricket Association since its foundation in 1903 I Zingari (Australia) has always had a crowded Fixture List of games against fellow members of the Association, schools attended by I Z members, teams from overseas against which I Z (Australia) has played on tour, as well as naval and army teams (when these have been able to field representatives), as well as its own competition for the Belvidere Cup.

This magnificent trophy, an engraved two-handled silver cup, surmounted by a lid with a figure on top, featuring a batsman at the crease, was originally the New South Wales Cricket Association's Second Eleven Trophy presented by W B Marks, a prominent New South Welshman, in 1888-89. It was won by the Belvidere Cricket Club and stayed with Dr. P C Charlton, one of the members of that club taken over by I Zingari (Australia) when Electoral Cricket was introduced. In 1936 Dr. Charlton, now long dead, but Patron in Perpetuity of I Zingari (Australia) presented the Cup to I Zingari for competition between its own teams.

My first, last, and only experience of playing for the Belvidere Cup was a personal disaster. Opening for the B team against the A team I was bowled first ball of the match by E S White. I learnt the hard way why Bradman was so pleased to have him along with the Australian XI on the team to England in 1938.

I averaged 24 for the season and did not bowl.

I found my work at HMAS *Watson*, the Navigation Direction School for the RAN at South Head, most rewarding. In addition to training officers and ratings I was also responsible for recommending the posting of sailors who'd qualified in radar and plotting duties. Although my predecessor, David Stevenson, had been on the Long N Course with me in 1944, he hadn't been involved with aircraft direction. As a result the training courses were in need of updating to prepare operators for the arrival in Australia of HMAS *Sydney*, the first of two aircraft carriers to be acquired.

Just as there were certain fixed attitudes concerning the size of the Army needed in Australia, so there was for Navy. Fundamentally, it was aimed at the two-ocean concept, so the number of ships required to meet it must be in multiples of that number. As with socks and underpants, this enables a one on and one in the wash philosophy to be followed, the theory being that even if one ship is under refit, the other will be available to meet whatever emergency may have to be faced.

For ships built in Australia there is a slight variation to this basic philosophy that I've called, for convenience, the rule of three. One is built at Cockatoo, one at Williamstown and a third at either Cockatoo or Williamstown depending on which dockyard finishes first. The modern practice of having ships for the RAN built in the United States has modified the basic concepts somewhat, but when all else fails the two-ocean concept can always be relied upon for rationalization if needed.

Every now and again some bright officer is given the task of producing a way ahead, or some such study, which purports to look into the future to decide what ships will be needed. Whether this is done periodically, or as we're led to believe on a continuously updating basis, the answer is fundamentally the same. We'd like two, or multiples thereof of such and such a ship, but can only afford one or such other reduced number.

On the one occasion that this exercise was supposedly carried out with the greatest objectivity, what started out to be a Light Destroyer suitable for building in Australia completely from our own resources finished up as a Super Dreadnought, one that was so full of eggs that the basket could never be risked in any battle at sea less its loss would mean the loss of the war.

During this time ashore I Captained the *Watson* Cricket Team in the I Z Shield competition making 50 odd in my first game, thus securing my place in the Navy team to play the Army and Air Force every season thereafter until going to sea again. I was concerned about getting back to sea as quickly as possible, as I could see that competition for promotion was particularly fierce and a seagoing recommend would be essential.

The Naval Board had decided to reintroduce the Examination for Command of Destroyers, with the proviso that any officer actually in command, or who'd been in command of a seagoing ship for a period of three months would be exempt from the examination. I presented myself to the Board of Examiners and duly satisfied them on the extent of my knowledge in all of the required subjects. Other candidates tried their hand at one or two with varying degrees of success, but I had to do the lot.

The Flag Officer Commanding the Australian Fleet reported the progress of the examinations to the Naval Board commenting on the high standard shown. The Naval Board then proceeded to appoint to command not the officers who'd passed the examination, but in some cases those who'd actually failed in the subjects they'd attempted. After three months in command these officers were exempt from further examination. Some system. It gutted me.

Late in 1949 I was appointed to HMAS *Sydney* as Navigating Officer. As the ship was flying the flag of Rear Admiral J A S Eccles, I was Master of the Fleet.

It had been eleven years since I first stood on the bridge of HMAS *Canberra* and saw Commander H A Showers in that role. I could perhaps be forgiven for thinking then that my career was coming along quite well. However there were clouds gathering over the horizon and the first rolled in even before I joined the ship.

— 18 —

The Summer Cruise of 1950

The Summer Cruise of 1950 was to be a flag showing exercise on a grand scale with visits to Melbourne, Hobart, Adelaide and New Zealand. For each visit a morning city fly over had been planned just as people were on their way to work, followed by the normal pattern of social calls in the Forenoon.

I was faced with two problems. Firstly, making myself known to the Second-in-Command, then Commander Otto Humphrey Becher DSC and Bar. I'd been told in no uncertain terms that in view of my junior status he'd given the occupancy of the Navigating Officers cabin in the Bridge section of the ship to the RN Commander (Air). My cabin was aft under the Flight Deck, about where aircraft touch down when landing. There was no bunk in the Chart House as in *Norman*, so officers during the night watches had no ready contact with the navigator.

The second problem was the tight scheduling of the planned flights over the cities in the mornings of arrival before the official calls. This seemed to have been done without any navigational input, such as where the carrier might be in relation to its berth when the last aircraft was to have landed.

The navigator I relieved had left the ship before I joined and to my knowledge hadn't served in an aircraft carrier before. When I first met him he was doing his Long N Course at *Dryad* while I was standing by to commission *Norman* in 1941. His attitude towards me then had been one of superiority that I'd found rather offensive. All in all it looked as though, as Shakespeare said in Hamlet, I may well have set myself up to be 'Hoist with (my) own petar.' Time alone would tell.

Our Melbourne visit started out quite well. Port Phillip Bay offered ample sea-room for operating aircraft and berthing starboard side to Station Pier, stern first, with tugs was a successful manoeuvre, with a couple of catamarans keeping the ships side from the wharf.

However, when the time came to leave only one tug was available forward, with a strong breeze coming in on the port bow. Lines were cast off, the tug taking the strain, but it had insufficient power to pull the bow clear. The wind took charge and because of the slight headway the point of pivot came off the forward catamaran and the ships side rested on the end of the pier. It was a classic case of being in irons.

The Captain went aft, the Admiral came down from his bridge to the Compass Platform and as the tug managed to pull the bow clear I decided to try to stop the stern from swinging in to starboard using the engines. This worked sufficiently, but unfortunately part of the aft superstructure touched the wharf side crane and derailed it. We finally got clear taking the tug with us. Our Shipwright Officer sorted things out with the harbour authorities and we heard no more about it.

The passage around the west of Tasmania was uneventful. In the early part of the Middle Watch I took the ship through the passage between Maatsuyker Island and the mainland, watching the echo sounder as closely as I used to do while surveying in New Guinea waters, comparing the depths being recorded with those charted by Matthew Flinders.

As in the previous visit to Hobart with the Fleet in 1938, the Flagship was to provide the manpower for the Debutantes Ball at Government House. As Wardroom Mess Secretary, or because of my poodle-faking propensities, or my friendship with the proprietor of the *Hobart Mercury* who was sponsoring Margaret Hughes, the newly crowned Miss Australia, I was given the task of organizing the partners for the young women making their debut. With so many 20th Carrier Air Group pilots it really became an easy thing to do. I formed two lines, one line tallest on the left, shortest on the right and vice versa on the other, facing inwards and partnerships for the introduction to their Excellencies before the obligatory dance was decided. Simple you might think.

After the rehearsals the littlest girl came to me in high dudgeon with the complaint about 'Shorty' her partner. It seemed that the one she really fancied was the tallest of the pilots, which wouldn't do at all. As the chaperone and mentor to the debs and my partner for the night, I enlisted Miss Australia to calm the situation, while I told the men to lay off the booze and smoking until after the performance on the night. Thankfully all went to plan.

Then Adelaide brought about the very situation I'd envisaged — our aircraft took off for the morning flight over the city without incident, but when it came to landing, the first plane was waved off. The ship's speed to get sufficient head wind for the landings was 18 knots, but by the time all the aircraft, except one, were onboard there was only enough sea room to turn hard a-port and complete a circle while reducing speed to eight knots on the leads for entering Outer Harbour. The lone aircraft landed at Adelaide airport and the car to take the Admiral on his calls was waiting as the ship berthed. It was a close call.

Then it was on to New Zealand. Combined exercises with New Zealand Navy ships were designed to give them experience at sea with an aircraft carrier and its fighter and anti-submarine aircraft. On one occasion Jas Eccles came down from on high and said to the Captain, "Dowling you have just sunk my Flagship."

Sydney had been taken out of the protecting screen to fly-off aircraft that in war in the likelihood of attack by submarines was always a no-no. I'd pointed this out to both the Captain and Boff Stevens, the Commander (Air), but they went ahead and did it anyway.

On approaching Auckland for an early forenoon arrival I briefed the Officer of the Watch on the situation that *Sydney* was leading the combined line of ships in Hauraki Gulf towards the harbour entrance and went aft to my cabin to shower, change and have breakfast. I was quite pleased when the ships address system called, "Would the Navigator come to the Bridge." I made it my business to be seen walking from the stern, along the flight deck to the entrance of the Bridge structure and take control of the ship from the Officer of the Watch. It was as good as saying, 'Up you' to Boff for taking my cabin and letting the Captain know how much he really was relying upon my skills.

Once again berthing ships became important. HMAS *Warramunga,* whose commanding officer had been Roy Dowling's second-in-command of HMAS *Hobart* at the end of World War II, was to go alongside ahead of Sydney. He succeeded in making a meal of the manoeuvre and kept us waiting the best part of 30 minutes. Once more Jas Eccles came to the Bridge, telling me to convey his displeasure of the ship handling that had resulted in him being late for all his morning engagements.

Although I did this with great tact and understanding, I'd made another high-ranking enemy in Allan McNicoll, who had his revenge when as Second Member of the Naval Board, some ten years later, he reverted me to the rank of Commander and appointed me to oblivion in the Department of Defence.

The next port of call was Lyttelton. Here Roy Dowling and I had a confrontation ... and just the preliminary of a series to come. He was all for putting the ship into the hands of the Pilot we were obliged to take.

I pointed out there was no way we could transfer responsibility for handling the ship, even producing the Kings Regulations and Admiralty Instructions to prove my point. Commander (Air) had offered his aircraft secured to the flight deck, to assist in turning the ship at rest inside the small harbour to enable Sydney to berth stern first starboard side to the wharf, the better to leave without assistance. In the event the manoeuvre went like clockwork, the Pilot was relieved that he didn't have to control the pinwheel performance and even the Captain acknowledged that I'd done what needed to be done quite well.

We spent an extra day in Christchurch when the weather deteriorated, before leaving Lyttelton under our own steam.

The highlight of our time in New Zealand was undoubtedly visiting Milford Sound and the ships company taking a shower on the Flight Deck under the waterfall.

As far as joint operations went, the most successful exercise was a night encounter. *Sydney* despatched its accompanying destroyer some ten miles to seaward and crept close to the coast to confuse the 'enemy' radar. Sure enough the destroyer did its best to engage the 'enemy' and the carrier lived to fight another day. One up to me as it was entirely my idea.

Returning to Australia both the *Sydney* and *Warramunga* encountered an unusual phenomenon of the Tasman Sea, the East Australian Current. Usually this runs from north to south along the coast of New South Wales before turning to run south to north off the South Island of New Zealand.

With clear weather astronomical navigation would normally make position keeping a certainty, but we had two days without star sights and the current had turned almost due west with increased speed. Early sun sights showed that *Sydney* was considerably behind schedule, so much so that Boff Stevens asked, "Water pilot, would you like me to fly an aircraft off to let you know where you are, relative to Jervis Bay?"

I told him not to worry himself about that because I had authority to increase speed and he would soon find the Jervis Bay light dead ahead. So it transpired.

The 20th Carrier Air Group transferred to HMAS *Albatross, Sydney* received a new Captain, D H Harries RAN, and I prepared to take the ship to Britain for the last time as Navigator. The Naval Board had decided to make use of my D Dagger experience and to get an RN Commander as Navigator on loan when the ship arrived in the United Kingdom. However I never got my cabin on the Bridge.

On 29 July 1950 while I was navigating *Sydney* to England our first child, a boy, Leigh Mackenzie Graham Wright, was born. He was named after the first husband of the famous British actress Vivien.

Jean and our son Leigh

Crosby-on-Eden, the Mackenzie family residence

Apart from doing shore training in the United Kingdom, I visited Jean's parents. They were then in Achnasheen, some forty miles by rail to the west of Inverness where *Sydney* was anchored for the weekend. Her father, Captain J S Mackenzie, was now Laird of the Manor having retired from his Dental Practice in Carlisle. With winter coming on, the house routine was to rise with the sun around ten in the morning, then hunt the deer until sunset just after two in the afternoon.

Jean's mother and a couple of her friends drove me back on the Sunday and were impressed when I signalled the ship, the boat came. We went onboard for a celebratory drink as the bar was open and they were then landed by boat back at the jetty. Outwardly it seemed that Jean's parents were contented that Jean had come through parenthood of her own, on her own.

Back in Australia in December 1950 two things had become paramount. Jean had no car and with a baby, Kingsley Hall was too small. Somewhere else to live had to be found. Unbeknown to me, my career was also slowly being undermined by Jean who was discontentedly airing her thoughts and problems to the mother of one of the officers a couple of years junior to me.

Meanwhile I was showing my prowess as a Direction Officer in getting the aircrew of the two Sea Fury Squadrons (805 and 808) and one Firefly Squadron (817), ready for joining operations in Korea.

— 19 —

In Command

As the only RAN Officer to have qualified for command by Fleet Board examination, I was appointed to HMAS *Culgoa* in command. It was July 1951. One hurdle in advancement had been cleared at last. A benefit was to accrue.

No words of mine can equal those of Herman Wouk in 1951:

'Naval command is the greatest strain that can be brought to bear on a person.' — The "Caine" Mutiny, Jonathan Cape, London 1954 p. 424

Having moved from HMAS *Sydney* which was about to work-up in preparation to relieve HMS *Glory* in Korea in late August 1951 I was to have an independent command with the responsibility of training Naval National Servicemen to sustain the complements of RAN ships in the Far East Strategic Reserve.

With a reduced complement of 101 (down from 140) sea training of six weeks was achieved on a regular basis from the Recruit School in HMAS *Cerberus,* formerly Flinders Naval Depot, Westernport in Victoria. I was given ample scope in planning venues for harbour training in boat work in which no shore leave would be given. These included Wilsons Promontory, Twofold Bay, Broken Bay and Port Stephens.

Melbourne was invariably a weekend event in the football season berthing at a wing on the southern side (never at Williamstown), Port

Adelaide, Devonport, Launceston, Hobart and Sydney our home port where normal leave to the ships company would be given whilst national service trainees were required to be back on board by midnight. Never once was my proposed itinerary not approved.

Early in 1952 I agreed to a suggestion that *Culgoa* should extend sea training in the Great Barrier Reef as far north as Cairns. Incidentally, once approval had been given for a cruise north a call at Gladstone was to put my ship handling capability to the test. Whilst in Cairns I was asked to load the Queensland black bean timber for the pews in the Chapel of St Mark being built for HMAS *Cerberus*.

On 6 February His Majesty King George VI died. I cleared Lower Deck and conducted a non-denominational service on the Quarterdeck underway in the evening to mark the occasion and the ascension to the throne of Queen Elizabeth II.

As Captain of HMAS Culgoa I hand over HMAS Emu after an epic tow of 1200 miles at 12 knots from north of Cairns to Sydney via Brisbane for refit

Whilst in Cairns I was ordered to proceed further north and take HMAS *Emu* under tow to Sydney. This proved to be great training for the entire ships company as at sea we followed war routine with darkened ship and Action Stations at dawn and dusk daily. Naturally we had to use steaming lights and particularly those for ships towing and being towed. Moreover the visit to Brisbane was an excellent test for seaman-like ability, particularly as the Captain of *Emu* decided that his crew should embark in *Culgoa* leaving him to cope with things his end. In the event we were able to maintain an economical speed of 12 knots and only parted the tow once, and that was as we cleared the Brisbane River. The photograph shows the arrival in Sydney recovering the tow to enable *Emu* to proceed to Garden Island dockyard for its planned refit.

There were also occasions on which *Culgoa* was selected for special duties. During the Montebello atomic test in 1952 we were stationed off the coast of Western Australia as a weather reporting ship. One morning the Sick Berth Attendant reported to me that a national serviceman with suspected acute appendicitis needed an emergency operation. As Geraldton was the nearest port I set off immediately at best speed while raising steam for full speed, informing all concerned of my intentions.

At evening stars my navigator was able to observe the correct star to get a position line for a safe approach into the harbour. We berthed alongside at 23:45 where an ambulance was waiting with a doctor in attendance.

By midnight we departed heading back to our original station and weather reporting, having also landed the mail for the mainland which my officers had censored. Only one letter needed some blacking out. It contained the following: *'It ain't gorn off yet.'*

One further special event which was to have a significant effect on my future career was to fly the Naval Board Flag and to Dress Overall for a Fleet Review in Port Phillip Bay.

Early on a newspaper photographer was onboard during individual exercises off the East Coast. He took an excellent photograph of a depth charge explosion at 50 feet and offered his Edgecliff apartment to me in such a way as to avoid the payment of 'key money' to the owner of the building.

This greatly improved our living conditions, but the demands on my time were even greater than before. My wife's lack of understanding of a warship captain's responsibilities didn't make our time together at home full of sweetness and light.

On one particular evening, with a baby-sitter looking after Leigh, we decided to walk to the cinema in Double Bay. On leaving our building a young man introduced himself, as a neighbour from just around the corner. At the time I thought nothing more of it.

In April/May 1952 *Culgoa* took command of two Corvettes for a Training Cruise with National Servicemen to New Zealand. The main activity was a parade through Napier followed by a Sunday church service. Unfortunately, the 100 or so bayonets needed for the armed marchers had been covered in black paint to prevent them from rusting. I was in no mood to set some sort of precedent by mounting a guard without glistening bayonets, so for the next 24 hours each man polished his own bayonet. At the church the rifles were stacked and guarded by sentries. It was a sparkling success.

Auckland, Christchurch and Dunedin were visited, also Milford Sound. The weather forecast was not favourable and fuel was in short supply. *Culgoa* shared its fuel with the Corvettes and dispatched them to Hobart, while remaining in the Sound to do the traditional things, like putting the forecastle under the waterfall and so on.

Leaving at sunset and setting course for Bass Strait brought the ship right into the path of a developing storm. Early in the Middle Watch the roll of the ship caused one whaler, which had to remain outboard of another whaler stowed on deck, to ship water and for the Upper Deck to become too dangerous.

On the Bridge taking charge of the ship, I had the Upper Deck cleared. Then all electric power failed due to a flooded alternator in the Engine Room. The auxiliary alternator had been dismantled for servicing. The gyro compass stopped, the Coxswain took the wheel and I ordered, "Steer roughly west by magnetic compass."

Meanwhile the Engineer Officer and his team worked feverishly to put the auxiliary alternator together in the dark. As the storm centre approached the barometer started dropping. I decided to run before the wind, keeping it on the starboard quarter, as the course being steered moved steadily to the southward. The barometer stopped at 954mbs, the storm centre passed and by now it was safe to alter course to starboard and reduce speed to ride out the rest of the storm.

Several senior officers reading my account of the return passage questioned why I didn't heave-to in the beginning. Undoubtedly they'd never bothered to read *The Caine Mutiny,* or *Slocum,* and had never served in the Australian built River Class Frigates with a propensity to dip the entire forecastle into a head sea and flood the whole bow section via the chain lockers. *Culgoa* returned to Sydney having weathered that severe storm in the Tasman Sea, resulting in only a short period in dockyard hands.

It was becoming clear to me that Jean was extremely unhappy and was concerned about her family in England. Claiming loneliness I allowed her to acquire a small dachshund, Mitzi. But she then began seriously considering another child. I knew this would only make life more difficult without me being home on a regular basis.

Time in command was coming to an end. With four years seniority as a Lieutenant Commander on 1 September 1952 and considering the success of my previous appointments, I expected promotion to Commander in the near future.

One Sunday afternoon in September I threw a farewell party for my officers and friends. John Dowson my old No.1 from *Norman* and Philip Stevenson, a fellow frigate captain were invited. But to my amazement my wife turned up with the neighbour from around the corner. It was obvious they were clearly more than just friends.

Late in 1952 *Culgoa* was restored to full complement for service in Korean waters and I was posted ashore to HMAS *Rushcutte*r to take charge of Reserve training. I took accommodation on Beach Road, within walking distance of Edgecliff Road. By now the marriage as such, was over and time would decide what was to happen next.

From the shambles I'd also inherited at work, I was able to institute training classes for the senior executive officers to enable them to sit for the Destroyer Command examinations. The Reserve Division was placed on a proper footing with Captain Stanley Darling OBE DSO ** VRD (seniority 31.12.52) authorized to correspond with Navy Office, Melbourne on all matters affecting his men. I established a Divisional System paralleling that in operation in PNF (Permanent Naval Forces) Ships and Establishments. Captain's Requestmen and Defaulters were seen on a regular basis on established training nights.

May 1953 saw my promotion to Commander, albeit on an acting basis. I took over as Master Attendant, Garden Island Dockyard and Deputy Captain of the Port, Sydney. While still retaining the occupancy of the flat in Edgecliff Road, I moved into the East Australia Area Headquarters in Potts Point for the next two years.

In the normal course of events I would've expected to head the list of promotions to Commander on 30 June that year, but the long slide down the seniority list was only just beginning. It had nothing to do with professional performance.

At that time RAN affairs were controlled by the Naval Board, consisting of a Minister of State for the Navy, a Vice-Admiral as First Naval Member, Rear Admirals as Second, Third and Fourth Naval Members and a civilian secretary from the Department of the Navy. The centre of control and administration was in the Victoria Barracks, St Kilda Road, Melbourne, with financial control largely in civilian hands at Albert Park.

Anyone interested in the conduct of naval affairs throughout the mid-to-late 1950's and early 1960's should read *Where Fate Calls* by Tom Frame, first published in 1992 by Hodder and Stoughton (Australia) Pty Limited Chapter 1 pages 2, 3 and 4, bearing in mind that some of those senior RAN officers lost during World War II would undoubtedly have filled senior positions during the post-war period.

It was evident now that by spending so much time as a junior officer on loan to, or exchange with the Royal Navy, I was largely unknown to my seniors in the RAN. Captain G C Oldham CBE DSC, Captain F N Cook DSC and Captain K McK Urquhart CBE were close associates at Garden Island, while the Flag Officer-in-Charge East Australian Area, Rear-Admiral H A Showers OBE, had been Commander of the RAN College when I joined in 1934, then Navigator of HMAS *Canberra* when I'd served as a Midshipman and Captain of HMAS *Adelaide* from who I'd gained my Watchkeeper's Certificate and promotion to Lieutenant. All these officers supported my promotion to the senior ranks of the RAN in some way.

Throughout my active service I'd always sought to train a subordinate to do what I was doing myself. This served two purposes. Firstly, I wasn't indispensable and was always able to move up the promotion ladder, and secondly, I always had the respect of my juniors. This latter fact was to sustain me in the dark years of the late 1950's and early 1960's.

Although Jean and I had separated during 1952, she waited till her second son, born in June 1953, was six weeks old before leaving Australia. Along with Leigh, Anthony and the dog Mitzi, she joined her sister's mother-in-law in the ship bound for England.

— 20 —

Other Adventures

My years at Garden Island were very different and outside of my regular work I was able to thoroughly enjoy other pursuits — rugby, ocean racing, game fishing and snow skiing.

I qualified as a NSW First Grade Rugby referee under Dr. Roger Vanderfield, Arthur Tierney and Bernie Freeman; navigated in the first ocean race from Sydney to Nouméa and enjoyed the thrills of the first of my Sydney to Hobart races for the Livingstone brothers, first in the ketch *Kurrewa III* and later the sloop *Morna*, which they renamed *Kurrewa IV,* after purchasing it from Sir Claud Plowman; I formed the RAN Game Fishing Club with Ricky Morrow and Philip Berry-Smith; and became a Founding Father of the RAN Ski Club with Geoff Hood, Guy Griffiths and Philip Stevenson.

Yachting and cricket are both time consuming team sports in summer and as much as I love cricket it's not possible to do both at the same time.

The most adventurous time I had was with the Livingstone brothers — chiefly because I was back on the water. They'd bought a ketch that had been ferrying supplies around islands in the Northern Australian waters of Torres Straits during World War II. The eldest Frank and his brother John, a few years his junior, were keen to make their mark in Sydney yachting circles.

In August 1953 the first race from Sydney to Nouméa was to take place. Organizers wanted to attract boats not usually entered in the Box-

Game fishing for which I held the World Record in 1953

ing Day Sydney to Hobart classic. I was fortunate in being asked to join the crew as Navigator. Having been Captain of my own ship HMAS *Culgoa* and a specialist navigator to boot, plus I was due enough leave from my post as Master Attendant at Garden Island Dockyard, I jumped at the opportunity to make the return trip.

HMAS *Hawkesbury*, with my friend Bob Scrivenor in command, provided escort for the race. He also carried my full dress uniform and sword, so I could finish what I'd started on New Year's Eve 1940 at Government House Nouméa.

In preparation for the race I checked on many factors needing consideration. Given the position of Nouméa on the island of New Caledonia, I discussed my view with the sailing Master that we should always aim to sight land to the north of Nouméa and come down to the finish with the wind well abaft the beam.

Many of the contestants from the Lake Macquarie area of New South Wales, because of their similarity, could be expected to remain in sight of each other throughout the race. Halfway through *Hawkesbury* came from over the horizon on our starboard side, obviously looking for us. It was fairly clear that our strategy was correct and we were doing as well as could be expected.

Our landfall was good and the run to the finish saw us come third. This was remarkable, taking all factors involved in ocean racing into consideration. It whetted the brothers' appetites. We were off to Hobart on Boxing Day.

Normally the Sydney to Hobart followed the same pattern each year. Leave the harbour, pass three lighthouses, then to starboard and cross the line. In the 1953 event, *Kurrewa III* approaching Gabo Island had a good stiff breeze coming in on the starboard quarter. We were making such good headway with night I persuaded the Master to hold our course, reminding him that I could be relied on to find exactly where we were when out of sight of land. We went 190 nautical miles to the east of Gabo Island and picked up the southerly ocean current and favourable wind.

Having avoided the horrors of Bass Strait with its shallow waters compared with the open ocean, and with the majority of the contestants becalmed off Bicheno, I roared past Stan Darling just finishing his morning star sights and we came into Hobart Bay to a decent finish for such an ancient craft.

The appetites were even more than whetted now; they were voracious. It wasn't long before Claud Plowman was persuaded to sell *Morna*, a 65-foot sloop and past performer in ocean racing, which was proudly re-named *Kurrewa IV.*

The build up of a dedicated racing crew then had to start. The forward hand was a great sailing identity, Rubber Kellaway, his first name acquired way back in the early days of flying when he took off from the top of a cliff in a home-made aircraft and crashed, bouncing like India-rubber. He soon had a team of experts able to handle all the intricacies in getting the most out of a spinnaker and finding the correct foresail when changes were needed.

I remained with the racing crew, largely because of my cooking ability for the return sail from Hobart to Sydney. On one of the races we had a professional cook who joined before the start. Off Bradleys Head he hit his bunk and stayed there until we docked. As we docked at the pier he jumped off with his bag, to get the first plane back to Sydney. The Livingstones always said that the meals on the way home were better than any at the Dorchester in London, even though I had to cope with the inevitable 'all hands on deck' to change tack always when I was about to serve dinner.

It was a fairly chequered event each year. *Kurrewa IV* was heavily handicapped, so to win outright was never likely. We came close on one occasion, when in sight of Tasman light, the wind turned southerly after 18 hours and ensured we wouldn't break any records. However we did get Line Honours in 1954 in a time of 5:06:09:47. Followed again in 1956, 57 and 60, but I wasn't a part of the team then.

Line Honours for Kurrewa IV Sydney to Hobart 1954

During 1955 the decision was taken to re-rig the boat. This involved putting pressure on the mast far beyond the ability of the keelson to take the additional strain.

My last ocean race became a disaster. Once past Gabo Island and into Bass Strait we started to pump. Pump and bale we did, all through the night and into the next morning. The brains trust met and the decision that pressure had to be taken off the mast was taken. Once this was done it was clear that we were no longer racing and the correct action would be to retire and return to Twofold Bay. The sea and I parted company once again.

Taking advantage of air travel from South Australia to Britain and return to Singapore in January 1955, I met and discussed a possible end to the marriage with Jean's legal representative and her mother. In those days there always had to be a fully established and usually substantiated reason to grant a divorce. Their proposal to me was on the grounds of cruelty. This wasn't true or satisfactory and I refused to settle. A further five years passed before I was able to obtain a divorce on the grounds of desertion.

I maintained both boys financially until they were 16. Leigh returned to live in Sydney in the 80's and Anthony became an Aircraft Technician in the Royal Navy. During a recent meeting, Anthony told me that his mother now refers to her time in Australia as 'the happiest time of her life', although she missed her family terribly.

The thrill of skiing has always captured me on land and more so since my time at Mount Fuji in Japan.

The RAN Ski Club was the brainchild of three officers serving in the aircraft carrier HMAS *Sydney* in 1951, Lieutenant Commander (E) G P (Geoff) Hood, Lieutenant Commander J P (Philip) Stevenson and Lieutenant Commander G R (Guy) Griffiths DSO. The latter was the

Gunnery Officer and the three met in his cabin. It was September and I'd left the ship to take command of the frigate HMAS *Culgoa* earlier that year, otherwise I would certainly have been there then.

A Commonwealth Navy Order No. 50 on 3 February 1953 stated that a Ski Club had been formed. At that time I was at the original meeting in Sydney.

Getting the Club onto the snow fell to a group in Melbourne that met regularly at a Toorak pub. With accommodation provided by the University, Monsanto and the Youth Hostels Association Ski Clubs, cadets from the RAN College at HMAS *Cerberus* took part in regular three-day visits to Mount Buller in the Victorian Highlands during the winter of 1954.

How we acquired the original lodge on Breathtaker Point is a tale well worth re-telling.

In November 1954 Geoff Hood chose one of three sites on Breathtaker Point on which to build a lodge. In 1955 Aurel Forras was commissioned to build a canteen for Harold Cumming, the operator of a commercial lodge at Dump Inn well below the main skiing area at the time. For some reason never disclosed, this appeared on the very site chosen by Geoff Hood for us.

However fate intervened. When Dump Inn burnt down in December of that year the operator quit and returned to Tasmania, offering the partially completed building to the RAN Ski Club. As it was on the site that Geoff Hood had wanted in the first instance we had to have it.

I'd taken over as Secretary from Philip Stevenson. The asking price was in dollar terms 4,400. The Central Canteen Fund gave the Committee a loan of 2,000. Debentures from members doubled this. The 1956 Club subscriptions all went into the pot. We were still 100 short, but pay-day covered my cheque for the remainder. The RAN Ski Club was in the snow in its own accommodation at last — flat, stony, motherless broke, but we had our own building.

But I'm pleased to say that today we have assets, we have a booking organization that works well and have experienced management in place. We also have a reputation as a reliable contributor to the skiing areas in which we operate — Mount Buller, Perisher Valley and Thredbo. The RAN Ski Club has lasted the years and only continues to get better. I, even now at 93, partake in skiing every winter.

During 1956 to 1962 I was an Office Bearer and because of sea postings for the other three principal founders and me either at *Cerberus* or Navy Office, Melbourne, I often found myself solely in charge of all Club proceedings.

When Geoff Hood was posted to sea in 1957, I took over as President and management of Buller. One of the more pleasurable tasks that year was to give Wran Collins, our Secretary, hand in marriage to a Fleet Air Arm member. Losing her as Secretary, and with no money to speak of requiring a Treasurer, I reverted to the stratagem of the mirror. This involved me consulting the mirror when an important decision was required to be made. I looked left for the Secretary and right for the Treasurer – I always received an affirmative.

While serving at Navy Office I asked Ken Urquhart, then the 3rd Naval Board Member with whom I'd served when Master Attendant at Garden Island Dockyard, if he'd take over as President from me. This was a masterstroke of luck, as he was great mates with Charles Anton, the skier behind the development of Thredbo, and was in the position to calm the disquiet of those senior officers whose daughters were enjoying the pleasure of skiing at the RAN Ski Club.

Given the steady increase in membership and the fact that the volunteer handymen had done just about all that they could be expected to do, it was decided to call in the professionals to turn the hut into a lodge.

An upper sleeping area was evolved after much juggling with drawings and cut-outs to fit in the equipment the Club already had. The accommodation was certainly greatly improved, however it was still rudimentary, but the massive stone fireplace and fitted gas lamps gave the lodge a character all of its own. Masonite over the floorboards stopped the wind and snow howling through and finally carpet was laid wall to wall, or almost.

The improved accommodation brought with it some problems. Who will ever forget the scion of a noble Italian family who drove from Melbourne to spend a weekend with the lady of his fancy in, as he thought, the luxurious surroundings of the best lodge at Mount Buller. After parking his Ferrari, (or was it a Maserati?), in the slush at the side of the road, he was forced to walk untold kilometres in the dark to a wooden hut at the end of nowhere, there to share his bed, such as it was, with another man. Next morning he took one run down Bull Run and without so much as a word of farewell to anyone, returned to Melbourne. Soon after that he left Australia for good. He and the young lady were married in Italy, and as far as we know lived happily ever after.

On St Valentine's Day of 1958 Philip Stevenson went to the altar, although one cannot claim any credit for the RAN Ski Club for that, there was a great cast of supporting actors and actresses who made the whole production possible. Without them the RAN Ski Club could never have survived.

— 21 —

What Future?

My posting in June 1955 was to HMAS *Cerberus,* in Victoria, as Training Commander, relieving my term-mate Ian Cartwright, who remained as Executive Officer.

Taking up residence in the Wardroom I joined in the life of the mess. The Commodore Superintendent of Training occupied an official residence, as did a number of senior married officers and their wives and families. Neil Mackinnon made it very clear to his wife Rachael, that under no circumstances was I ever to enter his house, or to be invited to any social function organized by her. This antipathy can be attributed largely to the fact that he joined the RAN in the year that I was born and now I was just one rank junior to him.

My contemporaries had known the Flinders Naval Depot community life style in the mid 1930's and were intent on recreating some of its successes. Alex Townsend, Marcus Cheadle and Bryn Mussared, to whom I was vaguely related through the husband of one of my father's sisters, had formed a drama group. I was invited to play the part of the Commander in *'The Middle Watch'* about to be produced. I had four weeks to learn my part and join the cast for the final rehearsals and performances. It turned into a lot of fun, as well as being successful.

Two magnificent churches had also been built. The timber for the Anglican Church pews was Queensland black bean that I'd picked up in Cairns while in HMAS *Culgoa.* As an old Church of England choirboy,

I joined the choir that practised next Sundays hymns every Thursday evening and was able to look down on all the young sailors who were marched into church for the good of their souls. Among other things this was something that really ruffled the feathers of the top brass.

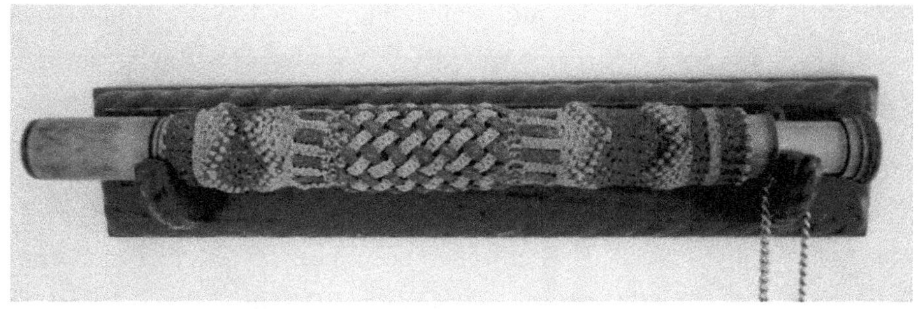

My decorated telescope which still takes pride of place at home

One action is sufficient to show just how ridiculous this attempt at social ostracism was in the circumstances. On leaving Garden Island the riggers in the Rigging Shed had combined to decorate my telescope that I'd won as the Otto Albert Memorial Prize for Seamanship. This procedure usually comes from your crew with promotion. But this showed how much respect they had for me through supporting them for two years in their struggle against Terry Gordon, the Communist leader of the Ship Painters and Dockers Union. Another group undertook the refurbishment of my son's rocking horse that I presented to the Play School at HMAS *Cerberus*.

The cricket season started with a major tragedy. Playing against a local team on the oval at Mornington I was looking around the field to decide who was to be next to come on to bowl when the field was struck by lightning from an approaching storm. A Frankston solicitor running towards the wicketkeeper was struck directly as the bolt passed to earth through the metal caps on the stumps. All the other players on the ground collapsed as if we were being photographed in slow motion. As soon as I got to my feet I realized that the batsman who had been struck was in a serious condition, so I covered him with a greatcoat and started CPR while one of his team rushed off to get professional help. It took forty minutes to get an ambulance and medical team from Frankston Hospital where emergency surgery failed to get his heart restarted. His funeral the following week was a sad event.

For me personally, being adjudged LBW on fifteen successive occasions of opening the batting marked my experience of the Mornington Peninsular Cricket Competition. The opponents on each occasion brought their own umpire to the ground and although I moved my guard from middle to middle and leg and finally to leg stump whenever the ball hit my pads anywhere at all up went the finger. This became so prevalent that I asked George Thoms who was then opening for Victoria in the Sheffield Shield having done the same for Australia against the West Indies in 1951.

Apart from the fact that opposing sides were keen to see me leaving the crease as early as possible he had a good look at the way in which I gripped the bat. To him it was obvious that not being a natural opener I was driving at the ball in such a way that instead of meeting it with the full face of the bat 4.25 inches at the widest part I was presenting only the edge, less than .25 of the width. Change the grip and the problem solved. Find another opener and drop myself down the order.

The advent of 1956 saw Melbourne as host for the Olympic Games. The Recruit School was to provide manpower for the security of the Melbourne Cricket Ground, the main stadium for the Opening and Closing Ceremonies and the venue for all track and field events. Having led the march through the city that preceded the opening of celebrations, I was surprised to be telephoned one Friday morning in May by Captain

R T Power whose conversation I recall, followed, "Graham, you'll be coming up here to Navy Office at the end of next week. We want your job for someone we have to promote."

The officer in question was Duncan Stevens, son of Bob Menzies' mate Sir Jack Stevens. I was to take over as the Deputy Director of Manning, in a position then held by one junior to me, who'd also taken over from another officer also my junior, though two years older. Both had performed their duties in a markedly ineffective manner, so much so that the RAN was facing a manpower crisis due to the unwillingness of sailors to re-engage on completion of their current commitments to serve.

For two years, one month and seven days with an excellent staff, I addressed the problems being caused by ratings seeking to remain in shore postings on compassionate grounds. Captains of ships who were losing key members of their crews were demanding replacements, particularly for the ships proceeding to the Strategic Reserve in the Far East. The 'pier head jump' was the bane of every rating's existence. No one was exempt from the possibility of having to pack up and get to sea at less than a weeks notice.

The professional head of the RAN for the years 1955 to 1959 was Vice Admiral Sir Roy R Dowling KBE CB DSO RAN, who'd been my Captain in the Aircraft Carrier HMAS *Sydney,*1949-50. His nominated successor was Henry Burrell, my Captain in HMAS *Norman,* 1941-43. Both of these officers were to have a profound influence on my future.

It was decided that I should lead a small group from my staff and visit all ships and establishments to address officers and ratings concerning the manpower crises and announcing the measures I'd designed to overcome the current problems. The essence of my solution was to forecast changes in postings six months in advance and to limit the chances of 'pier head jumps' to a specified number of personnel who hadn't been to sea for some considerable time. If those on the stand-by for sea service roster weren't required during the six-month period, they were guaranteed a further six months in their present posting before going to sea in the normal course.

The success of the work of the Re-engagement Team comprising an Executive Chief Petty Officer, a Chief Writer, two Leading Seamen and myself, were acknowledged in a Letter of Commendation from the Naval Board. A number of senior Captains weren't so thrilled to have me come aboard and talk to their Ships Companies, pointing out in particular the breakdown of the traditional Divisional System which had resulted in men simply following one another into civilian life without weighing up fully whether this was in their own best interests. Little did I realize that within the next five years my principles would become applicable to me.

The Royal Navy at that time was having great problems with collisions between ships, groundings and other minor disasters, attributable to the lack of sea experience of the captains of ships. Hence they decided to introduce a system first employed in the time of Nelson. This would create among captains and commanders a Post List and a General List. Those on the Post List would exercise command at sea and those on the General List would compete among themselves for promotion. The RAN, which had long followed the RN because of the interchangeability of their officer structures, decided that this was a great idea and set about instituting a similar system. Rear Admiral Burrell was appointed Flag Officer Special Duties to bring this about.

A conflict arose between CNS, Admiral Dowling, who desired a secret list, to which names could be added or subtracted and Burrell's insistence on a published list. As Burrell said to me, "Graham, the chaps will understand."

To which I replied, "No, sir the chaps will not understand."

When my name headed the list of Commanders destined never to go to sea again, and as a consequence, sixteen officers who'd been junior to me throughout my career passed me over for promotion to Captain on a permanent basis, I had to consider my options for the future.

In Navy there are traditional times for spending in certain ranks. A Cadet Midshipman spent four years at basic training before going to sea as a Midshipman for two years. Time as a Sub-Lieutenant depended upon time gained for promotion in the junior ranks. I spent nine months before promotion to Lieutenant; others spent up to three years. Eight years as a Lieutenant were served before promotion to Lieutenant Commander. After four years as a Lieutenant Commander one entered the zone for promotion to Commander that extended to eight years. Accelerated promotion usually came to those with four years seniority, the average was six years, and in exceptional cases some waited up to fifteen years.

A four to eight year zone also governed promotion of Commanders to Captain. Captains could expect to serve for 10 years in times of peace before being considered for Flag Rank. Promotions on the Flag List, particularly in Australia, were very much a form of political patronage.

With the political control of the nation in Canberra and the headquarters of the Navy in Melbourne, the Admirals who formed the Naval Board at the time were very closely involved with the Melbourne Establishment, their wives particularly so. In the corridors of Navy Office in Victoria Barracks, St Kilda Road it was impossible not to notice some of the antics come the half-yearly promotion time.

Lists of names for promotion to the ranks of Captain and Commander would be formed drawing on material provided in Confidential Reports (Forms S 206). The Chief of Naval Staff would appoint all Captains with the advice of his secretary, a Supply and Secretariat specialist, and the Second Naval Member, also with the advice of his secretary, another Supply and Secretarial specialist all Commanders.

Two significant issues came to my attention by chance, one as I was discussing an issue with Commander John Peel, the Director of Manning. Commander Richard Peek stormed out of an office brandishing a report by Captain J C Morrow on his Executive Officer in HMAS *Australia*, Commander J McL Adams. Peek was ranting and raving on the inordinate adulation being heaped upon his contemporary. Before entering the office of the Second Naval Member he proclaimed, "This is utterly ridiculous. They are just good drinking mates."

The second issue was even more serious. Dowling one morning took the proposed list of promotions of Commanders to Captain, and Lieutenant Commanders to Commander home to lunch to be vetted by his wife Jess, Lady Dowling. The first name on the Captains List, I H Macdonald was scrubbed through because, as she said, "His third wife is on my doorstep two or three times a week complaining to me about him."

The leading name on the list for Commander was D A H Clarke, also deleted in similar fashion for reasons that had nothing to do with his professional competence, but rather to do with some manner in which he'd unwittingly offended her. In 1960, as Naval Officer-in-Charge, West Australia Area and Captain of HMAS *Leeuwin* I was able to put Clarke's career back on track with an honest recommendation for promotion to Captain in due course. This particular piece of bastardry had set him back at least five years.

The Dowling antipathy to me had a long history. It had begun in 1937 at RANC, when I'd won the Athletics 440 yards open race in the time of 56 seconds. At the age of 17, I'd run this time over the distance against all opposition from those of my age in Victorian schools. The RANC record was set by R R Dowling in 1918, at 53 seconds. It was common knowledge that the timekeeper, a civilian instructor, was observed after the starting gun had been fired, vigorously shaking the only stopwatch at the event to get it started. Daffy Davis, who'd won the event in 1936, had not only given me his old running spikes, but also his training schedule for the cinder track, firmly believing that this so-called record could never be broken. In the 1988 publication *Work Hard Play Hard,* on page 154, the Dowling Shield is listed as the Award for the 400 metres.

In January 1946 HMS *Argonaut,* in which I was the Navigating Officer, relieved HMAS *Hobart*, in which Roy Dowling was then Captain, in Tokyo Bay as part of the Commonwealth Occupation Force in Japan. Allan McNicoll was the Executive Officer of *Hobart* at the time. Neither the Captain or Commander bothered to acknowledge my presence as the only other Australian involved in the hand-over of responsibilities involved. I found it quite strange that in the *Hobart* wardroom I had to introduce two of the Australian officers of that ship to one another.

A further rift developed in 1954, when at Garden Island I'd formed the RAN Game Fishing Club. The Dowling's elder daughter had joined the Club along with the daughters of other Senior RAN officers. Regular outings at weekends were features of our activities. Roy Dowling was then Flag Officer Commanding HM Australian Fleet based in Sydney. I lived in Kings Cross on return from England in 1948 and attended the Anglican Church of St Mark's Darling Point on a regular basis. My firstborn was baptized there in 1950. When this Church established its

Friends, I became one of the Founding Friends. One particular Sunday morning I was startled to hear a very angry fatherly voice behind me query, "Where's my daughter?"

In between responses to the Service of Holy Communion I was able to reassure both father and mother that I simply had no idea.

It transpired that unbeknown to me she'd been conducting a liaison with the man she was subsequently to marry, using me as a smokescreen to explain some of her absences from home. When her planned wedding was to take place some three years later I was expected to attend, however her parents told her that I wouldn't be welcome, to which she replied, "If Graham Wright is not invited to my wedding I will not be there either."

But there was no way to escape the hostility of the Melbourne Establishment. In 1958 my time in Melbourne was coming to an end. The Second Naval Member, Rear Admiral W Hastings Harrington, offered my services to Lady Dowling as Secretary to the Naval Ball Committee. This event had been part of Melbourne Cup Week in November from time immemorial and was a fully uniformed affair to which anybody who was anybody in Melbourne Society was invited to attend. At the first meeting of the Committee I suggested that with the changing nature of the political structure of the Defence Force, the impending move of control of the Navy and Army in particular to Canberra at the insistence of Prime Minister Menzies, we could possibly make the event a truly memorial farewell and should perhaps ensure that some senior ratings and their wives be invited to share the event.

Harrington duly informed me that Lady Dowling had accepted my resignation.

Responding, "I haven't resigned."

He firmly stated, "Wright you don't seem to understand. She has accepted your resignation. However, you will be going back to *Cerberus* as Executive Officer next week and no doubt will be very pleased to put the facilities of that establishment behind the event." End of conversation.

In the normal course of career development after five years ashore, although not on the Post List, there was one sea-going appointment for which I was eminently qualified, that of Fleet Operations Officer, definitely regarded throughout the history of the RAN as a 'Promotion Job'.

Some time later I learnt that when Henry Burrell was to be relieved as Flag Officer Commanding Her Majesty's Australian Fleet by David Harries, who'd been Captain of HMAS *Sydney* during my time as Navigator and Direction Officer, my name had been put forward for this posting. Harries, notwithstanding an appreciation of my ability, was adamant, "I wish to command the Fleet myself. I do not want Wright doing the job for me."

This from one who'd always maintained that I was more sinned against than sinning.

Returning to Flinders Naval Depot and my cabin in the Wardroom, I established my position as President of the Mess, re-instating the magnificent Presidential Chair in its rightful place in the centre of the high table; shades of my time at the College, when as Chief Cadet Captain I presided at all meals.

Once again I faced the hostility of the 'Fender Club', a group of old men, some of them four-stripers and all cronies of the Commodore, John Plunkett-Cole. His wife Betty had a brother who was very keen on a very good friend of mine, a Sydney artist divorced from her husband and living with her elderly mother. The Commodore's house was again out of bounds to me, but didn't worry me to any extent. I'd maintained my activities with the drama group throughout my time in Melbourne and starred in one of their major productions *On Monday Next*. It played to enthusiastic audiences in the Drill Hall Theatre and privately to a civilian group in a boutique theatre, And, I resumed singing with the choir and reading from the scriptures on those occasions when Plunkett-Cole didn't attend church.

I led by example on the sporting fields, refereeing Rugby, particularly those matches in which the RAN College First XV were involved.

Interservice cricket in Victoria in 1956 held some interesting realities. The RAAF had one player starring in District Cricket in Melbourne and the ability to fly in key players from other States. The Army had great strength because of Queenscliff, Victoria Barracks on St Kilda Road and Puckapunyal. Navy relied entirely on those at *Cerberus* (Flinders Naval Depot). It did, however, have a trump card in Frederick Mozart Murray. But there was a problem. Every time Fred played he would make a hundred and Navy would lose. The answer was one I found when serving at Navy Office in Melbourne while heading the organization responsible for posting sailors to ships and establishments throughout the RAN.

While in Melbourne I'd entered a Naval team in the mid-week cricket competition that played on two successive Wednesday afternoons on the grounds of the Saturday District Competition. Players in these matches were of an extremely high standard, unable because of their occupations to play at the weekends. Silver Top Taxis, the Milk Distributors and many others gave our Navy team the competition that we needed to meet the Army and the RAAF on an equal footing in the annual Services matches.

I was able to step down from captaincy of the Naval Team in Victoria as Vic Bonnett, an Instructor Officer at FND, had gathered together some excellent regular players, enabling me to concentrate on my own game and the general administration of nets and fielding practice. All this paid off handsomely in March 1959 at Wangaratta when, on the ground expertly prepared by Ernie McCormick who'd started his test career for Australia on 4 December 1936 under Bradman as Captain, Navy beat both Army and the RAAF to win for the first time ever. Plunkett-Cole, who'd played Rugby for the Royal Navy at Twickenham in 1928 was not impressed, urging me on return to *Cerberus* to 'get about my business.'

After such a mean-spirited attitude to something that had lifted the morale of our naval township I became more and more convinced that Harrington's sending me to *Cerberus* fulfilled some hidden victory over one of the people who'd joined the Navy with him. He'd seen how successful the confrontation between Mackinnon and me had turned out and now he was inflicting the same on Plunkett-Cole.

What they'd all failed to realize was, when I was a Midshipman in HMS *Malaya* before World War II I'd been one of the first Australians to serve in that ship since many of the 1920 entry of Australian Cadet Midshipmen, serving from October 1924 to September 1926. I could've sworn that the Gunroom bulkheads still echoed with the words of Arnold Green, Bunny Hodge, Max Clark, Yank Lewis, as Hastings Harrington grew his bugger's grips and developed his character of 'Ming the Merciless' as he lauded it over his fellows in the absence of Neil Mackinnon, then serving in HMS *Ramillies*. There was no love lost between those of the 1920 entry to the RAN College.

It's very easy to convince oneself that one can become the victim of a conspiracy. The traditional theory is that there must be a combination of persons intent on depriving an individual of something that in the normal course should rightfully be theirs. In October 1959, when I was in a posting from which Commanders had always been promoted, sure enough I became an Acting Captain and was appointed to relieve a Commodore old enough to have been my father. I took up my position as Naval Officer-in-Charge West Australia and Commanding Officer HMAS *Leeuwin*. When I left Victoria to take over in Western Australia my services to Navy Cricket were acknowledged with the award of a barometer suitably inscribed.

At the same time Commodore Plunkett-Cole was appointed to London in the rank of Captain as the Australian Naval Representative. These appointments were the last throw of the dice by Harrington, who then took Command of the Fleet.

On St Andrews Day, Monday 30 November 1959, I attended my first official function in Perth, to be greeted by my host with these words, "Thank you for coming to represent the Naval Officer-in-Charge West Australia."

To which I replied, "I'm sorry, but I am the Naval Officer-in-Charge West Australia." The look on his face was a delight to see.

However the talk was received well, albeit with some astonishment. The local press next day was very informative, while Rigby produced a cartoon which highlighted my main interests: Naval Command, cricket, rugby, game fishing, skiing.

The Governor of Western Australia at that time was General Sir Charles Gairdner, who placed great reliance on his Service Commanders, myself for the Navy, Bob Knights Army and the Commanding Officer RAAF Station Pearce. One of us was expected to accompany him on each and every official occasion. In one period of three months I attended ninety engagements that had nothing to do with my naval duties, while seeing the successful introduction of the Junior Recruit Training Establishment, Fremantle, due to start business with the first intake in July 1960.

Rigby's cartoon of me as the incoming Naval Officer in Charge West Australia

It was also my good fortune to be the start of the 1959-60 cricket season and particularly to be asked by His Excellency Sir Charles Gairdner to play in his team on WACA ground and at other venues around the State. Tours to Albany and Geraldton were delights as was the company of some of the best players of the time. Bob Knights, the senior military officer in WA, was also an occasional player until promoted to Major General and appointed to the Royal Military College, Duntroon as Commandant.

The year 1960 was to prove prophetic for me in many ways. When I'd berthed *Culgoa* for the last time in command alongside Garden Island in 1952, I had the feeling then, that it would probably be the last time I'd handle a ship as its captain. I'd qualified for command of destroyers through examination, but other officers were being appointed in command without this qualification, some in fact had failed the subject in which they'd presented themselves.

My marriage, which had been over for eight years, was in the process of being ended legally and I had every reason to believe that as far as life in the Navy was concerned, I was on the way up. However, a decision by the Chief of Naval Staff, Sir Henry Mackay Burrell KBE CB, convinced me that I was in fact on the way out.

Although I'd joined the navy to go to sea and to go as far as I could as fast as I could in February 1960 I received a private letter from Vice Admiral Sir Henry Burrell, CNS, which signalled the virtual end of my naval career. His Supply and Secretariat Secretary, Captain W D Graham, had just shown him the latest report on me, obviously written by Plunkett-Cole. This, combined with other reports, had decided that I would not be going to Sydney as Captain of the Port in my next posting, and the Second Naval Member, Rear Admiral McNicoll would be posting me later in the year as a commander. It was almost inconceivable that my replacement as Captain of the Port, Sydney, was Captain W D Graham, Burrell's own secretary.

Official reports on naval officers were documented confidentially on Forms S 206. It wasn't obligatory to write a report on an officer who'd served with a superior for less than three months. In the case of an adverse report made by a captain on a junior officer, those remarks, after being conveyed to the officer in question, were highlighted in red. The reporting officer deeming that it was within the capability of the one being reported on to make an improvement. Damning with faint praise became a traditional form of disparagement for an officer whose progress one wished to impede. In addition, there was a numerical system from nine down to one, for a series of qualities every naval officer was expected to possess.

During World War II much of the traditional paperwork went by the board. Ship's Captains were far too busy fighting the war. Mail was being lost and Australian Naval Officers serving in Britain were often employed on tasks in which they were considered expendable. When promotions to senior ranks were being considered a typical RN expression was, "Why waste a brass-hat on a Digger?" One can only wonder at the source of the 'other reports' to which Admiral Burrell was referring.

With my next appointment being taken by Burrell's secretary, Captain W D H Graham, who'd been a Sub Lieutenant in the Gunroom of HMAS *Canberra* when I was a Midshipman in 1938, I was to be shunted off to the Department of Defence in Canberra for the last two years of my time in the zone.

The reaction to this sentence of death on my sea-going career was to enroll as a mature age student at The Australian National University, starting a five-year course in 1961for the degree of Bachelor of Arts. My chosen subjects were Political Science, Public Administration, Philosophy and for good measure Australian History.

— 22 —

Interesting Times Ahead

During July 1960, His Honour Mr. Justice Dovey, granted me a divorce from my first wife, Jean, so I was finally free to marry again.

I'd met the lady who was to become my second wife in 1958. People talk about unusual weather patterns and global warming now, but this particular November Show Holiday Weekend we were skiing at Mount Buller. It was bitterly cold with blizzards and a young group of woman gathered around the fireplace in Arlberg Lodge. Naturally, as a founding member of the first Navy Ski Lodge I introduced myself.

Twelve months later, when I was transferred to Western Australia, Miss Margaret Lorraine Wheeler had no intentions of letting me out of her sight and actually relocated herself, setting up her business in Hay Street, Perth, even before I'd arrived. After a year in Perth she travelled across the Nullabor Plains back to Melbourne via train with me.

When I'd left Victoria for Western Australia I'd sold my car, as my appointment was not for a period for which there was an entitlement to transport it across at Government expense. Although I had an official car as NOIC, manning restrictions precluded the appropriation of a driver. I overcame this problem easily enough by driving myself with my official flag flying, on appropriate occasions. I also acquired a private car for non-official use. When the time came to take up my next appointment to the Department of Defence in Canberra, I was confronted with the Catch-22 argument, that transport for my car from Perth to Canberra couldn't be a Government expense because the Government hadn't paid to take my car from Melbourne to Perth.

Fortunately, Mr Bill Kenny the civilian Director of Personnel at Navy Office, with whom I'd had a good relationship during my time there, saw through this nonsense and my car went on the train at Kalgoorlie and off at Port Augusta.

On 10 December 1960 Margaret and I were married. We'd originally planned to have the ceremony at HMAS *Cerberus*, with a long-standing friend, Commander N H S White, as best man. The introduction of the Wet and Dry Lists to the RAN had resulted in the appointment as Commodore Superintendent of Training at *Cerberus* of an Engineer Officer, Frank George. He'd made it very clear that if White valued his career he wouldn't stand up for me and in no circumstances would I be permitted to marry in his church. Thereafter, I always regarded the Chapel of St Mark at Flinders Naval Depot, as the Parish Church of Frank George.

I wasn't the only naval officer to be barred. Chaplain John Were was forbidden to marry Captain A S Rosenthal to the divorced wife of Admiral Ken Urquhart, but to his credit he did so anyway, late one afternoon when no-one was taking any notice.

Our Melbourne wedding took place at the bluestone Presbyterian Church, East St Kilda, followed by a reception at the George Hotel, Fitzroy Street. It was a traditional naval occasion. My best man was a true friend, Commander A F Sallmann, who'd just transferred to the Emergency List of the RAN, as I was to do also on 18 October 1962.

We immediately moved to Canberra and became the first residents in an apartment on the top floor of the newly constructed Stuart Flats in Manuka. The Nation's Capital was nothing more than a big country town then. The lake wasn't developed and wouldn't be until a few years later.

As a member of the Joint Intelligence Staff in the Administrative Building which Defence shared with the then Department of External Affairs, my immediate superior was a senior diplomat, Harold Eastman, my colleagues an Army Lieutenant Colonel, a RAAF Wing Commander and another diplomat, Frank Cooper who was to figure prominently in my future in two years time.

The Cold War was upon us and the Official Secrets Act was our Bible. I'm a great believer in Sir Humphrey Appleby's contention that the Official Secrets Act was not designed to protect secrets, but to protect officials.

My work in Defence required a Top Secret clearance and close contact with the then Department of External Affairs. Our shared building, the Administrative Building, had originally been designed to house employees of the Australian telephone system. Due to the Great Depression it wasn't built until after World War II, with the entire interior being re-developed for its new function.

My colleagues and I spent many lunch hours walking to see the progress of work on the Kings Avenue Bridge leading to the site for the Russell Offices, being built to house the Headquarters of the Navy, Army and Air Force when the move from Melbourne was implemented.

Back in Canberra during the 60-61 and 61-62 cricket seasons (October to May) I was playing regularly in the Navy team in Canberra. In one season I also appeared for the Manuka 1st Grade side over the Christmas break following a 75 not out innings at the Forestry Oval during a Sunday match between a Defence team and a good local team.

Canberra was a shock for Margaret, who thought it would be endless days of coffee and cocktail parties. Becoming bored she decided to start another modelling agency in town. The same week it opened she was asked to write a regular column, *'Out and About with Margo'* for the first weekly newspaper, *The Territorial*. It covered the Capital's diplomatic and social scene.

My university examinations at the end of my first year were successful. In my second year decisions had to be made determining the direction I'd take if a Naval promotion was to become effective on 31 December 1962. These would be announced on 30 June 1962.

While playing bridge at the American Embassy in early June, after bidding a grand slam, I had to play Margaret's hand, as she began experiencing severe cramps. Others present, with more experience in childbirth, insisted it was indigestion, as the pains weren't in the right spot. I wasn't of any help, this was also the first birth I was experiencing. At 22:30, after winning the bridge, we sped to the old Canberra Hospital and at 02:00 on 7 June 1962, Margaret gave birth to our daughter, Victoria Lyall Wright. At 08:00 Margaret was sitting up in bed with a typewriter on her lap, tapping out her weekly column, which was due that day. Of course the column was all about having a baby.

The senior officers I'd been working with in Defence were all civilians and accepted me as their equal. The Chairman of the Joint Intelligence Committee, Harold Eastman and a Deputy Secretary of Defence, Sam Landau, together with the Director of the Joint Intelligence Bureau, Harold King, were all impressed with my performance over the first year of my tenure. The then current Chairman, Alan Loomes and another senior diplomat Lew Border, were also impressed with my work. None of these, however, were in any sense obliged, or even able to report in the manner accepted by the Naval Board.

Shortly after 30 June it was made abundantly clear that the Navy intended to post me, on completion of my time in Defence, but it was to a position that would in effect deprive me of eleven years seniority. Not having served at sea as a Commander and having been passed over for promotion to Captain by sixteen officers junior to me on the General List, spending two and a half years seconded to the Department of Defence, I was in no mood to hang around in the hope that some changes, which clearly had to be made, would be in my favour.

The three years seniority I'd lost could never be regained. To add insult to injury, the appointment offered to me on completion of my time in Defence was one to which an officer of Lieutenant Commander's rank was to fill as an Acting Commander, in effect a back classing of almost ten years. My answer, in Shavian terms, was, "not Pygmalion likely."

In August, when Alan Loomes asked me if I'd be prepared to go to Bangkok instead of Frank Cooper, an External Affairs Officer of the Joint Intelligence Staff who they wanted to be the first Australian Ambassador to Taiwan, I saw this as an offer I couldn't refuse. I was to head the Research Office in the South East Asia Treaty Organization (SEATO).

My letter of request to transfer to the Emergency List was drafted during a skiing visit to the Navy Ski Lodge at Mount Buller in Victoria. I made no bones about my opinion of the posting and promotion policies then being followed by the Naval Board.

Early in 1962 I'd bought a lease on the highest building block in the ACT and after some slight hiccups along the way Bob Warren, a leading Canberra architect, acquired a builder and construction had begun at 14 Holmes Crescent in Campbell.

In September my wife and I moved into our new home, still minus a front door. We lived in it for a grand total of six weeks. My friend Senator Reginald 'Spot' Turnbull, the newly elected independent from

Tasmania, took over my Stuart apartment in Manuka, and on 18 October 1962 I drove to HMAS *Harman* to return my gas mask, which had been part of my essential equipment since leaving the Naval College in December 1937.

Next morning, with a baby in a basket and leaving a car to be sold by a friendly garage owner, it was to Sydney by plane to board an Italian passenger ship for Singapore, and then by train to Bangkok. The Department of External Affairs had consigned our travelling luggage some time previously, but it didn't connect with us until the ship arrived in Adelaide. Such was our euphoria that this seemed a very small inconvenience.

— 23 —

Bangkok

On arrival in Bangkok a very friendly Brit met us with arrangements for me to start work the next morning. In November 1962 the first of my many articles from then until the end of my two-year term as an International Civil Servant appeared in print.

My time in Bangkok was, in many ways, the antithesis of my personal and professional humiliation at the hands of the Naval Board. The Deputy Secretary General of the South-East Asia Treaty Organization was an Australian, Bill Worth who'd been a Flight Lieutenant in the RAAF during World War II. He was an extremely capable administrator and an avid supporter of the Royal Bangkok Sports Club, held in high regard by most of the members of the Thai meritocracy. Like him and his family, we lived in Samsen, in a typical Thai house on that side of the SEATO Headquarters remote from the area populated by the Americans and most of the other 'farangs'.

As was the requirement in 1962, I bought a Mercedes-Benz and supported a live-in domestic staff of Thai Cook, a wash girl and the Cook's daughter, along with a part-time male gardener and handy man. We also inherited two extremely beautiful cats from the couple leaving to return to New Zealand. At the end of my two-year appointment all these were handed on, except the Benz.

At 42 I was washed up on the beach, married to a beautiful woman 13 years my junior, father of a lovely six month old daughter who was given the nickname Tookie, which remains with her to this day (as all babies in Thailand are Tookata), and driving a blue Mercedes to and from a splendid home at No.2 Ronachai Song, Samsen, Bangkok to the SEATO offices adjacent to the Dusit Zoo, lunching every Friday at the restaurant opposite the Thai First Army Headquarters and allowed to continue as a part-time student of the Australian National University (ANU) in Canberra for one unit a year one in which, perhaps, I could be forgiven for thinking I'd been particularly favoured.

My wife had intended to retire, but in usual form she couldn't sit still and established the first modelling school in Asia, The Margaret Wright School of Grooming and Deportment. The highlight was when Malaysian Airways invited her to produce a South East Asian fashion flight. The tour would take three weeks and her specially chosen Thai models, only one was pure Thai, became known as the 'Maids of Siam'. She was also pregnant with our second child, eight months in fact, but assured me she'd planned it so the baby would be nearly two months old and able to travel with her. This time she went three weeks over and our son, Matthew Wheeler Hanford Wright, was born on 4 June 1964.

With only three weeks before her grand fashion tour, her mother joined her to help with the baby, travelling to Penang, Kuala Lumpur, Singapore, Hong Kong and back to Bangkok.

While in Hong Kong my wife celebrated her 32nd birthday. HMAS *Melbourne* was also in port. The Captain was David Stevenson, whom she'd first met with me while in Perth in 1959, when I was Naval Officer-in-Charge West Australia Area. He invited her and her mother onboard. Needless to say the tour was a success in more ways than one.

Margaret also continued to write for *The Territorial* back in Canberra, her weekly column now titled, *'Margo's Bangkok Postcard'*.

There were of course other advantages. Bill Worth and his wife, Lila, were overjoyed to have the only other Australians in the organization living close by. One of our near neighbours was the mistress of Thai strongman, Field Marshal Sarit, whose visits to the area were marked by an extraordinary exhibition of reverence by all around us. Love in high places was only one step down from devotion for the Thai Royal Family.

Also during 63-64 my services were needed in the cricket being played at the Bangkok Sports Club. As there were only 24 actual players the matches were contrived to be different from the usual 12 against 12, like Married Men v Singles, British and Colonials against the rest. A great event was a match between E W Swanton's Visiting XI against the Royal Bangkok Sports Club. I was needed as Umpire and managed to give the Nawab of Pataudi out LBW on 30. Richie Benaud guided a young Etonian, Nick Preslick to his first 100.

When I arrived the Australian Ambassador to Thailand in Bangkok was very interested to learn of my application for the position of Deputy Secretary to the Department of Immigration, which had been advertised in a recent Gazette. As it hadn't been filled, he subsequently applied and was selected. His replacement as Ambassador was Alan Loomes who'd been Chairman of the Joint Intelligence Committee in Australia and my superior in Department of Defence, and instrumental in getting me this job. It was good working with him again.

Some members of the USSR Embassy were aware of my work as Naval Officer in Charge West Australia Area and the visit I paid to a Russian ship in Fremantle in 1960. When Kruschev's son-in-law visited Bangkok I was invited to a party to meet the Editor of *Is Vestia,* a companion newspaper to *Pravda*. At around 21:30, after the consumption of vast amounts of Vodka by all concerned, Arjubai, in the company of his minders said to me, "Commander, what is the real reason you are here in SEATO? People are led to believe that I'm simply a newspaperman married to the President's daughter, but really I'm a Major General in the KGB."

My reply was true to the fact, "I head the Research Office which reports regularly on the trends and highlights of Communist propaganda."

Next morning I reported our conversation to the representative of the Australian Security Intelligence Organisation (ASIO) and subsequently received thanks from Whitehall in London for confirmation of what had been suspected.

I was very fortunate in having a United States Foreign Service Officer, Frederick Zerban Brown, on my staff. He volunteered to examine the Sino-Soviet dispute that was then in full swing, enabling me to range over the other issues of interest to the SEATO members, Britain, France, USA, Philippines, Australia, New Zealand, Thailand and Pakistan. My collection of articles written from 1962 to 1964 has little relevance now, but one from 1963 entitled *'Exposure of Communist Method'* remains as a reminder to those who may be exposed to the activities of global terrorism now and in the future. Most of these are now available through the Freedom of Information Act.

Thailand often took advantage of the SEATO Research Office to provide three months experience for officers from other branches of the civil service. Pote Sarasin when Director General of SEATO, was particularly interested in the performance of Thai Nationals in the organization and those on permanent or semi-permanent employment were exceptionally qualified. Some were members of the minor royalty from way back. On only one occasion was I to fail with a trainee, who after three months departed with this final statement, "My time here has convinced me that the communists may be right."

I was reminded quite forcibly of the World War II stance taken by Thailand with Japan — avoid occupation by a foreign power at all costs.

Membership of the Royal Bangkok Sports Club was essential. Inside the racetracks there was ample space for full sized cricket and rugby grounds and numerous tennis courts were adjacent to the magnificent Club House. The British Club also welcomed membership from citizens of the Commonwealth. Its facilities were not on such a grand scale, but Club indoor functions were always well attended.

I was in great demand as a rugby referee, particularly for matches between Thai teams where great rivalry existed, such as between the Army and the Police. One of the games I controlled was played at the height of the wet season and resulted in a nil-all draw. I returned home still in my football gear, which had started out white but was now jet black in drying mud. My Thai cook and her mate the wash-girl, looked at me in amazement asking, "Master been playing tennis?"

As a relief from the oppressive heat and humidity of Bangkok many weekends were spent in the hills at Nakorn Nyok, close to Princess Chumpot's garden, famous for being one of the classical gardens of the world at that time. The Australian Embassy also had a cottage at Pattaya, then a small fishing village on the coast. Nowadays it's one of the world's high-rise resorts, popular with jet setting tourists.

On one occasion at Nakorn Nyok, when accompanied by Brian Worth, I demonstrated my ability at pistol shooting with a perfect score right handed and then followed up similarly left handed. As a Midshipman ashore in Palestine during HMS *Malaya's* stay in Haifa, cut short by the Munich Crisis, I'd been seconded to the Royal Marines and decked out as a Second Lieutenant because of the lack of any junior marine officers in the detachment embarked. A service revolver was my principal weapon. My father had been a rifle shooter, but not in the King's Cup class. On some occasions when giving dinner I'd control the evening with a trophy he'd won in 1937 with the 30th Battalion NSW Scottish Regiment Rifle Club.

Nearing the end of my time in Bangkok I seriously considered whether I should perhaps try to do what other Australians from SEATO had done and join the United Nations in New York. Particularly in view of the parlous state the RAN had fallen into as a result of the *Voyager - Melbourne* collision, with the loss of so many lives, and the fact that this was the culmination of a period of disasters that had started in July 1958, when Captain R J Robertson was lent to the Williamstown Naval Dockyard to conduct sea trials for the newly built destroyer, HMAS *Vendetta*, (see *Where Fate Calls* by Tom Frame Hodder and Stoughton 1962 p. 36).

I gave serious consideration to applying to join the United Nations and went so far as to fill in the voluminous application form. I had a vivid recollection of the offer that'd been made to me in March 1940 by Claud Schuster, to transfer to the Royal Navy if I didn't wish to leave the active war zone in Britain. Back then I believed that, as my father had promised, I would serve in the Royal Australian Navy for 12 years after the age of 18, it was my duty to fulfill that promise. After all I'd done so well in the courses for the rank of Lieutenant I couldn't expect my RN contemporaries to accept me with any enthusiasm.

Moreover, I believed that I couldn't live on my pay alone, as many of the others were heavily in debt to Gieves all the time. Once again my Australianess won out. After all, I had a home to go to back to in Canberra, a Mercedes Benz to drive and some first class Thai furniture to live with. Plus my wife's business had done so well in South-East Asia and would have more impact in Australia than in New York.

Myself, Margaret, Tookie, Matthew and Pintuma (the cat)

The Benz came home to Canberra and the house in Holmes Crescent, Campbell. Our neighbours were now the Head of the Tariff Board on the left and on the right the Chief of the Air Force Staff. Down the hill and close to the Campbell shops were two Deputy Secretaries of the Department of Defence, one soon to be Secretary to the Department of the Navy in a small 'Guvvy'. With the move of the Navy Office from Melbourne to Canberra the houses allocated to the Admirals of the Naval Board were so small that all hell was raised to little avail. One CNS, Henry Burrell, had married for the second time and his wife, as one of the wealthiest women in Australia, had no qualms about building a mansion in Mugga Way and acquiring a nearby country property for their retirement.

The move to Canberra of the controlling elements of the three Services foreshadowed the end of the Navy as the Silent Service and in particular the influence of the Melbourne Establishment on promotions to senior rank.

— 24 —

More Skiing

The Club had long realized that although Buller offered a wonderful introduction to skiing for Naval personnel it was difficult for those serving in the Fleet or in the Sydney area to make use of Breathtaker. Moreover, many skiers were 'Birdmen' to whom HMAS *Albatross* was home. Added to that, the return of the RAN College to Jervis Bay and the movement of a large part of the Navy Office to Canberra shifted the focus away from the Victorian snowfields to Kosciusko.

Inevitably the debate polarized, Thredbo or Perisher. The better skiers were invariably Thredbo supporters. Those with the experience of introducing sailors and WRANS to the sport came out in favour of Perisher on the grounds that no matter how bad the weather, nor how poor the skier, it was always possible to find somewhere on the slopes to enjoy the snow.

Then too there was always the problem of money. Whether it would be ethical to use the profits from Buller to support a venture in Kosciusko or not was a question frequently posed by the more conservative element. Thredbo itself was strictly a commercial venture. Would a club like the RAN Ski Club really fit in?

In 1962 the decision was made for us. The RAN Ski Club was invited to inspect the last remaining sites for allocation as club lodges in the Perisher Valley.

Guy Griffiths had done the spadework with the Kosciusko State Park Trust. At the time I was performing my last action as a Club official before leaving the Active List of the RAN. We walked the sites and opted for the one on which the RAN Ski Lodge now stands. The choice was decided on the basis that good skiers would be able to run down to the bottom of the chair lift to start their day and the beginners would have an easy run to the nursery slopes. Coming home ... well that was a problem no matter where one spent the day; and the nearer your destination the more you are slip sliding away.

Once again the Club faced the problem of financing the building of a lodge. This time without the option of starting with a modest structure and by dint of ingenuity developing it into a worthwhile asset. The conditions imposed by the NSW Government and the Kosciusko State Park Trust required a building of the highest quality, properly sited and constructed to withstand the worst that the Perisher was capable of providing.

The name Perisher was given to the valley by the old sheep minders who, with the approach of bad weather, took their charges out of the direct path of the biting wind (the Perisher) that came in from the west and buried them in holes in the snow (the Smiggin Holes). How different from today when it is snow bunnies who are wrapped in continental quilts in the area still called Smiggin Holes.

Guy Griffiths and Geoff Hood were given the tasks of selecting an architect, a builder and raising the necessary finance. Once again the Central Canteens Committee was prepared to back the Club.

Guy Griffiths, with the support of an understanding wife, undertook the project. In the years that followed he became famous as 'they'. Night after night, visitors to Perisher were heard to ask, "Why didn't they do so and so? What were they thinking about when they did that?"

In the event the Lodge was open for business in time for the 1964 season; the credit for this belongs to him and to Carla for her forbearance.

With the assets of the Club being added to and with their value increasing, it became increasingly difficult to appoint new trustees for the property every time a Club official received a new posting. The Club was incorporated as a non-profit making company and on 21 November 1963 the then Minister for Defence, the Hon. Athol Townley, consented to the name subject to the condition that it remains under the control of serving members of the RAN.

After 40 years not only had the original members aged, but so had the Perisher Lodge. For a time the RAN Ski Club owned the Halgapa Lodge at East Jindabyne that had three self-contained flats, a real water frontage, land galore and a magnificent view of the mountains. This worked well from 2 May 1980 but there remained a need for more accommodation on the mountain itself.

During the 1980's the Army Ski lodge behind the Fire Station at Thredbo became the purview of the Senior Officers of the Australian Army and was managed by the Warrant Officer of the Army during the snow season. Eventually there were financial problems which were not improved when one of the senior Generals and the Head of the Department of Defence fell out over the meetings of the Defence Committee being called for at 14:00 on Saturdays during the winter ski season. This resulted in the staff car being stopped at Berridale by police in time to turn back to Canberra to be on time.

The RAN Ski Club was the beneficiary. Army sold the building to it in April 2000, and it has now become the alternative accommodation in the snow to the new Navy Ski Lodge in Perisher Valley which I was privileged to open on Saturday 9 June 2012.

We have retired Brigadier Adrian Stuart d'Hage to thank for convincing previous army skiers that their old lodge now welcomes their continued support. Sixty plus years later the RAN Ski Club can now boast of three truly comfortable well managed and well run lodges with special thanks to the tireless efforts of so many volunteers. Long may it be so.

— 25 —

Canberra and Public Service Life

The end of my contract with External Affairs was brutal. It was made abundantly clear that as all their foreign service officers were four year graduates, and I'd only completed two years work of a BA, my services were no longer required. When I finally completed my Honours year part time, I had absolutely no desire to join the Department of Foreign Affairs and Trade. Fate had called me elsewhere.

Christmas was coming and extensions to the house in Holmes Crescent, Canberra were on the way to rejuvenate the Margaret Wright Modelling School and Agency. Like a good friend of mine in Sydney, I drove my Benz to the unemployment agency to register as an applicant. At the same time I pursued further sea-service with commercial ventures looking for capable officers, only to be told that I was too highly qualified for their requirements.

My priority was to continue my part-time studies at the ANU and gain some income from employment in the private sector to supplement the successful business being run by my wife.

Early in 1965 I accepted an offer to manage the Park Royal Motel that had just opened on Northbourne Avenue. After four weeks 'training' in Melbourne with free accommodation provided by the Joint Managing Director of the parent company, but no salary, I returned to Canberra as both the Night Manager and daytime Front Desk Manager. My days began at 07:00 each morning and didn't finish before 22:30 each night. My salary was the same as that being paid to the Head Housemaid.

At 14:00 precisely I was required to telephone the takings for the previous 24 hours to Head Office. My employers were Rockman and Rothwell, who insisted that I should park my Mercedes prominently out front as an indicator of the standard of occupation passing visitors could expect.

My first problem was to cope with over-booking for the Easter weekend, followed a week later by the Anzac Day long weekend. I did this by calling in favours from other places with vacancies and free dinners at Park Royal to unhappy people we couldn't accommodate.

Rothwell, who'd gone overseas to play a Bridge tournament, returned to Australia to find that the expected motel to be built in Sydney wasn't going to be ready on time. So naturally he wanted his Canberra job back. I had to go.

The Rockman family had just been to Canberra and on leaving had expressed their appreciation of my attention to their needs by giving me, of all things, a pair of socks. Rothwell turned up one Monday morning and gave me two hours to clear my desk and leave. So much for private enterprise. I retaliated by leaving him a couple of bottles of a good red and a solicitor's letter for unfair dismissal.

Shortly after I answered an advertisement for a secretary at the Federal Golf Club, Red Hill. A committee member of the Club, Air Chief Marshal Sir Frederick Scherger, then Chairman of the Chiefs of Staff Committee in the Department of Defence, took this up with the Secretary, Sir Edwin Hicks on the basis of, "what a waste of talent and experience, that would benefit the Department greatly".

The result was that one Saturday morning at the Campbell shops, L G Poyser of the Defence Planning Division in the Department, always regarded as a great 816 elevated to the Second Division, approached me with a suggestion that I might wish to return to the Department, not at the same level that I'd held from 1960 to 1962, but one below that. This would avoid the need for getting someone else from the Services for the position.

Not wishing to be beholden to anyone for such a deal, which my instinct told me would be a complete dead-end, I applied to enter the Commonwealth Public Service at the bottom of the Third Division. I sat for the examination and passed, still leaving five of the numerous questions to be answered in the time allowed. I learnt from my examiner, who'd been my civilian psychological adviser when I was Training Commander at Cerberus in 1956, that no one ever completed the whole thing anyway.

On 1 September 1965 I joined the Intelligence Branch of the Department of Defence and spent the first six months of my new working life filing the papers I'd written in the years I'd been there as a Class 8 Officer, seconded from the Navy to be Joint Secretary of the Joint Intelligence Committee. With that done, Thursdays were Gazette Days and I applied for and received promotion to the level of the Campbell Shops offer in my own right.

Three years later there was a vacancy notified in the Commonwealth Gazette in what was euphemistically called 'The War Book', headed by a Principal Executive Officer. On my return to Australia in 1940 I'd seen the results of implementing what was The War Book in Australia in the latter part of 1939. Instead of all officers remaining in the positions they were holding, many were shifted to the positions to which they were to take up according to The War Book. Trains from Sydney to Melbourne and vice-versa were filled to capacity. Efficiency suffered. In my estimation the work on such an activity in 1968 was nugatory.

I made my request under Section 52(1) of the Public Service Act 1922-1968 not to be transferred. L G Poyser had by that time returned from attendance at the Imperial Defence College in London and was very miffed that I had not taken up his offer of 1965. He was even more miffed that I'd been able to forestall an attempt to shift me to an even deader-end than the one I was in already. I let it be known, none too subtly, that with an Honours Degree (along with Des Ball) from the Australian National University, a rarity in the civilian staff of Defence, I was no longer going to work for peanuts. I was looking for macadamias at least.

In 1969 I applied to lead an Antarctic Mission for a six-month period before reaching 50 years of age, after which I'd no longer be eligible. I reached the final hurdle, being one of only two to qualify. At the final day-long interview my leadership abilities were acknowledged as outstanding, my skiing prowess adequate for the task, but I was to learn that one of my referees, Rear Admiral W J Dovers RAN, then Director Joint Staff under General Sir John Wilton, Chairman Chiefs of Staff Committee in the Department of Defence had used these words to my examiners, "Wright, yes. A well-balanced chap. He has a chip on each shoulder."

In the end, despite a glowing report from my next-door neighbour, Head of the Tariff Board, the fact that I had Arts and the other fellow had Science swung the job his way.

It seemed like everything was crumbling towards the end of the 60's — both at home and at work. My marriage was ending and I was even unhappier at work.

During 1968, six years after I had transferred to the Emergency List of the RAN both David Stevenson, two years ahead of me at RANC, and David Wells, only two and a bit months younger but destined to go through his life in the Navy always the best part of a year behind, became Rear Admirals. I also completed my BA Honours Year at The Australian National University.

Graduating with Bachelor of Arts (Honours) from ANU

On 3 June 1969 in the South China Sea the collision between HMAS *Melbourne* and the American destroyer USS *Frank E Evans* raised the spectre of the *Melbourne/Voyager* collision of 1964 and the legal hiatus that had followed.

This time there were some changes in the dramatis personae. The professional head of the RAN was Vice Admiral Sir Victor Alfred Trumper Smith RAN, the Flag Officer Commanding HM Australian Fleet Rear Admiral Gordon John Branston Crabb RAN, and the Commanding Officer of HMAS *Melbourne* Captain John Philip Stevenson RAN, no relation to David Stevenson then a Rear-Admiral who was to command the Fleet in January 1970. The captain of the *Evans,* Commander Albert McLemore was asleep in his bunk throughout.

Retired RN Admiral Harold Hickling, the author of *One Minute of Time,* again put his oar in and gave his opinion that in the *Melbourne/ Voyager* wash-up the first Royal Commission made a mess of it and this time there should be a board of enquiry, then a court martial if necessary because the Americans were practical.

What transpired was a USN-RAN Joint Board of Inquiry with representatives of both navies. The president was Rear-Admiral Jerome King USN and five members, David Stevenson, two RAN captains and two from the USN.

Every effort was made to reduce any blame attributable to the American destroyer captain, although in private the USN accepted full responsibility.

The Naval Board considered the report of the Joint Board of Investigation and passed it to the Flag Officer Commanding Australian Fleet for necessary action. This resulted in a court martial. Philip Stevenson pleaded not guilty and was honourably acquitted and really had no case to answer.

But the ploy that worked to cause me to withdraw from the rat-race of promotion to flag rank, and was successful in getting rid of Captain R J Robertson was used in Philip Stevenson's case. He was offered an appointment in leaving HMAS *Melbourne* that lowered his status considerably.

His resignation was accepted on 3 April 1970. When some years later he wished to be placed on the Emergency List of the RAN it was done with his seniority adjusted to 31.12.1966. He had, in fact, been promoted on 31.12.1960. This loss of six years should be compared with my loss of 11 years and one rank that was finally restored to me in 2008.

David Stevenson went on to be Flag Officer Commanding the Australian Fleet from 6 January 1970 to 14 April 1971 and again from 24 January 1972 to 1 April 1972. He then reached the top of the tree and served as Professional Head of the RAN from 23 November 1973 to 22 November 1976.

After his wife's death in 1978, my second wife, Margaret, and he married on 13 March 1979. David died on 26 October 1998. His funeral at the Duntroon Chapel on 6 November with full honours was a fitting tribute as was my eulogy of him. Margaret lived another 13 years, until 3 August 2011.

David Stevenson

— 26 —

Lucky 70's

Many say 50 is the hump year, with everything going downhill after that. Well not in my case. 1970 saw leaps and bounds in both my work and personal life. .

With the prospect of serving another 15 years before compulsory retirement I set about getting a living wage to support myself and the two children of my first marriage and the two children of my second marriage.

Arthur Tange also became the Secretary Department of Defence. He was 55. He was an intellectual and an effective executive head of the civilian side of the Department of Defence and became one of the most influential people in the Australian Government for nearly 30 years. His main objective was to reform the Australian Department of Defence.

At the time the Department of Defence was of little consequence in the Commonwealth government; each service (Navy, Army and Air Force) had its own separate department with its own minister. Further, the Ministry of Supply, responsible for military logistics was also a separate portfolio with yet another minister. The respective services and departments were in competition, each group jealously guarding its own budget and powers against the others.

I was appointed Executive Officer in the Special Studies Branch to work with Tange on the preparation of the merging of the departments of Army, Navy, Air Force, Supply and Defence into one.

With his career background in diplomacy and international affairs Tange was the ideas man and advocated a wider view of defence policy than the civilian members of the Defence department and the uniformed members of the armed services.

Our work culminated in a 1973 report, formally titled *Australian Defence: Report on the Reorganisation of the Defence Group of Departments,* but was widely known in the press and in government circles as *The Tange Report*.

With the support of the Barnard and Whitlam government, the proposed changes were enacted and since then the uniformed services have been known as the Australian Defence Forces (ADF), the civilian arms as the Department of Defence (DoD), and the whole as the Australian Defence Organisation (ADO). The Prime Minister and Minister of Defence are now advised by both the uniformed Chief of the Defence Forces (CDF) and the civilian Secretary of the Department of Defence (SECDEF), in a unique (in Australia) arrangement known as *the diarchy,* with overall defence policy being developed and enacted co-operatively between the uniformed and civilian staffs.

Another aspect of Tange's work was a desire that the three services should work together in the Defence of Australia at all levels, rather than as feuding tribes. To this end he was instrumental in the decision to set up a primary tri-service college for the joint training, academic and military, of all officer recruits in the services, known as the Australian Defence Force Academy (ADFA).

Neither of these reforms were easy and they were both accompanied by enormous resistance and press clamour. Tradition within the old service departments led to fights over these issues in the press, the ministries and the parliament in the 1970s. Tange's role in the changes saw him regarded as both a forward-looking visionary and a wrecker of Australian security, on a grab for personal power.

Tange having succeeded in the re-organization of Defence with the reluctance of the Service Chiefs, then had the problem of selling the changes to the Services. There was no way that T*he Tange Report* was going to be read by Service personnel, so he had me condense the main points of my thesis into a special document published under my own name to be distributed to each of the Staff Colleges of the Navy, Army and RAAF for study by their students.

Organisation for the Administration of Australian Defence Force Policy 1958-1974 - http://books.google.com/books/about/Organisation_for_the_Administration_of_A.html?id=HTWGNAAACAAJ

In addition I conducted educational seminars in Defence Canberra for Service personnel — *Command and Control of the Australian Defence Force.*

Until he retired on 17 August 1979 we had an extraordinary working relationship much as there'd been between John Jervis and the younger Horatio Nelson. On one occasion sitting opposite Sir Arthur and dealing with a problem involving Defence personnel in visits overseas he said to me, "I will do the thinking — you do the arithmetic."

But the one that went the rounds of the Department concerning the briefing of a Rear Admiral to represent Defence in London was when I said to him, "It is no good you ranting and raving at me. Take it up with CNS if you want more time."

Books on Sir Arthur Tange AC, CBE include the independent biography, *Arthur Tange: Last of the Mandarins* by Peter Edwards, published in 2006 and Peter Edwards personal memoirs in *Defence Policy-Making: A Close-up View, 1950-1980,* released in 2008.

On 10 December 1970 I met my match.

For some months I'd been moonlighting for Canberra Taxis, driving on Wednesday evening after work until early next morning and again from 07:30 on Saturdays until there were no more calls on the Sunday mornings.

It was 12:45 when the Base called to go from the rank by the Administrative Building in the Parliamentary Triangle to the Department of Foreign Affairs to pick up a fare. Five minutes later a young woman who I remembered from several years earlier appeared. But it was her opening statement that bowled me over, along with her looks.

"I am so sorry that you and Margaret have split up."

My earth shook.

When dropping her at her Lawley House destination, without any hesitation I blurted out, "Would you like to go to dinner on Monday night?"

When she accepted I was done.

The dinner was interesting to say the least. Marie Patricia Anson had just returned from four years working at Australia House in London and arrived at the restaurant in the company of an old boss, a RAAF Wing Commander. Small talk was all England, Europe, Northern Lights and people some who I'd known way back. I knew, however, that a connection was developing between us quite rapidly and poor old Ras Berry was not in the race, no matter what his aspirations may have been.

A few weeks later, again at another restaurant on a Monday, I tied a piece of string around the third finger of her left hand. For me it was important to get an accurate measurement. A work colleague was heading to a SEATO meeting in Bangkok and I wanted him to get me a black star sapphire ring surrounded by diamonds. I was already planning for a proper proposal of marriage to take place when my divorce came through.

Here I must reminisce.

Marie, also an only child, was from Townsville. She'd moved to Canberra in 1965 to work with the Department of Treasury. Living at Lawley House, a Commonwealth hostel, in order to broaden her horizons, she'd replied to a newspaper advertisement. Accepted immediately, she soon found herself with a full diary and some extra money.

The advertisement was for my wife's modelling agency and during the five years Marie worked for her, she became one of Margaret's most lucrative models. For quite some time she was the Waltons Department Store model, appearing there most Friday nights and Saturday mornings. She was also the Queensland Latin American dance champion in 1964, but I certainly didn't marry her for her ability to dance!

One evening when Margaret was sick and unable to conduct a meeting with a group of her models I arrived at the class, delivering the news to the girls assembled. Unbeknown to me, Marie was immediately impressed, but knew I was married and out-of-bounds. Our paths seldom crossed during the next couple of years but we met up again within weeks of her taking up a four-year appointment in London. My memories of this meeting are that she talked incessantly about her forthcoming trip but interestingly she doesn't remember the meeting at all. So much for being impressed those couple of years before.

My divorce eventually materialized in June 1972 and we married in Townsville on 12 August 1972.

Saying goodbye to hostel living, we moved from our respective abodes in Macquarie and Lawley Houses to an apartment in Queanbeyan. Hostel living was gradually going out of fashion anyway and group housing was now on the increase.

Living in Queanbeyan was always a stopgap before buying something suitable in Canberra.

Marie and I on our wedding day in Townsville 12 August 1972

With our age difference of 25 years, friends and even my ex-wife were giving the marriage about six months. In fact Margaret had told Marie rather matter-of-factly, "Take him for all he's worth, but don't marry him."

Proving them all wrong, we're still together after 42 years and life couldn't be happier for either of us.

Finally we found the right home in Curtin and moved in. Marie's mother was still living in Townsville, but had a hankering to be closer. My mother was getting on in years, but doing quite well in Sydney. She was delighted when we visited her, but couldn't help calling me Bluebeard and similarly affectionate names. She was extremely happy with her new daughter-in-law though — the only one of my wives who ever called her 'Mum'.

The time hadn't come for us to start a family. Marie was keen to complete her education that had been interrupted by joining the workforce and time overseas. I was fully behind her. It was all systems go.

Just before midnight on 21 March 1973 in Deakin a chap who'd charged full pelt down the hill on my left, bowled my vehicle over. He'd just dropped his girlfriend off and was still enraged from their heated argument. Fortunately my seat belt held, but upside down the roof split my skull, requiring 19 stitches and bed rest for a week.

Marie had just become Model of the Year and spent her week in Hobart doing Fashion Shows at the Casino.

During Marie's studies for a Bachelor of Arts degree and ensuing testamur in 1980, more often than not she achieved Distinctions and some High Distinctions. During a practical map preparation on the south coast of New South Wales and partnered with an ex-Army Brigadier, she was using a prismatic compass to ensure an accurate map of a particular location would be produced. Positive she knew exactly what

Marie – Model of the Year

she was doing, Marie took an accurate bearing of a dark object in the distance to ensure a faithful reproduction would result. Only to be told later by the expert, that it was in fact the backside of a cow!

Marie was unsure about having children. We were extremely happy and she maintained that I had enough children and that it wasn't fair to me at 56 to become a father yet again. I finally convinced her that it was something a woman should experience at least once in her lifetime and give Marie her due, to this day she still says how lucky she was that she listened to me.

On 19 April 1976 our daughter Jennifer was born to the absolute delight of both of us. By this time we'd also settled into our house in Weetangera and had a swimming pool installed. Marie's mother had decided to sell up in Townsville and move to Canberra to do her grandmotherly care while we both continued working.

When I was on Paternity Leave after Jennifer's birth my then boss, Sir Arthur Tange needed me. When told where I was his reaction was, "He's a bit old for that isn't he?"

We all combined to buy Marie's mother a town house in Hawker, a pram ride away and were lucky enough to be allowed to have our daughter all to ourselves at weekends. The arrangement with Marie's mother worked perfectly, enabling us to travel overseas almost every year.

— 27 —

My Other Love

Our travels often involved a cricket tournament followed by extended touring of the region where the game had been held. I've always had a love for cricket and have luckily been able to incorporate it into my naval career and life afterwards. During the latter years I've been able to thoroughly enjoy I Zingari (I Z) and the Golden Oldies matches even more.

My wife Marie, who loves me dearly, maintains that there are two things for which I will never be late — church and cricket. Perhaps it is because of religious fervour — beginning at ten when I was convinced I was Don Bradman and maintained right up until my last I Z game in London 2011.

In 1977 the I Z tour was in England. I played on some outstanding fields during the month of June — the Royal Military Academy at Sandhurst, Hugh Friends's XI at Bryanston School, Old Merchant Taylors at Croxley Green, Windsor Great Park, Rickling Green, The Guards at Burton Court in London.

Over the years I Z tours have opened many doors for me and Marie which otherwise would have remained closed. The privileges extended to I Z cricketers and supporters were amazing and included places and events that would not normally have been accessible.

In 1977 we were billeted in a Queen Anne stately home. A bus was hired for the cricketers and a couple of cars for the women. In each new town a notice board heralded suggested day trips or visits to nearby places of interest, particularly for the women. To join they simply added their name to the list.

For example thanks to Ros Eldershaw with her horticultural interests, there were organized trips to nearby open gardens with a personal guide. Other outings were to stately homes and palaces, or picturesque villages.

Marie more or less went to everything from Blenheim Castle, Jane Austin's family home, Windsor Castle, Anne Hathaway's cottage, Glastonbury and the Lakes District, plus enjoying the splendour of a personalized guided tour of Arundel Castle by Lavinia the Duchess of Norfolk. Other activities that year included a tour of the library at Lords for her (because she was working on her final thesis on Bradman). She certainly doesn't remember watching too much cricket, but it was almost an unwritten rule that those who went walkabout during the day should turn up for afternoon tea and the last session of play.

One day while watching a last session E W Swanton was standing beside her. Discovering she was Australian he commented, "Thanks to Packer we are about to see the end of cricket."

"Cricket is not just about the players," she argued. "Money and spectators also must be considered!" She was right.

In the earlier days when fewer women worked there were less lunches but more dinners and receptions after the days play and more scones and jam. These occasions needed more long frocks and formal attire. We packed two large and two small suitcases, overcoats over our arms plus the kit. A vast cry from 2011 — if it didn't fit into one large suitcase (plus the unwieldy kit), it didn't come.

In 1977 there was parity between Sterling and the Australian Dollar. Marie wasn't the only one who hit the shops, with some people paying excess for additional baggage on the way home. No names!

After the I Z tour we saw more of England and then travelled around Europe. Having come through World War II the most startling event for me was in Heidelberg when our German guide took us to look at a valley, her instruction, in her very best English, was, "You will enjoy the view!" Delivered more as an order rather than a pleasant statement, I felt like adding 'Heil Hitler!' and saluting her, but Marie stopped me just in time.

— 28 —

Working with the Commonwealth Ombudsman

Returning to Canberra after the England Tour with I Z (Australia) and our European holiday I was pleased that the officer chosen to stand in for me in Defence had been doing his job to everyone's satisfaction.

The Commonwealth Ombudsman, Professor Jack Richardson, had asked some of his mates for assistance with administration in setting up his office in Canberra. The Deputy Secretary to whom I'd been responsible offered my services for the best part of a year, even though I'd not specialized in Law.

It proved to be a good deal all round. Both Marie and I were working in close proximity and our daughter Jennifer was with Marie's mother from Monday to Friday in Weetangera. Jack and I got along really well because of our differing views on some of the knotty problems for an Ombudsman. In one particular instance, a complainant clearly had a case to put before a Court which would have required him to start with an investment of $500 and the additional expenditure needed to be represented legally, the better to secure satisfaction. My view was that the complainant expected a High Court judgment for the cost of an 18 cent stamp. Jack's view was that he was the complainant's last hope, and he would give it all that he could. In the end the complainant was found to have tried to make a financial gain from buying up land, which his position had enabled him to forecast would be required for government activity.

The matters coming forward were many and varied and can best be described by some of the responses that were sent following detailed examination of the complaints. A few examples along the lines of many received are interesting in that many complaints received by the Ombudsman were against the laws passed by Parliament which required Departments to follow with enforcement.

In many cases the Ombudsman was only able to inform the complainant in these terms:

'Your complaint to me is not one that I am empowered to investigate and should more properly be directed towards those who make the law as it is: the members of the Federal Parliament. Perhaps you should take this matter up with your local member.

I am sorry that I am unable to assist you.'

However the following example shows how a complainant can misconstrue a departmental action by failing to acknowledge some failure on their part to give facts of which the department being called to account has no knowledge. This letter is to Mrs. A. N. Other:

Ombudsman

77/0123

31 November 1977

Dear Mrs Other

It has taken longer than I had expected for the reports on the matters about which you have complained to me to be prepared and examined. The enquiries I have made have been thorough and what I now have to say will show in detail the reasons why you have to pay $10 a fortnight from your age pension until such time as you *have paid back the money which the Government has paid you in excess of your entitlement on account of social security benefits and why you owe the Department of Veterans' Affairs $109.72.*

Firstly let me take you back to 1974. On 8 November 1974 you applied for an age pension from the Department of Social Security. You were then in full-time employment, but it seems that you neglected to tell the Department about that. Your late husband was at that time receiving an age pension free of means test which had been granted on 21 February 1974. On 25 November 1974 both you and your husband applied for a service pension from the Department of Veterans' Affairs. It was made clear to you that one of the conditions of eligibility for a service pension was that a person cannot be granted a service pension in addition to an age or invalid pension payable by the Department of Social Security. In your husband's case he was granted the service pension from 22 November 1974 and his age pension from the Department of Social Security was cancelled on 16 December 1974. Your husband therefore satisfied the conditions under which the service pension could be paid.

You have maintained that you did not apply for both the age pension and the service pension. The records show that you did. Moreover in answer to the question on the application form for the service pension: "If you are not receiving age, invalid or widow's pension, have you at any time made a claim?" You answered: "No", but two weeks previously you had lodged a claim for age pension with the Department of Social Security. At the same time as giving a negative answer to this question on the Income and Property Statement you filled in a form requesting the cancellation of the age pension.

Accepting that there was some confusion in your understanding about the status of your claim for an age pension from the Depart-

ment of Social Security, we come to the situation in January 1975. On 24 January 1975 the Department of Social Security notified you that it had awarded you an age pension and reminded you that you were obliged to notify it if in addition to the Social Security pension for income combined with your husband's income became greater than $94.03 a week.

When you received the service pension your income exceeded the sum of $94.03 a week, but you did not tell the Department of Social Security.

It is clear to me that both the Department of Social Security and the Department of Veterans' Affairs were at fault in accepting your statements at face value, and that their checking procedures left a great deal to be desired. At the same time I find difficulty in accepting your contention that you thought you were receiving a part pension from both Departments, when in fact each was paying you a full pension and your total receipts from the Government greatly exceeded the limit specified.

I note that your view has been investigated by the Social Security Appeals Tribunal, and I can find no grounds on which to disagree with the Tribunal. You received $632.50 from the Government to which you were not entitled; so far you have paid back $32.50 plus $10 per fortnight which will continue until the Department of Social Security has been repaid in full.

We now come to 19 September 1976 when your husband died. The Department of Veterans Affairs granted you a war widow's pension and domestic allowance. In addition it paid you what is known as readjustment allowance for the period 23 September to 15 December 1976. Readjustment allowance is a benefit payable where a married couple were both in receipt of income test pensions and, where one of them dies, the surviving partner will receive for the next six fortnights the same amount that they had both been receiving previously.

Notwithstanding your previous experience, you accepted at the same time as you were receiving these benefits from the Department of Veterans' Affairs an age pension from the Department of Social Security. As a result of doing this it was necessary for the Department of Social Security and the Department of Veterans' Affairs to get together to reconcile the payments each had made, as the Readjustment Allowance cannot be paid at the same time as the social security benefit is being paid. On this occasion the amount that you received to which you were not entitled was $109.72, and it is this sum that you owe to the Department of Veterans' Affairs. There is no question that this amount has been overpaid because of any departmental error.

The present situation is that you are receiving an age pension free of income test with effect from 23 December 1976 and a war widow's pension of $118.20 a fortnight. Although service pension and age pension cannot be paid at the same time, war widow's pension and age pension can.

I am sorry that I have not been able to help you more, but in the circumstances I believe that the Department of Social Security decision to recover the amount overpaid by installments from your Social Security benefit is fair and reasonable. I urge you to come to some such arrangement with the Department of Veterans' Affairs concerning the smaller amount of $109.72. I do not intend to pursue the matters you have raised any further.

If you have difficulty in understanding why I have come to this conclusion I suggest you make arrangements to see the Assistant

Ombudsman NSW when he sets up office in Sydney early in the New Year. I am sure that he will be pleased to see you.

Yours sincerely,
(Kant B Fuled)
Ombudsman

Another frequent source of complaint were Telecom charges particularly for STD calls. I became the primary expert on this and hit upon a way to test the complainant. I'd ring them and start a conversation about what had been written. When the matter had been discussed ad nauseam I'd then ask the complainant how long their conversation had taken. Invariably the time estimated by the complainant was in the region of half the time I'd recorded, thus resting my case.

In one instance the duration of calls made by the complainant on STD had been altered by whiting-out the original figures and substituting a figure much lower than the original in such a way as to make the complaint more favourable. This case got the treatment that it deserved.

Perhaps the most extraordinary complaint on record is this:

Case History (77/662 Folio 23)

Out in Moonee Ponds Dame Edna Everidge ... so if your long-haired layabouts are still studying, are under 25, and still have their feet under the mahogany, Ma, Be in it!

Who said working in the Australian Public Service was dull?

— 29 —

Welcome the 80's

Life was pretty much the same on my return to Department of Defence. Sir Arthur Tange retired in 1979. I spent my final seven years in Special Projects in the Industrial Division concerning the research and development of policy and operational aspects of administrative services. Mostly, as it turned out, the difficult things that no one else could or wanted to do! One such project was setting up the Defence National Automatic Telephone Service (DNATS), which meant continual liaison with security, Telstra and everybody else.

In 1982 a five-match cricket tour of South-East Asia with I Z took us back to my old stamping ground of Hong Kong, Bangkok and Singapore. We added in Penang and Kuala Lumpur for good measure. The team won all games, but unlike the 1979 tour of New Zealand I did nothing of distinction to equal the two sons of my old antagonist Commodore Neil MacKinnon.

Just as 1984 was good for George Orwell, Marie and I had a great year.

Christopher Turner, who I'd last seen as a pupil at Winchester in 1943, wrote to me in February telling me of his mother's death at the end of November 1983. We'd been promising to visit her the next time I Z toured England, but as this wasn't to be until 1988, even Mrs Turner, obviously sensing her tenuous hold on life, had suggested that we shouldn't leave it too long.

Hence we decided to make a visit to her grave the first call on arrival in England. By some stroke of good fortune we landed at Gatwick on 31 March 1984, picked up a car and drove south. After a night at the Botley Grange — where I couldn't afford to stay in 1941, and the leeks were served with sand still in them — we headed straight to the cemetery at Lulworth Cove. Staying a night there, we set off the next day for Stowe School where Christopher was the Headmaster. It was wonderful being able to stay with him as it allowed us to reunite with the whole family at various times and various places, with the one exception, Jennifer after whom our daughter was named. She preferred to keep her memory of her teens intact.

After his retirement Christopher and Lucia came and visited us in Canberra in January 1997. Kate, their daughter, had stayed a couple of years earlier, as had Louise, Michael Turner's daughter.

Farewelling London in fine tradition, we enjoyed Afternoon Tea at the Ritz, before crossing the Channel to the Netherlands and spending the weekend in Paris. Followed by a week in Croatia with the family of a nephew of Marie's father. This over the Easter Week included a visit to Dubrovnik and across the bridge at Mostar to Sarajevo and Belgrade, then flying to Athens. From here we relaxed on a long cruise around the Eastern Mediterranean in TSS *Atlas* — not to be confused with the coal carrying ship I piloted in Hong Kong.

As luck would have it, on the first night out we met a close friend of the Captain which assured our status throughout the cruise and accompaniment during onshore visits to Rhodes, Egypt, Israel, Patmos and Kusadasi. As a grand finale I won the prize at the fancy dress party on board for my performance as a dissolute Frenchman with his girl friend. Marie stayed well out of it, as did the Captain's friend, instead his companion obliged by accompanying me.

Back in Canberra Marie and I had barely recovered from our tour when we set off for outback Australia with Jennifer and some of her classmates. In all there were 24 children, 21 parents, three teachers and a staff of four.

Travel was by coach. The longest distance on any one-day was 752 kilomtres. Overnight stops were in tents. Leaving from Canberra on Saturday 25 August 1984, by the time we reached Wagga Wagga each child had used the microphone to tell the assembled company about their parents. Jennifer, at eight years of age, proudly announced that I was a cook, and thereafter every meal prepared by the staff was presented to me for my approval.

On the second night at Clare in South Australia the foul weather rolled in. Jennifer in a tent by herself slept through the night even under the collapsed tent, a feat for which she was presented a certificate at the end of the trip.

On reaching Ayers Rock, now Uluru, Jennifer, Marie and I climbed to the top. It was well worth the three hours of effort, not just for the reward of a Climbers Certificate, but the outstanding panoramic vista that we witnessed. Camel riding in Alice Springs also earned us a certificate from the Emily Gap Camel Farm.

The return journey took in the Birdsville Track, Maree, the Flinders Ranges, and Broken Hill where I took a photograph of my old 1924 classroom at the Burke Ward Public School, established in 1893.

Looking back, this trip remains one of my family's best memories. Not just for the family sharing, but because Australia's inland is unique and I believe everyone, even Australians, should experience some part of it during their lifetime. I guarantee it will be unforgettable.

— 30 —

Golden Oldies Cricket

The year 1984 was an outstanding one, especially for the First International Golden Oldies Cricket Festival in Auckland, New Zealand, that I took part in gleefully.

The format for the event hasn't varied over the years. All the planning for venues and invitations to send teams is done by an organization that covers where to play, who will play whom, and accommodation for players and umpires. Matches are scheduled for Monday, Wednesday and Friday, with an organized tour of attractions on Tuesday or Thursday.

Players have to be 40 years of age or older, batsmen must retire when they have scored 40 runs, but may return if there are still overs to play within the set limit for each innings generally 40 overs. It didn't take long before experts would get to 39 and then hit a six and hope that nine, ten and jack wouldn't hang about but give them a chance to bat again.

There were also restrictions on bowlers, six in each team had to be used and a maximum of eight overs for any one bowler, but generally most of the bowling was military medium, with the occasional off break more by good luck than intention. A maximum of 10 metres run up was all that was allowed.

I Zingari was very fortunate to have Ron Archer as a player. He had to give up Test Cricket at age 24. I lent him my bat at one game asking him to hit a six with it. In all my cricketing days I'd only scored one six and that was almost accidental, with my old Gunn and Moore, not my present 1977 bat which was meant for Derek Underwood, a left-hander. As the bat was for a right-hander I got it for 38 pounds sterling and it stood me in good stead right up to my last innings in 2011.

I played twice in New Zealand, once in Canada and on one occasion went from Canberra to Sydney to see I Zingari play Canada. On arrival at Rawson Oval in Mosman, Sydney, I looked in amazement at the wicket with four I Z's all in full batting dress at the wicket. It was the Wednesday game and each batsman had a runner. The Captain of the Canadian team was in the same dire straits when he asked me, "Graham, is there any chance you could play for us on Friday?"

I just happened to have my cricket gear in the boot of the car, so I was happy to accept. I fielded quite well and batted so far down the order that my three runs ended in a Not Out.

To show how popular the Golden Oldies Cricket Festivals have been, the number of clubs participating the 1992 Festival in Christchurch, New Zealand were: Australia 26, Canada 3, USA 2, New Zealand 51, United Kingdom 5 and the Organizing Committee numbered 25.

To all cricketers there comes a time when one is no longer able to field – then it is time to play one's last innings. On my 1994 cricket tour of England I'd declared that I would play my last-ever cricket innings the next time I Zingari went to London, thinking then that it would probably be before the end of the century.

At the I Z Annual General Meetings in August of each year a tour of England was always discussed but the timing was never quite right. On two consecutive occasions I was totally incapacitated, having had my right foot reshaped one year and my left foot the next. At that time I had a world record for the time taken to put ski boots on — 28 minutes.

Now it only takes eight minutes in what may be regarded as a complete oxymoron, comfortable ski boots.

Finally a tour of England was scheduled for 2011. From the Diary of the Tour you could be forgiven for thinking that the whole event was staged for my benefit — I topped Don Bradman's final score!

— 31 —

Retirement and Third Career

At age 65 on 10 March 1985, my second career ended with compulsory retirement from the Australian Public Service. I'd already moved from the Emergency List to the Retired List of the Royal Australian Navy on my 60th birthday, but now I'd joined the world of women.

I enrolled in the nearest Health and Fitness Organization to Weetangera comprising a pool and gymnasium in Kippax, owned by Mrs. Liangis. My daily attendance was to participate in Aqua Aerobics, where I was heavily outnumbered 29 to 1 by women.

My wife, who is very wise and thoughtful, said that as a precaution I should consider some place from which I could be buried. Having ex-communicated myself from the Church of England on account of divorcing two wives and marrying again while they were still living, I fronted up to the Anglican Memorial Chapel of St Paul at the Royal Military College of Australia, Duntroon and asked if they'd have me as a parishioner, unaware that I was about to embark on a third career. One in fact that has proved to be most rewarding.

After six Sundays I was asked if I'd consider becoming a Lay Assistant, as help was needed behind the altar rails. When asked if I knew the words I rattled them off without hesitation, only to be told, "They are the old words."

So it was new words and cross dressing on Sundays for me.

After a few months I was invited to become a non-voting member of the Trustees of the Chapel. When the Treasurer of the Trust was posted away from Canberra I took over as Treasurer.

My time with the Commonwealth Ombudsman had made me realize that my thought processes and those of the lawyers with whom I'd dealt were attuned differently. With retirement I saw an opportunity to discover why this was.

I approached the Australian National University in Canberra to see if I was eligible to enrol in the Law School. The first hurdle came when I couldn't study for the LLB as I already had a degree. What about the Diploma of International Law then? Well I couldn't study International Law because I didn't have a degree in National Law. So I asked whether changing my name to Yosarian would make any difference. That did it! Thanks to Joseph Heller, the day before the beginning of the academic year I was told to front up to the Law School and join the group starting the Graduate International Law Programme.

There were no textbooks. At a price there were 'materials'. The first volume of many contained 256 pages and reproduced material from nine bodies ranging from the Commonwealth Attorney-General to the United Nations. In all ten volumes were involved, some with two or three appendices or addenda. The cost was considerable, the lectures told me much about what I wished to know. I finished the year convinced that being a lawyer is a hard way to earn a living.

The best part was the visiting exposition of an American economist dealing with international monetary affairs. Before this, as opposed to Marie, I had difficulty deciphering the Business pages of *The Australian*. Using four-dimensional diagrams with coloured information on a white board the economist had predicted the break-up of the Soviet Union. Above all it convinced me that the Parish Trust, that I was to manage for the next 25 years, was in no way adequate for the purposes for which it had been created.

The first and most important requirement was to satisfy the Australian Taxation Office that the two chapels were not running a business. The second was to clarify the status of the Honorary Treasurer as the sole person with authority to declare that the tax invoice requirements have been met to qualify for refunds for GST on quarterly Business Activity Statements. Posting turbulence among Service Chaplains and the frequent replacement of Command of the Royal Military College made this an essential step in good financial management.

My first task was to establish the level of inescapable annual expense for maintenance and regular tuning of the two pipe organs, plus insurance for moveable items needed for conducting religious services. Maintenance of the building owned by the people of Australia and built on Commonwealth land was governed by scales and standards laid down for Service establishments.

The use of the Chapels for weddings and funerals attracted cash donations in line with similar usage by all other religious establishments in the ACT. The bi-annual meetings of the Trust considered reasonable sums for these activities.

My target for self-sufficiency was set for $100,000, which at 5% per annum would cover normal expenditure. When I finally reached this in December 2007 I was told to make it $150,000. The need for this was clear considering the World Financial Crisis and the effect this was having particularly on interest rates. For four years running our expenditure exceeded our receipts. We needed a playground in the Chapel grounds to increase interest in weekday meetings with chaplains in the Family Room, and as our Anglican Chaplain was a mother herself.

If you need a playground you have to use an expert to ensure the structure will be safe for those using it and that wasn't cheap. Given the target I'd hoped to reach before too long I've had to consider an additional three years before I can hand the responsibility to someone else.

On a number of occasions I've been asked to take committal services at the Norwood Park Crematorium by the widows of friends, the widows of Naval comrades and in some cases to be a Naval presence alongside Army Chaplains in the Chapel. This has been a very personal reward for the years I've spent in Choirs when serving in HMAS *Cerberus* and conducting Services while in command of HMAS *Culgoa*.

— 32 —

Family Life After Retirement

Retirement also meant I could enjoy much more time with our daughter and enjoy a true family life.

Jennifer's 10th birthday in 1986 became a milestone in my life. Her party was marked by a change in her relationship with Marie's mother, whose place in her life had been taken by the friends she'd made at school. For us, it posed the question of her further education. Her name was down for Radford College, still to be opened, and also Canberra Girls Grammar School, which had well established traditions. My preference was Radford, it was co-ed and more easily accessible. Moreover, one of the members of the Board of Directors was Tom Millar, younger brother of one of my Cook Year Cadets of 1934 entry.

I Z had planned a Centenary Tour of England for June-July 1988 and I'd agreed to be one of the supporters. With 21 games to be played over 28 days, Marie and I decided that Jennifer should fly over with the children of Bill and Gail Douglass and join the party.

The record of the Tour had this to say:

'The grounds ranged from charming village greens to immaculately groomed school ovals, to the private grounds of old country houses. In all it proved to be the most wonderful introduction for Jennifer to what used to be called 'the mother country.'

As I write I've just spoken to Jennifer about this visit and the surprises she found: 'the difference between houses in the streets of Brighton from those in Australia, her looking down on the white cliffs of Dover, sliding down the grass bank at the Lancing College ground in Sussex, famed for its Chapel, the largest school Chapel in the United Kingdom if not the world.'

In the brochure for the tour Rodney Tubbs, the Tour Captain wrote:

'By Australian standards, the maintenance of traditions and the observation of certain formalities have been atypically important in the evolution of the Club. I Zingari (Australia) is a very successful and competitive cricket club, but … witness the following pen portraits ... care is always taken to ensure that we don't take ourselves too seriously!'

My entry read as follows:

'WG Wright: Formerly a Commander in the Royal Australian Navy. An enthusiastic member since 1948 and regular IZ tourist since the mid-1970s. In spasmodic, but invariably brief appearances at the crease over the past forty years, he has accrued 569 runs (av. 8.49). You probably suspect that these are the batting figures of a highly successful bowler ... but alas no ... he's never bowled and is an equally appalling fielder! A pleasant bloke with an even more pleasant wife!'

Nothing could be truer than the last sentence.

There was one outstanding incident during the match against the Free Foresters at Henley-on-Thames. One of the opponents was Richard Hutton, son of Sir Leonard Hutton, England's first professional captain. I'd been Umpire when, as one of the tourists with EW Swanton's

Eleven, he visited Bangkok in 1963. I'd given him out under somewhat controversial circumstances on that occasion and during the interval between innings I reminded him of the fact. On coming out to bat he made no bones about reminding me on this occasion, and in the purest Yorkshire imaginable for all on the field to hear, "Umpire. Keep f'ing finger in your pocket." He made 50 but the match ended in a draw.

Ever since my wartime west to east crossing of Canada I have always wanted to go back. The opportunity arose in mid 1990 with the I Zingari team, playing in the Golden Oldies Festival in Vancouver. I was also eager to use my knowledge of the French language again. It hadn't failed me when Marie and I had been travelling the French countryside with another French Canadian couple and they'd had difficulty in ordering lunch because of lingual variations, I'd stepped in and saved the day.

The rest of the I Zingari team were Sydney based and our travel organizer, Jack Sedgwick, a renowned travel agent, secured United States visas for the team members. However on arrival in Los Angeles to

Marie and I

change planes for Vancouver, both Jack and myself were placed under arrest and confined to the airport in custody. He'd forgotten our visas. So while the other team members spent a couple of hours sightseeing, we enjoyed the company of our custodian, who turned out to be a pleasant companion and a fountain of knowledge about LA.

Vancouver proved to be a delight for sightseeing on the Sunday and next morning I held the IZ banner aloft while carrying our IZ flag in the team procession. Our first match against Bermuda Cricket Club was a disaster. We lost the toss and chasing 189 to win finished our 40 overs losing four wickets for 143. The difference was that in the first 10 overs Bermuda had scored 70, while we'd only scored 17. Next day, however, we beat New Zealand by 19.

The following day we were introduced to Canada's best-kept secret, Whistler. This is probably the best skiing village in the world.

On 17 July 1990 there was snow on the hills and down to where we'd lunched above the village itself. Skiers were being lifted off in helicopters to the highest slopes. In the snow season the longest run downhill varies from five to seven kilometres, and even the fittest skiers can only manage one complete run in the forenoon.

My one regret now is that my skiing days are limited to the runs at Perisher with which I'm familiar, and Fridays Flat at Thredbo, where during my last day of skiing for 2013 I was bowled over by a female snow-boarder who didn't even bother to see whether she'd done me any damage. She was obviously late for lunch, fortunately my safety gear worked perfectly and the bruising from cheek to ankle on my right side only lasted six weeks.

On the Friday I Z played British Columbia on the Upper Brockton ground, called one of the world's most picturesque by Don Bradman — and he'd played on more grounds than most. I was fortunate to get into double figures largely because the bowler from whom Garfield Sobers scored 36 from one over (six sixes from six balls), always put every ball in the same spot on the wicket. In my case he actually moved the fieldsman I was beating and I changed my shot, which had me caught in slips. I had a drink with him on Sunday before leaving for the airport to go home.

Jack Sedgwick also came good. To make up for Los Angeles he asked Air New Zealand to upgrade his 'old father' (me), for the return flight as far as Auckland.

Nearing the end of the 1992 winter I was skiing at Perisher Valley with Jennifer on a Saturday afternoon in an absolute whiteout. Marie had decided not to come to Perisher with us. While being quite good, she's a fair weather skier and will only venture out if conditions are perfect, unlike either of us who'll go out in anything. Marie rarely skis now as she says, 'après skiing was always far more interesting and it's better to be curled up with a book by the fire than wet and cold on the slopes.'

Anyway during this particular ski trip, Jennifer and I had just taken the chair lift to the top above my favourite ski run and were discussing where we should meet, as we'd certainly not be taking the same track together going downhill. Before we could even complete our discussions I began slipping sideways left. In countering this movement I fell on my right side breaking the top of my shoulder and dislocating it. Incapacitated, there was nothing either of us could do but to head back to the chair lift and get to the bottom to the medical centre.

Two muscular attendants administered a hearty dose of nitrous oxide prior to putting my shoulder back into place and my right arm in a sling. Their bit done we were sent on our way. Jennifer wasn't old enough to drive, so via my instructions she controlled the gear lever while I steered with my left hand. Fortunately both my legs and feet were working normally and off we went back to Canberra.

Arriving home Marie asked Jennifer how dad had managed, to be told, "Very well. He laughed all the way back to the roundabout at the south end of the city." It had taken that long for the laughing gas to work its way out of my system!

In March 1993 I went to the Golden Oldies Cricket Carnival in Albury-Wodonga as a playing member of the I Zingari team. Marie never missed an I Z tour, but this Golden Oldies Carnival and several other Golden Oldies events coincided with her working in South East Asia.

During the first match at Albury-Wodonga I was surprised when handed the ball to bowl. I wasn't sure whether my right shoulder would be up to the task. However much to my amazement, the first ball went exactly where I wanted it to go. With just enough spin on it to pass the inside edge of the bat and graze the off stump, it successfully removed the bail. The captain of the batting side came down the pitch towards me and was startled when I said, "I'm sorry, but I've bowled you out." Now I know how Warney must have felt when he bowled Mike Gatting with the miracle ball of the 20th Century at Old Trafford in June 1993.

After the game I handed the opposing Captain one of I Zingari's city ties, not the out of darkness, through fire into light Club ties, but the blue one with the I Z insignia coloured black, red and gold and date 1888. The Club tie has a tradition – Club members only may wear the tie, old men may use it to hold up their cricket trousers, and those totally fed up may end their lives using it to strangle themselves. Fortunately these latter occasions are extremely rare.

On the way back to Canberra we stopped at a farm outside Albury owned by the Knox family and I was invited to take over the role played so elegantly by the late Jack Hoyle. He'd died three months after the 1988 tour of England. His version of the Australian Cricket classic, *'How McDougal Topped the Score'* by Thomas E Spencer is a difficult act to follow, but I never left home to play cricket without my *Collection of Bush Songs, Ballads and Other Verse*.

Jennifer's final year at Radford was 1993 and everyone was predicting great things. As sometimes happens in Higher School Certificate examinations, the overall results often reflect a difference between those who set the papers and those who prepare students. Jennifer did well, but not well enough to get into the Australian National University immediately. Thankfully, she'd already decided to take a gap year and go to Britain to prepare herself for doing what her mother believed she would be good at – teaching.

In January 1994 we said goodbye to a schoolgirl at Canberra Airport. In June a sophisticated young woman welcomed us in London, joining us on what turned out to be the final I Zingari Cricket Tour of the 20th Century. She'd frequently accompany the younger members of I Z to the nightclubs, arriving back at our room around 04:00 to be up again at 08:00 and on the bus an hour later for the next game.

I played quite well and helped one of our star batsmen to a century in the match against the Old Merchant Taylors at Rickmansworth in NW London where we fielded two teams and won both games. It was then that I made the fateful decision to play my last innings on the next IZ Tour of England believing then that it would take place before the end of the century.

In 1995 Marie and I had proof that John Milton (1608-1674) had it right when in Samson Agonistes he wrote, as I know I have told you before:

All is best, though we oft doubt,

What th'unsearchable dispose
Of highest wisdom brings about,
And ever best found in the close.

Jennifer was accepted for her Bachelor of Arts at Southern Cross University, Coffs Harbour Campus beginning in 1995. The English Department had just been strengthened by the appointment of a new Director from Sydney University. Although he wasn't one of her lecturers, his example rubbed off on his fellow tutors. I saw her installed in an apartment half way between the town and the harbour, an easy bike ride to University. Later when one in the same building came up for sale, Marie bought it. This allowed her to stay there till graduating in 1998.

The year of 1997 started in grand style. Christopher Turner's son Matthew married his New Zealand girlfriend in Auckland on 11 January and Marie and I went over for the week of that event. After the wedding we travelled north to the Bay of Islands and I renewed contact with Peter Cumming who I'd not seen since skiing at Mount Buller back in the 60's. He'd won the King's Medal in 1947 and like me his had been stolen. He was in the process of getting a replacement at no cost to the Crown. We agreed to keep in touch, neither of us realizing that it was to be ten years before he was to finally receive his replacement medal.

Jennifer's 21st birthday on 19 April was a gathering of the clan. It heralded the last big bash we would host in Weetangera.

All in all five years passed in remarkably quiet times in suburban living and my investment account for the Anzac Memorial Chapel of St Paul, Duntroon had grown from $25,000 to $41,000 (Australian dollars) and I continued to be an Anglican Reader in the Defence Force.

— 33 —

The Final Move

Both bad and good filled 1997. Or as they say, out of bad often comes good. One morning while changing a light globe in the kitchen I slipped and dislocated my right shoulder again. So I was rushed off to casualty at Canberra hospital, where they had me lying on my back with my right hand down holding a bag laden with house bricks. After nearly an hour of this my shoulder gradually took up its proper position and they placed my arm in a sling. It was to remain this way for several days.

With nothing else to do I cozied up in the dining room's most comfortable chair. One day Marie stood in front of me and announced, "I'm moving you."

My reply reflected how pleased I was to have four bedrooms upstairs, a pool out the back which I'd learned to service about a half-hour each week and I was fine.

Determination all over her face she repeated, "I'm moving you. If I don't do it now it will be too late."

So in my immobilised condition we drove out to Lexen Avenue, Nicholls, elegantly called 'Dream Street'. Here seven leading Canberra builders had built their ideal 21st Century home. Stopping outside the first one, we ventured inside.

The entrance was not impressive. There was a very small room on the left and to the right the doorway led to a sitting room of reasonable proportions but with a split level floor. However the next room was an absolute revelation. A kitchen/family room with a thirteen and a half foot long granite bench in a room twenty-three and a half by twenty-four and a half feet, plus a nine by six foot dining alcove to the right of the kitchen and a view onto a courtyard which was accessed by a large sliding glass door. The pièce de résistance was the walk in pantry. At eight and a half by seven and a half foot I was in heaven. All my married life I'd been the providore and cook. It was superb, with only one small imperfection – the ceiling was one foot too low.

The other houses were also inspiring, but hadn't as many winning features as the first. When the builder assured us he could build this place on one level, with higher ceilings and a decent sized entrance we signed on the bottom line. Marie paced out the frontage – twenty-seven of her paces. The only problem now, was where to build!

Canberra is renowned for the number of heritage houses in its inner suburbs. With many of these the streetscape must be maintained, while the inner design can be modernized. Both Marie and I were determined that having lived for so long in Weetangera with a house facing west and no windows on the north side that location was paramount.

As the shopper, for me it had to be close to where decent shopping could be done easily. Having built my first Canberra house in Campbell close to the Defence Centre where I worked for so long, this time my preference was for south side. I'd always had an eye on Yarralumla, while Marie had enjoyed hostel living and fancied the Kingston/Barton closer to Manuka area. Saving marital stress, we handed the problem to the estate agents who'd been dealing with our investment properties.

On a Tuesday in August 1997 an agent rang Marie at work and said they were putting an ad in Saturdays paper to sell a Guvvy in Yarralumla that might interest her.

Marie saw it that evening. An attractive workman's cottage between two well built builders originals and exactly twenty-seven paces across the frontage in a street with only twelve houses.

Next day at noon I went to trace the daily passage of the winter sun. It shone clearly down the left side. I rang Marie, the deal was clinched and the advertisement never went public. To add spice to the sugar, our agent asked if we could hold off for a few months and rent the cottage to a family building in the area facing a delay in completion. Not a problem. Deal done.

This also allowed us time to organize ourselves in temporary accommodation. Our only problem was Henry the cat. He spent the first three days holed up in Jennifer's wardrobe and then looked longingly at how to jump the fences and go westward from where we'd brought him. Eventually he, too, settled down and found great interest in the club across the street.

One of my favourite aphorisms is, *'truth is stranger than fiction'* and during this period it was to become reality.

An organization in Murrumbateman had a very successful business in moving wooden cottages from Canberra to new locations in New South Wales in particular. Generally it involved splitting the house in two equal parts and the move to the new location, on huge semi-trailers, being supervised by police.

So as soon as the tenants moved into their house we were ready for the old Guvvy to be moved to a property in Forbes. Smooth as silk, the operation took place, the only casualty being a Prunus tree on our nature strip. But we now had a clear block for building to begin. For many years my mother's ashes had been in the garage waiting to be taken to Molong and placed with her mother who'd been buried in the cemetery there in 1951.

The Monday after the old house left Yarralumla Marie and I took off for Molong. Arriving at four in the afternoon in pouring rain, I headed straight for the railway station to show her where the line had been moved away from the platform, as trains no longer stopped there. The buildings are now being used for community purposes. Leaving there, the rain still hammering down, we sought shelter inside the first open shop on the main street.

Lo and behold it was a furniture store and directly in our path was the perfect dining table and six chairs for our alcove. When the proprietor came from a back room to make the sale, Marie noticed he had white plaster in his hair. This led to the explanation that he made cornices for the ceilings of all the renovations this side of the mountains. Marie announced we wanted the table and chairs for our new house in Canberra, to which he added, "My brother and I have just had an old house from Canberra brought over in two parts."

Startled, Marie asked, "What's the wallpaper like in the smallest room?"

His answer saw the three of us get into our car and drive to the suburbs of Molong. Sure enough it was our Canberra house, joined together and with the same letterbox on the pavement. Just two streets away from where my family lived when I was away at war. Apparently each part had been too large to go down the Forbes driveway, so the house went to the next buyer here in Molong.

Next morning while doing the honours for my mother at the cemetery, a utility pulled up. The driver greeted us. He was the brother of our furniture vendor. In the conversation about how small the world really is and what a coincidence etc, he mentioned he'd just received the bill for clearing the asbestos from the Yarralumla site. Quick off the mark,

Marie responded, "Don't you pay that. I've already settled the account for that."

It just goes to show that some people will do anything to make a buck!

On 13 March 1998 the slab was poured at the Yarralumla block and for the next four months our new next-door neighbor, Jack Sparkes, a retired building inspector kept a close eye on Steve Planinac and his team of workers, providing a detailed monologue whenever we visited.

By 23 July 1998 all was complete for habitation. Marie enjoyed the spring season developing the garden she'd planned meticulously. Henry the cat created his usual shenanigans inside and out, while Jennifer revelled in her quarters — a bedroom, sitting room, ensuite and own courtyard entrance. Even the architect received an award for the design.

At intervals throughout the next year, jars containing five cent pieces were left at the front door until a total of fifty dollars was reached to cover our cost of the Prunus replacement. Now each year Marie fights the white cockatoos for the delicious small plums.

As the 21st Century loomed I took stock of my ability to make the most of the years ahead. I was fortunate in having Tom Gavranic and Marie-Ange Nambiar both General Practitioners who were able to put pressure on me as far as my general wellbeing was concerned.

After returning from a cricket tour of England followed by a cruise, I'd spent a week in hospital with my first bout of pneumonia, which presaged the five yearly injections prescribed for those of my age.

Moreover in November 1998, a visit to the plumbing doctor threatened emasculation, which Dr. Nambiar was keen for me to avoid. She encouraged me to apply for a Department of Veterans' Affairs Gold Card and when this was granted my life was virtually in her hands. She would prescribe with the admonition; "You will take this for the rest of your life."

I've lost count of the number of colleagues, much younger than I am, who have died of prostate cancer, and or stroke, or have simply withered on the vine.

— 34 —

The New Century and My 80's

My 80th birthday was a milestone to stay with me for a good many reasons. First was the presence of the only two survivors with me of the 14 of Cook Year 1934, Ian Cartwright and John Bell. John had brought us together at Jervis Bay in 1987. I had decided that I'd accept the invitation of the Trust of the Anzac Memorial Chapel of St Paul to sponsor the stall for the Archdeacon of the Navy in the memory of all 14 of us.

Three Cook Year survivors L to R myself, Ian Cartwright and John Bell

Second, I acknowledged that I needed to review my athleticism in order that I should not become a burden to others in trying to do that for which I was no longer capable.

Third, the Hanford genes may well have ensured longevity, but incipient bunions and hammer toes were obviously going to cause me problems.

Fourth, the optometrist with whom I had been consulting over the years put me on notice that within the next five years I would need to have cataracts removed one eye at a time.

To celebrate my birthday friends from I Zingari, the Navy, skiing, the Chapel, the neighbourhood, gymnasium and my two children of the second marriage, Tookie and Matthew, gathered. But, what I found difficulty in admitting to myself was the gradual but definite loss of hearing which was not to be corrected for another nine years.

Colonel Peter Rose and I go back a long way. In the late 1970's we had offices on the second floor of the Army building at Russell Offices while I was working with one of the Deputy Secretaries of the Department of Defence. Our friendship developed through our involvement with the Anzac Memorial Chapel of St Paul, Duntroon and Marie's friendship with Peter's wife, Marion. They shared a mutual interest in travel, particularly to South-East Asia. Marie and Marion's first visit was to Vietnam in 2005, where they shopped till they dropped. In 2009 they also advanced their study of Italian together at a school in Italy. Their overseas travel became an annual event.

In 1989 I'd taken over the position of Treasurer of the Trust of the Chapel from Peter. A position I'm still holding until the capital invested becomes self sufficient to meet our annual expenditure.

A reader could perhaps consider that religiosity has more to do with my close relationships than true friendship, but when Tom Frame and his wife Helen are taken into account and the way in which we have grown together, there is so much more.

Tom left the RAN after a very successful appointment as Research Officer to the professional Head of the Royal Australian Navy Vice Admiral Michael W Hudson AC RAN (21.4.1985 to 8.3.1991). In his foreword to *Where Fate Calls,* Tom's book concerning the tragedy of HMAS *Voyager,* 10 February 1992 the Admiral wrote:

> *'Through publication of many articles, documentaries and other books, Tom has more than amply demonstrated a competence well beyond his years.'*

Before taking holy orders the Navy granted him study leave to complete the doctorial thesis on which the book was based. During that time I assisted him with fleet work in which he was not experienced. Having served with both captains, Robertson and Stevens, during my seagoing years, I was able to give him my appraisal of their abilities and attitudes. The preference in appointment shown to both of them in large part led to my decision to go onto the Emergency List in 1962 and embark on a second career.

It was Peter Rose who first convinced me that I needed professional help with my hearing. In 2007 I became Lay Minister to the Australian Defence Force and had to admit to myself that I hadn't heard a full sermon for some time. I was in no position to add anything in the way of relevant comment on the effectiveness of our weekly services, and at the meetings of the Chapel Trust I was clearly disadvantaged.

Throughout these ten years of my life I was fortunate in being a Life Member of the Naval Officers Club. Formed in 1946, it had suffered somewhat in support for membership in the 1970's and 80's, but came into its own in 1988. Here in Canberra after the funeral in Curtin of one of the early post-war naval aviators a group of his colleagues were outside the church. I was among them and it was clear that we all had something to talk about and some things led to laughter all round. I suggested that perhaps it was a bit unseemly to have the solemnity of the occasion diluted in this way. What if we were to meet regularly and lunch together at some suitable venue. Great idea — the first Monday of each month at the Canberra Club in Civic.

Then came the fateful day on which I turned up wearing a very expensive pair of white leather Italian shoes to be forbidden entry on the basis of my dress — sandshoes indeed! When those already gathered upstairs were told they decided to leave without lunching and we retired to the Yacht Club on Lake Burley Griffin, which then became our venue henceforth.

As far as my Chapel clerical duties were concerned I received promotion from Lay Assistant to Lay Reader during the early 2000s and became Lay Minister to the Australian Defence Force on 1 July 2007.

Soon after 10 March 2010 the then Bishop to the Defence Force, Leonard S Eacott AM, informed me that he could no longer insure me for what I was doing behind the altar rails. My licence was not renewed and my title lapsed. So I am back to reading the Scriptures and preparing the Book for others to read, making sure that they relate what they are reading to relevance to the now as well as the then.

Mike Taylor, who'd been at the Naval College in 1956 when I was Training Commander in HMAS *Cerberus* and often refereed Cadets v Officers Rugby Games, was persuaded to be our Club Secretary in 1999, and the Coordinator two years later. Mike's wife, Helen, and Marie had developed a strong friendship and the four of us shared dinners and birthday celebrations throughout the decade. Marie, unlike Mike and Helen, attends church C and E (Christmas and Easter), so most Sundays the remaining three of us sit in the same pews and spend an hour after the morning service with others of the congregation in the Fellowship Room for coffee and a chat.

Shortly after moving to Yarralumla I became a Zone Leader in the Neighbourhood Watch organization. It meets regularly for ten months each year and involves the distribution of newsletters to the community throughout the year. I'm also a member of the Yarralumla Residents Association, which aims to form and represent to the administrative branches of the ACT Government a view on important matters affecting the suburb.

It's with some regret that my views on retaining antiquities have been formed by such things as the pyramids of Giza and the remains of the three separate and distinct phases (Early, Middle and Late) of the Minoan civilization which I visited in May 1939 at Knossos in Crete. I cannot, therefore, accept that a collection of decrepit tin sheds at a brick-works that no longer makes bricks and a section of railway lines should be the subject of the expenditure of millions to preserve for the education of children. My view is if one wants to see bricks being made, get out of the train at Bowral and walk a few hundred metres to where it is all happening. Marie says, "Philistine — but at least keep the chimney."

No doubt there is no solution to this problem in my lifetime.

Two other friends have figured prominently in my life in the past ten years, Timothy Johnstone, a retired solicitor and barrister, and Desmond Woods, a serving RAN officer. Through one I met the other. Each has supported me in my efforts to persevere with my story, Timothy through Rotary and Desmond through his contacts in the British High Commission.

After much consideration of the possible ill effects of surgery on my general well-being Dr. Nambiar agreed to refer me to Dr. Miniter for surgery on my feet, right foot in 2004 and left foot a year later. This had an effect on skiing and non-attendance at annual general meetings of I Zingari in Sydney for both years. However it proved to be a bonanza for Henry the cat. Each day of the two six week periods in which I was confined to an easy chair with my foot up on another chair, Henry would lie across my ankle and assist in my early recovery.

In 2008 and 2009 I was glad when I had cataracts removed from each eye in turn. Sadly this time Henry was not feeling the best himself and had more to think about than helping my recovery. Henry's last day was nothing if not eventful. The vet had warned me that he was running out of time in June 2008, so I had him on a regular schedule, up at 07:00, outside for a good hour and then around the house until bedtime in the laundry after evening television.

When he did not come home by 08:00 on Sunday 18 January 2009 I suspected that something out of the ordinary might have happened. He was nowhere to be found around the garden, and I was relieved when the phone rang about an hour later. It was the RSPCA at Weston Creek.

Henry had been delivered to them wrapped in a towel having been rescued from a backyard pool in Yarralumla. His identity chip had done its job. Within ten minutes I had him home, dry and comfortable in the laundry and ready for breakfast.

Clearly he'd gone further than usual when checking out his territory at the back of our house. Thankfully someone with good sense had rescued him. He hardly moved all day and died quite peacefully around 18:00 that evening. He'd lived a full life that ended without the violence and uncertainty to which so many domestic animals are subjected.

I'm pleased to have been a supporter of the International Fund for Animal Welfare since 2001.

Next morning I buried him in my best shoe box on the boundary of our house and the one next door, as he'd spent many hours with this neighbour. Her two cats were extremely unsociable and like most males, he never minded the extra attention in the least.

— 35 —

King’s Medal Replacement

Finally at the end of 2007, Peter Cumming succeeded in having his stolen King’s Medal replaced at no expense to the Crown. It had taken him 13 years. Sending me a letter, he outlined the successful stages he’d followed, so I decided to follow the same process. Unfortunately my first attempt caused some confusion, as my documents, when received in the Defence Section of Australia House in London, were passed to a Fleet Air Arm Officer who thought that I was trying to get a replacement medal for Peter Cumming.

A Captain Martin received my next request. He was the son of D J Martin and grandson of W H Martin, a pre-war colleague of my father. Within a week he had Her Majesty’s approval for my medal replacement which he passed on to the Royal Mint. There it seemed to wait while the price of gold kept on rising. When the price had reached its highest, the exact replica was minted. Captain Martin then paid for it and sent it on its way, safely through the system. I then reimbursed him.

What had taken Peter Cumming 13 years, I’d done, with the help and understanding of Captain Martin, in 11 months.

On 21 April 1938, the Administrator to the Commonwealth, Lord Huntingfield had handed me my original King’s Medal. There’d been no fancy ceremony. In full dress, with dirk, I boarded a ship’s boat at No.1 Buoy Farm Cove, crossed the harbour to the steps below Government House, Kirrabilli, and walked up the lawn into the study. His

Excellency, seated at his desk, handed me an inscribed case and said, "This is yours."

I thanked him and retraced my steps back to the boat. Very simple.

As I now had a replacement medal, and a new Governor-General was to take over in Yarralumla in a week, I wrote to the Official Secretary suggesting that the new incumbent might consider a repeat performance.

I heard nothing, until one morning Marie answered the phone to be asked, "What does he want out of this? Money?"

She replied, "Absolutely nothing. He just thought it might be a good news story for the incoming Governor General."

What happened next was not just a chariot race, it became bigger than *'Ben Hur'*.

The Chief of Navy, Vice Admiral Russell Crane, who'd just moved into Navy House, Duntroon, would hold a grand reception at which Her Excellency would present Captain W Graham Wright RAN (Rtd.) with the replica King's Medal for 1937. This event would be followed by a Passing Out Parade the next day at HMAS *Creswell,* to which those of Years 1934 and 1935 were to be invited to join those whose 50 years since graduating were expected to attend.

On arrival at the Wardroom of the Royal Australian Naval College on the evening of the presentation, Philip Stevenson greeted us, announcing to the assembled gathering, "Graham Wright you've done it again. You've upped us all once more!"

I'd just been on National television that evening with a warts and all depiction of the entire morning's event.

One of the best things to come out of appearing on international television was a letter from Anthony Mackenzie asking very formally whether I was in fact the same Graham Wright listed as his father on his birth certificate. I had not had any contact with him since seeing him off to England as a six week old in 1953.

With my replacement King's Medal 2008

Once contact had been established we arranged that he would come and stay with us in Canberra for a few days early in 2010 on his way to New Zealand where he was going to stay with friends.

On 22 January 2010 we went through the correct legal procedure for DNA testing to establish once and for all the facts concerning his paternity, which then enabled him to make contact with several daughters of his natural father of whom he knew nothing. At 57 years of age I believe he had the right to know the truth, the result of which Marie and I have gained a friendship which will certainly outlast my lifetime.

In 2011 I went to England a week before the I Zingari team was to start the often postponed next Cricket Tour since 1994. As I arrived at Heathrow on Sunday 26 June 2011 I was met by Marie who had come from Italy and Anthony with whom we were to spend five memorable days narrow-boating in the Midlands travelling from near Lichfield to as close to Oxford as we could go. We spent the next weekend with Christopher and Lucia Turner during which I read the Gospel before Christopher preached his sermon at one of his Churches on Sunday. I then joined the I Zingari team, and was met by one of the players with whose grandfather I played when invited to join I Z in 1948.

Second, I acknowledged that I needed to review my athleticism in order that I should not become a burden to others in trying to do that for which I was no longer capable.

— 36 —

The Last Hit

To organize a successful cricket tour requires a good two years of correspondence to-ing and fro-ing between club officials of the two countries involved.

Anthony came to visit us for three days in January 2010 by which time we had the rough outline of the tour from 25 June to 14 July and with this information he planned our pre-cricket activity.

There was one problem about my resolve to play my last innings. I simply couldn't hold my place in the field. I did my bit by going to all games, and took charge of raising and lowering the I Z flag on all occasions. Moreover I ensured that all players on the ground should be able to follow the score, which tied me to the official scorers and the scoreboard.

That worked until the final match against the Guards Cricket Club at Burton's Court in Chelsea on 12 July 2011. I can do no better than to quote from the Diary of the Tour 2011:

'We then had a steady fall of wickets in search of our target of 200. At this point, Steve Martin, with a massive reversal in form after his last couple of innings, had back cut, square cut, square driven, late cut and pushed his way through point to 92. With only three overs to go, he needed support to ensure that he got to his maiden century. The Captain, again showing great vision, sent the Commander in to steer 'Mistoffelees' to his 100.

Having sat patiently since the team photo with his pads and gloves on ready for his Captain's call at the time of crisis, Graham strode to the wicket at the start of the 38th over. With great aplomb, the Commander achieved his first goal – to bat longer than Bradman did in his final innings in England. With that achieved, he turned a ball off his legs and scampered to a single to also out score Bradman. Alas, with the task achieved, the Commander was bowled for 1, leaving Steve on 97 with the last man to join him.'

My last innings with I Zingari (Australia) in London 2011

Steve finished with 110 not out and I Z won by 53 runs. The first time ever at Burton's Court. To celebrate this occasion the Guards presented two coffee mugs to Marie and me to commemorate the marriage of HRH Prince William and Catherine Middleton on 29 April 2011. For us this was a reminder of the marriage of our daughter Jennifer to Frank Pigott on Saturday 12 February 2011.

With my daughter Jennifer at her wedding 12 February 2011

It may perhaps be confusing to some readers to understand why a Naval Captain should be the 'Commander'. In a Cricket Club over many years, and particularly *I Z Australia 1888 – present day* there have been many team captains, particularly in the late 1940's and onwards when as many as three teams, Veterans, A's and B's were all playing each season.

Marie and I celebrated my last cricket match by plagiarising a verse by Thomas E Spencer:

How the Commander Topped Don Bradman's Final Score

A delightful ground is Burton's Court to the west in London town
Where the Chelsea Pensioners end their days and the Guards just fool around
Playing cricket if and when they can with Royal duties done
They often give IZ a game when on an England run.

Sometimes they even stack their game and savage us with mayhem
An Earl or Duke and maybe one who bats as well as Graham.
And there the Commander chose to play an innings to ensure
A farewell effort with the bat in a manner to endure.
He wondered how the Don had felt when he failed to make a score.
The Commander knew with nerves of steel he had to get one more.
Steve was in the nineties, the Commander was the same.
He stood his ground and ready to face whatever came.
The Commander hit the next ball and then he scored a run
A run in his last over – what Bradman hadn't done.
Having faced the balls he needed he could therefore do no more
That's how the Commander topped, Don Bradman's final score.

At the time of writing I have just returned to Canberra from Sydney having attended the Quasquicentennial Members Dinner to celebrate 125 years of cricket in Australia.

Myself, Sax White (centre) and Marie at the I Zingari Ball 2013

— 37 —

Finally Putting It Right

Throughout the writing of this book the last concern I've had is an article in the Naval Officers Club Newsletter No.58 of 1 September 2004. Titled *Man Overboard, N Class Destroyers* and told by Ken Cunningham, who retired as the Senior Chief of the RAN in 1965 after 27 years service. It kept on turning up among the papers I was considering.

One remark with which I have had difficulty refers to an account in my Journal for use of Junior Officers afloat of Tuesday 15 March 1938 in HMAS *Canberra* on passage from Hobart to Jervis Bay. A page of handwriting accompanied by a memorial drawing honouring the loss of leading Seaman H J Storer can be contrasted to:

'Many people, especially junior sailors, find it hard to understand how a man overboard can be left behind … like a Leading Seaman from an Australian cruiser in 1937. No attempt seems to have been made to rescue ... him though in the cruiser case, the survivor was seen in the water with a lifebuoy over his body.'

The truth, as I wrote it then, is this:

'Tragedy closed down upon us when, at 0824, a man slipped and fell in the Torpedo Space, going overboard on the port side. Immediately all ships stood by but were powerless to assist. The state of the sea made easy manoeuvring an impossibility and HMAS Stuart

came close to foundering, losing one boat, a skiff and damaging a whaler in an attempt to pick up our man.
The Canberra sighted him once more an hour later, but a heavy rain squall soon obliterated him.
On that occasion the ship was to leeward of Leading Seaman HJ Storer who was seated in his lifebuoy waving to us. We managed to get round again making allowance for the drift to leeward, but never saw him again.
The remainder of the day was spent in a fruitless search, in which hopes were raised only to be convincingly shattered on all occasion'.

Compare my account with: *'No attempt seems to have been made to rescue either sailor even though, in the cruiser case, the survivor was seen in the water with a lifebuoy over his body'.*

The errors in this shows that not only is the year of the event inaccurate, but also the facts of the case. But it is with an earlier part of the story that I have the problem. Headed *'Horn of Africa'*, an eyewitness is reported to have seen off the Horn of Africa on 29 June 1942 Stoker Donald Campbell washed overboard. The article says that the Captain, Commander Henry Burrell:

'evidently considered the rescue too dangerous or the chances of success too unlikely. Campbell was left to drown.'

All I can say about this hogwash is, that the eyewitness must have had exceptional eyesight, as the actual event took place off the southern end of the continent of Africa and a good nine months or more after this recording. It certainly didn't happen when I was the Navigator of

HMAS *Norman* off the Horn of Africa after leaving the Mediterranean in June 1942.

As Lord Byron (1788 – 1824) wrote in *Don Juan*:

'Tis strange – but true; for truth is always strange; Stranger than fiction.'

I can understand the reason for the invention of the Burrell account of HMAS *Norman* during the three days in the White Sea, but attributing to him the imputation that he would have left a shipmate like that, is certainly not the man I knew.

The true story of the event appears in Burrell's book, *Mermaids Do Exist*, on page 151. This is one occasion on which I'm glad to know that I'm putting it right.

And as for my life — I'm proud of it and my achievements. Even though I didn't go as far as I believed I would in the Navy, clearly God had other plans for me and on reflection he chose the Wright man for the right job. I have been truly blessed.

SYNOPSIS

Captain Graham Wright is a man ahead of his time. He saw life and work differently from others. However, speaking his mind brought him more trouble than good, as others didn't often agree with his point of view or vision. But during his current 93 years, he's seen many of his predictions and ideas come to fruition.

Putting It Wright covers his life to date, from joining the Royal Australian Navy at age 13, his experiences in Palestine, Malta, Turkey and adventures during World War II in the Mediterranean, Madagascar, South-East Asia and most importantly Archangel and the truth behind a secret meeting with Stalin in Moscow by Sir Walter Citrine, UK Trade Union Congress leader, under Churchill's orders in 1941. No other book in history has ever exposed this detail. This Naval career highlight earned him the Arctic Star.

His service continued during peacetime until 1962 amid major changes in the Navy and then all the Defence Forces. After 29 years of Naval service he accepted an offer from the then Department of External Affairs, spending two interesting years amongst the communist spy scandals in Bangkok, Thailand, as Head of Research in the South East Asian Treaty Organization Headquarters.

Later, after joining the Australian Public Service, his major achievement was working with Sir Arthur Tange in producing the well-known Tange Report. With his Bachelor of Arts Honours degree and his thesis work, the Tange Report amalgamated the administration of the three armed services and Supply Department, creating the Department of Defence as we know it today.

Even after being criticized by Australian National University gurus who believed that an insider couldn't be credited with writing about Defence matters, Wright proved to be right again — as history has shown that what we have today with the day-to-day operations of the three Services now controlled by the Headquarters at Bungendore — is just as he'd written it.

ABOUT GRAHAM

Born 10 March 1920 in Newcastle, New South Wales, Walter Graham Wright joined the Royal Australian Navy in 1934 aged 13, much to his mother's concern for her only child. After topping not only his academic examinations and being awarded the King's Medal for leadership, his sporting prowess also shone with Rugby Colours in his second year and as Captain of the First XV, plus the earning of his Cricket Colours in his fourth year. Then when one of his instructors said, "Mrs. Wright your son is going to be a future Captain in the Navy", she no longer worried.

Now 93 he's always lived by one rule, "I'm a very good team player, as long as I'm the captain." In fact the prizes he's won throughout life have had a profound influence and while he may not have reached the top echelon in his three main careers, he has certainly left his mark in the Navy, the Department of Defence and later as a Lay Minister to the Australian Defence Force, as well as the Navy Ski Lodges in Mount Buller and Perisher Valley, the Navy Game Fishing Club and the Australian I Zingari Cricket Association. While he played his final I Zingari match in England in 2011, he was still actively skiing in the Australian Alps during 2013.

Married to Marie his third wife for 42 years now, he has four children, seven grandchildren and six great-grandchildren.

www.ingramcontent.com/pod-product-compliance
Lightning Source LLC
Chambersburg PA
CBHW021826090426
42811CB00032B/2042/J

* 9 7 8 0 9 9 2 4 6 5 7 0 4 *